The Game Makers

THE GAME MAKERS

The Story of
Parker Brothers from
Tiddledy Winks to
Trivial Pursuit

Philip E. Orbanes

Harvard Business School Press
Boston, Massachusetts

Library of Congress Cataloging-in-Publication Data

Orbanes, Philip.
  The game makers : the story of Parker Brothers from Tiddledy Winks to
Trivial Pursuit / Philip E. Orbanes.
      p. cm.
Includes bibliographical references and index.
  ISBN 1-59139-269-1 (alk. paper)
  1. Parker Brothers, inc. 2. Board game industry—United
States—History. I. Title.
    HD9993.G354P376 2004
    338.7'61794'0973—dc21

                                                    2003010768

The paper used in this publication meets the requirements of the American National Standard for Permanence of Paper for Publications and Documents in Libraries and Archives Z39.48-1992.

This book is dedicated to all
who were "Parkerized"

It is in the blood of genius to love play for its own sake,
and whether one uses one's skill on thrones or women,
swords or pens, gold or fame, the game's the thing.

—Gelett Burgess, "April Essays,"
The Romance of the Commonplace

Contents

Preface

The Object of This Book

When I was eight years old, I was invited to play the *Monopoly* game for the first time. The experience was pivotal; I held my own against my favorite aunts and uncles. I fought back tears when forced to mortgage property; I beamed when Pacific Avenue earned me $900; I felt guilty when sent to jail; and breathed a sigh of relief when my top hat leapt over Boardwalk and I avoided bankruptcy. I'm hardly alone in harboring cherished memories of Parker Brothers games, which include blockbusters like the *Monopoly*® game, *Sorry!*®, *Clue*®, *Boggle*®, and *Trivial Pursuit*® as well as personal favorites *Risk*®, *Pit*®, and *Careers*®. Parker Brothers games are woven into the fabric of our American culture. When we were kids, playing one for the first time often marked a rite of passage; as adults, they continue to renew bonds within families and strengthen the warmth of friendship.

Founded in 1883, Parker Brothers is one of the most enduring brands in the United States, and around the world. Yet the fascinating story of this important firm—how it was conceived by the innate genius of a teenager, molded and expanded with help from his older brothers, and then, still at the top of the field, passed down and further grown by subsequent generations of the same family—is largely unknown.

George Swinnerton Parker was just sixteen years old in 1883 when he embarked on his lifetime career, convinced that games were not just about bolstering a person's "moral fabric," but about having fun. After persuading his older brothers Charles and Edward to join him in forming Parker Brothers, Inc., George led the firm to bring Americans everything from *Tiddledy Winks* and *Rook*, to *Mah-Jongg* and *Ping-Pong*, to the modern jigsaw puzzle and the *Nerf* ball. Two thousand products later, Parker Brothers is one of the best known and most beloved of all game publishers. And somewhere in the process, its games have gone from simply reflecting the values of the country to helping shape them.

A peculiar trail of events led me to the story of Parker Brothers and this attempt to tell it. After my first experience playing *Monopoly*, I persuaded my mother to buy a copy for our family. Next, I asked her for *Clue*. My sisters and I loved this great detective game, so I asked for a third Parker Brothers game. But this time she shook her head and said that two games would have to do until my birthday (three months away). Undeterred, I made up my own game (involving mines and oil wells, I recall). I soon discovered that I had a knack for inventing one whenever the mood struck. After graduating from high school, I founded my own game company (Gamescience Corporation). After a slow start, it helped pay for my education. In 1968, I sold Gamescience to a New York–based toy company and, following graduation from college, spent seven years working for small game companies in New York City before becoming director of the game division of Ideal Toy—then the world's third-largest toy company.

I became part of the Parker Brothers story in 1979, when the growing company recruited me to serve as director of new product research. In time I became head of research and development and remained with Parker Brothers until 1990. Shortly after moving my family from Long Island to Boston's North Shore, I toured Parker Brothers' Salem factory and was invited to enter the firm's well-maintained archives. The secretary who served as their curator unlocked the door and ushered me inside. There, surrounded by brick walls, under the third-floor eaves in the original part of the factory, was the collective output of hundreds, if not thousands, of Parker Brothers employees who had come before me. Steel shelves held neatly stacked copies of games dating back to 1884—legendary games I had only heard of, like *Pillow-Dex* and the *United States Game* and the Maxfield Parrish target game. Games that I knew, like *Pit, Flinch,* and *Pollyanna,* also caught my eye—but I was astonished to see how old their first editions were. As I walked the rows of shelves and touched their protective wrappings, I was struck by a desire to understand how these games came to be. Who were the people who published them? What factors led them to select these games over other candidates? How were they made? Where did their ideas come from? Why did they come to reside here, on the top floor of a clapboard building over one hundred years old, near the bank of the North River in Salem, Massachusetts?

Partial histories of the firm had already been published and answered some of my questions. *Seventy Five Years of Fun* and *Ninety Years of Fun* are lighthearted pamphlets, produced by Parker Brothers (in 1958 and 1973) to promote their games. *Playing by Different Rules* by Ellen Wojahn (Amacom, 1988) attempts to explain what went wrong after General Mills acquired the firm. "Parker Pride: Memories of Working Days at Parker Brothers," by Professor John J. Fox (*Essex Institute Historical Collections,* vol. 123, no. 2) is a delightful collection of oral histories of key Parker Brothers employees prior to the General Mills acquisition. Numerous magazine articles have described Parker Brothers the company, the most memorable being Pete Martin's "Game Maker" in the *Saturday Evening Post* issue of October 6, 1945. Other histories have focused on Parker Brothers' most famous products, like the *Monopoly* game. All of these were limited in scope, either by design or by lack of source material. My eleven years with the firm helped me to fill in some of the gaps in these published records.

But questions still gnawed at me: What was George Parker really like? What about the other Parker brothers? What stories preceded even the memories of the old-timers still at work in the firm? Robert Barton would come to my aid. President of the firm from 1934 to 1968 and George Parker's son-in-law, he graciously responded to every question I posed, relevant or not, for my first book, *The Monopoly Companion* (sparked by my experience as chief judge at U.S. and World *Monopoly* tournaments).

My curiosity about the company was further whetted by this effort. A few months before leaving Parker Brothers in 1990, I received approval to make a photographic record of every game in the archives and write a brief history of the company focused on these games. But after gathering all available information about the firm, published or otherwise, business reality intervened. The budget crunch of Parker Brothers' then owner, Tonka Corporation, caused the photography sessions to be curtailed and I stored away my research. In early 2002, after the *Harvard Business Review* published my article, "Everything I Know About Business I Learned from Monopoly," I decided to resume independent research on the Parker Brothers story, reflecting my views and not necessarily those of Parker Brothers or its parent, Hasbro. Randolph Barton and the heirs of the other two founding brothers led me to invaluable source material that had lain untouched for half a century. Packed away in 1952 by his wife, who survived him, George Parker's personal archives began to unlock the story of the firm during its first seven decades. Records, pocket diaries, photos, scrapbooks, and letters came forth from steamer trunks locked and shuttled about from family home to family home during the second half of the twentieth century. In addition to releasing these family archives, the heirs of the three Parker brothers consented to hours of interviews about their families and their company, as did many former employees.

As George Parker's business took root and grew, he came to feel passionate about the enduring and transferable values to be found in playing games ("Make it last" became his creed). "The older George Parker became, the more convinced he was that business itself was like a game," Robert Barton explained to me. "Mr. Parker believed that, with a reasonable amount of foresight and attentiveness to important rules, one could succeed in the world." George Parker was to settle on twelve such "rules" (principles, actually) that successfully guided his decisions for decades. But Parker Brothers endured and flourished armed with more than twelve principles. It made enduring products, cultivated devoted and capable employees, sank deep roots into a community that returned its loyalty, and fostered quality and customer service long before these became buzzwords in U.S. business.

George Parker not only proved himself a gifted inventor, he also distinguished his company from competitors by bringing an editor's eye to bear on the refinement of his games. He insisted on eye-catching and durable designs. And he continually sought innovative ways to make his

A Dollar's Value

To help put the monetary values of past years in perspective when they appear in the text, here is what one dollar in each of these years was worth (as of the beginning of 2003).

YEAR	PRESENT VALUE	YEAR	PRESENT VALUE
1880	$17.22	1945	$9.85
1885	$18.26	1950	$7.35
1890	$19.43	1955	$6.62
1895	$20.97	1960	$5.98
1900	$20.97	1965	$5.62
1905	$19.98	1970	$4.56
1910	$18.58	1975	$3.29
1915	$17.51	1980	$2.15
1920	$ 8.83	1985	$1.65
1925	$10.09	1990	$1.36
1930	$10.59	1995	$1.16
1935	$12.95	2000	$1.04
1940	$12.61		

Prices declined from the time of the Civil War until the turn of the century. Rapid inflation occurred during World War I, followed by deflation until World War II; prices have risen ever since.

SOURCE: S. Morgan Friedman, The Inflation Calculator, <http://www.westegg.com>

games known to the U.S. public. His principles and techniques were imbued in the members of his family who would run the company following his partial retirement in 1934 and his death in 1952: son-in-law Robert Barton, nephew Foster Parker, great nephews Edward Parker and Channing Bacall, and grandson Randolph Barton. They added their own management acumen and built the firm into a game empire.

My object in writing this book is to tell not only how the games made by Parker Brothers came to be, but also to show how the firm's values and George Parker's principles guided the way to its success and kept the company alive during many hard times.

The story of this family business is more than just a highlight in the annals of U.S. industry. Below the glare lies a study of contrasts: of self-limitation as well as expansion; rigidity as well as flexibility; and of a serious-mindedness among a few men that generated lightheartedness for millions.

But the best part of the history of Parker Brothers is that most of us were—and still are—part of the experience.

Acknowledgments

Many people made possible this telling of the Parker Brothers story. Most significantly, the years 1883 through 1932 (and beyond) could not have been written in detail without the discovery by Randolph Barton of the personal papers and photographs of his grandfather, George Parker—and the unlimited use of them he accorded me. I am also appreciative for the hours Ranny devoted to answering my questions about Parker Brothers' history, his ancestors, and his years with the firm from 1957 through 1984.

Channing Bacall's memory was crucial, especially regarding the period after George Parker's decline (in 1949) through the General Mills acquisition in 1968. Channing's attention to detail and commitment to accuracy helped me to get the story right. His recollections of his grandfather, Charles Parker, were equally valuable.

Edward P. Parker's daughters, Anne Parker-Pollack and Diane Bolman, were very gracious in providing memories, records, and photographs of their father and of their grandfather Foster Parker. I am also appreciative of the materials provided by Diane's sons, Edward and Shelley, especially with regard to Edward H. Parker, their great-great-grandfather (eldest brother of George and Charles Parker). My thanks also to Natalie Parker (d. 2003), widow of Edward P. Parker, and Maud Barton for their contributions.

In 1986, Professor John Fox of Salem State University recorded the oral history of nine Parker Brothers employees who witnessed seventy years of the firm's history. Fortunately, he made them available through the American Game and Puzzle Collectors Association, and I drew upon them several times in the narrative. These tapes supplemented and verified many of the comments made to me in 1988 when I was researching my first book, *The Monopoly Companion*. To John Fox I express my deepest gratitude.

Many of those we both interviewed have passed on, including Robert B. M. Barton, Louis Vanne, and George Fox. Their recollections were vital to the accuracy of the Parker Brothers story from 1933 through 1968.

My special thanks are extended to Craig Nalen. His memory of the acquisition of Parker Brothers by General Mills helped me to ascertain the facts of this pivotal moment in Parker Brothers' history. Bill Dohrmann's vivid memory, files, and photographs provided pinpoint detail from 1969 to my arrival at Parker Brothers in 1979. Bill's enthusiasm and generosity were without measure.

Many employees whose eyes saw history unfold from 1950 to the present also provided their wonderful memories to my efforts. These include Barbara McDonough, Fred French, Tony Lemone, Joe Marquez, Jack McMahon, Rene Soriano, Connie Knudson, Frank Ventura, Clara Sheehy, Laura Lemiesz Pecci, Bill Brett, Barbara Kenny, and Pat McGovern. My sincere thanks as well to Dave Wilson, who provided insight about his days in sales leadership at Parker Brothers and his current perspective, as president of Hasbro Games, on the Parker Brothers brand. I am also grateful for the insights provided by Cam Nixon and the early encouragement from Tom Klusaritz, both of Hasbro, and to Judy Flathers, Helen van Tassel, and Mark Morris of Hasbro Games for the materials they provided me.

I tip my hat to Bruce Whitehill, founder of the American Game and Puzzle Collectors Association, for his insights into early Parker Brothers games, and to Anne Williams—its current librarian and expert extraordinaire on jigsaw puzzles—for sharpening my facts about *Pastime Puzzles*. Inventor Charles Phillips kindly recalled for me his impressions upon his first visit to Salem in the early 1970s. Rev. Jeffrey Barz-Snell provided insights into the origin of the stained glass windows of his church and also the life of Mr. Getschell, gleaned on my behalf from Mr. Getschell's grandson, Jim Morrison. Patricia Johnson Beaulieu kindly shared her mementos and remembrances of her grandfather, Albert Richardson. I extend appreciation to Irena Strumpf of Winning Moves for the photographs of the games from my collection that appear in this book. Will Lemoy and staff at the Peabody Essex Institute Library were very helpful in retrieving Parker Brothers documents from their archives. I thank Alan Kirby for sharing his recollections of working at Robert Barton's home, and Joe Barnes for his kind assistance.

Background materials and comment on John Waddington Limited were graciously provided by Victor Watson and Penny Melling.

Sincere thanks go to my agent, Rob McQuilkin, and the great editorial staff at Harvard Business School Press, including Hollis Heimbouch, Jacque Murphy, Astrid Sandoval, Jill Connor, Sarah Weaver, and their consultant Connie Hale. Their belief in this book and their cogent advice made it far better than it otherwise would have been. In addition, Jennifer Waring, Sharon Rice, Zeenat Potia, and Laurie Ardito each graciously contributed their special expertise. I would also like to thank the anonymous reviewers; their suggestions greatly aided me in shaping the final manuscript.

Chuti Prasertsith designed the eye-catching cover and Ralph Fowler provided the sharp graphic design found throughout the book, while Steven Strumpf created the border design for the chapter title pages. I am very grateful to these fine artists.

I thank Michael, Beatrice, Phil, Sonya, Natalie, Jean, and Marion for that memorable first *Monopoly* game.

And a very special thank you to my wife Anna, whose patience and encouragement were golden during all the long evenings and weekends that this manuscript was written, and rewritten. Within you, like all the fine people mentioned above, shines the true spirit of Parker Brothers.

The Game Makers

Chapter One

First Moves

1883–1897

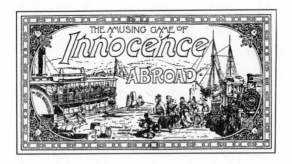

N THE SUMMER OF 1883 THE UNITED STATES, UNDER THE leadership of President Chester A. Arthur, was beginning to exploit its inventiveness. The Brooklyn Bridge had opened in May and was lit by the country's first city lighting system, now three years old. Telephones had recently linked the East Coast to Chicago. A national system of time zones was about to be adopted by the nation's railroads. People enjoyed a new concept called "leisure time." Buffalo Bill Cody's Wild West Show toured the country. Americans read Mark Twain's *Life on the Mississippi* and the new humor magazine, *Life.* But formality and tradition were still the norm. When in public, men wore stiff-collared shirts and bowler hats (price: $1.50 each); women's dresses ($2.00) were still full-length and touched their shoes. The typical family congregated in the parlor every evening to read (usually by candlelight), complete homework, and sometimes play games.[1]

Sixteen-year-old George S. Parker, the youngest of three brothers, was living with his widowed mother Sarah, an elderly uncle, and a spinster aunt in Medford, Massachusetts, a suburb north of Boston. Several years earlier, Captain George Augustus Parker had given up the seafaring life after the remains of the maritime trade at Salem, Massachusetts, moved south to the deeper waters of Boston harbor. At thirty, in 1850, he adjusted to life on solid ground, first as a merchant and then as a real estate agent. As bigger and better houses came within his grasp, he moved the family from Salem to Lexington and eventually to Medford. The panic of the early 1870s collapsed not only real estate prices, but the fortunes of the former captain as well. Unwilling to sell the Medford home at a loss, he hunkered down and struggled to make ends meet. In 1876, when George was just ten, his father died of Bright's disease.[2]

The big brown Parker family home rambled up three flights of stairs and consisted of eighteen rooms. Young George disliked all of them, save one. It was nicknamed the "Red Room" for the color of its carpet and furnishings. It was not the color George loved about the room; it was the collection of games on its shelves.

Board games were not commonplace in 1883. While a few little-known games dated from the 1820s, the first popular American board game had been created in Salem only forty years earlier: *The Mansion of Happiness.* Sixteen-year-old George played it with his older brothers when they came home for Sunday dinner. Like many games of the era, its purpose was to promote high moral value among its players. A spiral path of sixty-six spaces led to its goal, the "Mansion of Happiness" space. The path traversed to get there was highlighted by named spaces, such as "humility," "charity," and "generosity"—as well as "cruelty," "whipping post," and "prison."[3]

Although he enjoyed the company of his brothers, George played games more often with his close friends—Joseph Dyer (who would eventually join George in business) and Arthur and Louis Wellington (the former would one day run the U.S. Leather Company, while the latter would enjoy a successful career in banking).

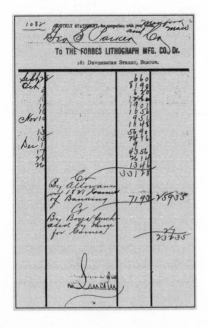

FIGURE 1-1
***Banking* Invoice**

Statement for 1,821 Banking games. Dated 1884, this is the oldest extant company document.

On a rainy summer day, in the Red Room, the boys were growing restless. They were tiring of the heavy-handed moral lessons of the games available to them. Their imaginations demanded a taste of adventure and the adult life they eagerly anticipated. Responding to his friends' complaints, George took action. He modified an old card game called Everlasting by adding lettered cards. He came up with a "borrowing" rule and renamed the game Banking. The old game gained new life. The new objective was to become the richest player by winning "speculations." A speculation began with the play of a letter card and ended when another card of the same letter was eventually played. The winner was the player who claimed all the cards, as in the game of War. To avoid defeat, players took the risk of borrowing cards from the "bank" to stay alive, paying back each such "loan" at 10 percent interest (borrow ten cards, pay back eleven). Partnerships could be formed and profits shared, which added to the excitement. George's friends wanted to play Banking nonstop. Here, at last, was the kind of no-holds-barred game the boys yearned for—one stripped bare of moral lessons and replaced by the thrill, however vicarious, of making a lot of money.[4]

In 1883 banking was a hot topic. Confidence in the nation's banks had risen dramatically following the establishment of nationally chartered banks—which were required to back their notes with federal securities—two decades earlier. By contrast, the volatility of the nation's unregulated stock and bond exchanges was dramatized daily in newspaper accounts of greed and ruin.[5] It comforted most people to know that their bills and silver coins were secure inside the four sturdy walls of the bank building that anchored their neighborhood. Cash was king; the banks held the cash. If one dreamed of riches, one dreamed of owning a bank and possessing the combination to its vault—as did George Parker and his game-playing buddies.

So convinced were George's friends that this was *it*—just the game that kids everywhere wanted—that they persuaded him to try to publish Banking. With the cautious approval of his mother, George took a train to Boston to make a proposal to the firm of Lee *&* Shepherd, publishers of books for boys. Mr. Lee, who headed the firm, brushed him off—his firm published books, not games. By chance, a successful playwright named Walter Baker was present. He took a liking to Banking and encouraged George to publish the game himself. As the evening train carried him past frost-covered fields back to Medford, this idea grew on George.

Sarah Hegeman Parker had raised her sons to be self-reliant. George quickly earned $50 selling currants picked from an orchard planted by his father. Armed with this cash, George decided to act on the playwright's advice. First, he carefully wrote the rules for Banking. He discovered that he had a knack for writing clear, well-organized instructions—a talent that would serve him well for the rest of his life.

Next, he contracted a printer in Boston—Rand, Avery & Company—to make five hundred copies of the game in return for the princely sum of $40. When it was delivered, George was pleased by the graphics on the cover, even if the top fit too tightly over the bottom of each box. Fortunately, the 160 letter cards and folded pamphlet of rules inside were nicely made. The games arrived just before Thanksgiving. George was momentarily glad that his home had rooms set aside for storage. The size of the stacks awed him. How could he possibly sell so many games? Endorsed by his mother and encouraged by his two older brothers, George paid a visit to his headmaster, Mr. Dame of Medford High School, and won permission to miss classes until after Christmas. (Mr. Dame, an avid game player, thought George might be onto something.)

The following Monday, George was back on the rails to Boston accompanied only by his mother's big suitcase, stuffed with copies of *Banking*. He went to several retailers he thought might be interested in his game, and then to the few wholesalers in town they pointed him to. Given the holiday season, his timing was perfect. He emptied his case at $4 per dozen to the retailers and $3 to the wholesalers. He asked for and was paid in cash.

On a subsequent trip to Boston, he did even better, selling no fewer than three dozen copies to upscale retailer Horace Partridge & Company, and two dozen to Richard Schwarz—brother of New York's leading seller of toys, F. A. O. Schwarz.

Notwithstanding his early success, it was clear to George that he would be stuck with a room's worth of games if he didn't go beyond Boston. Just prior to his seventeenth birthday on December 1, 1883, George went to Providence, Rhode Island. The Boston experiences had enabled George to perfect his sales pitch. He placed games in nearly every store he called upon, emptying his case in one day, and returned to Medford station that same evening.

Worcester, Winchester, and Salem were his next destinations. In Salem, his brother Charles, now twenty-three, was working his way up within a fuel-wholesaling firm. He allowed George to store a quantity of games in his room at a local boardinghouse. Charles was astonished to find the games had disappeared after just one day of George's peddling.

By Christmas Eve, George had sold all but a few of his five hundred copies. After expenses, he had cleared a profit of $80. Moreover, the intense selling experience had bolstered George's confidence. He was emboldened by what brother Charles had said upon seeing that no copies of *Banking* remained in his room: "You're quite a salesman, Little Brother."

At school the next year, George—now a minor celebrity—was elected president of the senior class. He published a second game called *Baker's Dozen* and then added a third, *Famous Men,* which had been invented by one of his teachers, Mr. Morrison. These games were not as successful as *Banking,* in part because George tried to sell them only in his spare time, but they hinted that there might be more than one game within George Parker.

Upon graduation, he turned down an opportunity to go to college in order to pursue what he and his family thought was his true calling: journalism. George knew he had a knack for writing. He had excelled at English, and he found it a joy to reduce the complexity of a game's rules to a few chosen words that almost everyone could understand. His oldest brother Edward, eleven years his senior and already an editor at Boston's *Commercial Bulletin,* had proven how rewarding a career in the newspaper business could be.

Sarah Parker was pleased when her youngest son was also hired by the *Commercial Bulletin* as a cub editor at a salary of $3 per week. On weekends, George continued to try to sell his remaining inventory of *Baker's Dozen* and *Famous Men.* But at this point, a career in the games business seemed unlikely. He wrote to his friends of how much he liked his job, observing and rubbing shoulders with "important men" people such as Curtis Guild, Jr., scion of the family that owned the *Commercial Bulletin* and a man destined to sit in the governor's office; Gaylan Stone, a powerful banker; Bill McNeary, a ward politician. As 1885 began, however, George's health and enthusiasm waned. He became bedridden with a bronchial condition that caused him to miss work. In June, his family physician, Dr. Sullivan, ordered him to quit his job and recover at home.

His mother, suffering from infirmities of her own, finally sold (at a loss) the big home in Medford. Like George, she disliked the place, despite its gardens, orchard, carriage house, and barn. Both Parkers would recover in a town they loved—Salem—after moving to a much smaller home at 8 Mall Street, without George's aunt and uncle.

The George S. Parker Company

During his recuperation, George decided to try the games business one more time. He added some new titles, published his first catalog (four pages, unillustrated), and began to earn a few dollars' profit each week.[6] Restless and annoyed by the challenge of making a living with so few products, he realized his business would only grow slowly unless, and until, he had a much broader line. From this frustration came inspiration. He packed his bag and headed to New York City (his mother had grown up on Long Island), where a cousin provided lodging. There, he struck a deal with a firm called E. I. Horsman, a local toy wholesaler, to sell their games throughout New England. The proposition suited Horsman as well as it did George.

The success of this venture made George hesitate when a new offer came from the *Commercial Bulletin*. If he returned to work, the amazing sum of $12 a week would be his. When he declined, a competitive paper

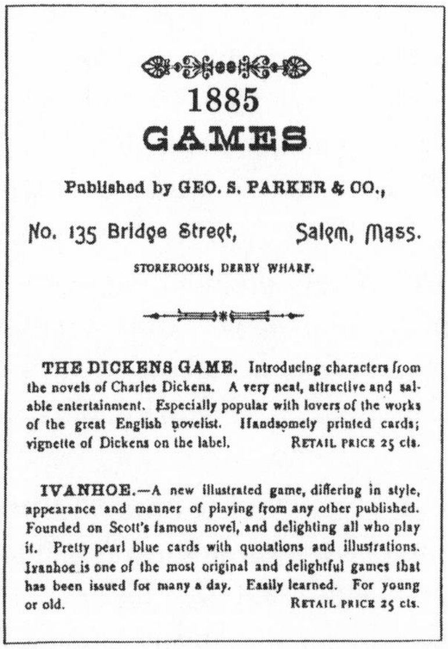

1885

GAMES

Published by GEO. S. PARKER & CO.,

No. 135 Bridge Street,   Salem, Mass.

STOREROOMS, DERBY WHARF.

THE DICKENS GAME. Introducing characters from the novels of Charles Dickens. A very neat, attractive and salable entertainment. Especially popular with lovers of the works of the great English novelist. Handsomely printed cards; vignette of Dickens on the label.   RETAIL PRICE 25 cts.

IVANHOE.—A new illustrated game, differing in style, appearance and manner of playing from any other published. Founded on Scott's famous novel, and delighting all who play it. Pretty pearl blue cards with quotations and illustrations. Ivanhoe is one of the most original and delightful games that has been issued for many a day. Easily learned. For young or old.   RETAIL PRICE 25 cts.

FIGURE 1-2
Parker Brothers First Catalog

Cover of first Parker four-page catalog, 1885.

offered him $16 a week—more than he was making by selling games. And with his mother's health again on the decline, he was contributing to her support as well as taking care of his own needs. What to do? Hunched over a table in Charles's apartment one night, he asked for his brother's advice. After waxing grandiose about the importance of satisfaction in a man's career, he asked George which career choice would satisfy his soul. The answer? Games.

George redoubled his efforts. By Christmas of 1886, he had the makings of a business. But he was again thwarted by the difficulty of growing it without capital and without leverage against established competitors. His little game company was insignificant compared to the Milton Bradley Company (at the time, primarily a maker of educational products) or Selchow & Righter, toy jobber and the maker of *Parcheesi*. And it was but an annoyance to the biggest, most powerful game maker of the day—the great New York firm of McLoughlin Brothers, headquartered on glittering Broadway. This publisher had covered the country with its children's color storybooks and broad line of games. It was as close to a household brand as any in the nation's embryonic toy and game industry.[7]

George contemplated how he could gain a foothold solid enough to start building a business, one that would last as long as he had the will to continue it. In June 1887, George Parker made his "first coup," as he would later characterize it. He returned to New York, this time to meet with Jasperate Singer, whose firm was a substantial competitor of McLoughlin Brothers. Singer was a born businessman and had enjoyed quite a bit of success before entering the games business in 1883, the same year that George had invented *Banking*. His financial resources had enabled him to build up a broad line of "ABC" blocks, sliced picture puzzles (cut into rectangular pieces, without interlocks), and games. On the night before his meeting with Jasper Singer, George again stayed with a cousin of his mother, Daniel Hegeman, in Queens and paced the floor, mentally rehearsing his next move. Confident, he couldn't wait to go to Manhattan in the morning.

Singer, bright and progressive, met George in his den on Thirty-first Street at nine o'clock in the morning. He later admitted to being amused by the young man's eagerness, but also swayed by his logic. Tall, thin, and pale, George looked much younger than his age. Towering and portly, Singer looked every bit of his fifty-odd years. While tempted to dismiss this baby-faced young man, he instead found himself impressed by the conviction written on the young man's face and in his blue eyes. The proposal was this: George Parker would buy items of interest from the Singer line and replace the firm's New England sales agent. In return, Singer would have selling rights to Parker games in the Mid-Atlantic states. In a few hours, the deal was hammered out. George carefully avoided disclosing how paper-thin his finances were; Singer didn't broach the topic. George's strategy had worked; he had persuaded the older, wiser man through words and gestures that his business was solid and much larger than it really was.

George couldn't wait to tell his mother the good news. He sent her a telegram: "Have closed an important deal which might mean a profit of $2,000 a year." George finished his other business in New York and then rushed, via horse-drawn omnibus, to see the marvel of the day—the Brooklyn Bridge, dedicated in 1883 by President Chester Arthur and former President Grover Cleveland. Next, he traveled to Battery Park to gaze across the harbor at the shroud covering the Statue of Liberty, scheduled to be unveiled in October.[8]

Once back home, he prepared his mother's basement for the inventory, already on its way from Singer. He quickly organized a selling tour of the largest cities of New England. The orders he received were "record-breaking," including a $350 order from a store in Fitchburg, Massachusetts.

Given the cash flow from the tour, he rented a storefront in the heart of Salem and hired his first employee. The store was in the Franklin Building (where the venerable Hawthorne Hotel now stands) and the employee was fifteen-year-old Harry Phillips, who would become a key salesman for decades. (George's Red Room chum, Joseph Dyer, would become its second employee.) The store rented for $12.50 a month; George and Harry soon had its shelves lined with Singer and Horsman items, their own, and a few other games they felt had merit. This particular address had seen failure after retail failure. A lady walking by several months later was overheard to say to her friend, "Well, he's stayed there longer than anyone else so far!"

Thanks to the Singer line, revenues far exceeded expenses, but the ensuing paperwork overwhelmed the twenty-year-old George. Charles

Parker, his business mentor, began to split his spare time between outings in Salem with his lady friend, Abigail Streeter, and evenings spent organizing his younger brother's records under a lamp in the back room of George's store.

In the fall of 1887, while George was in Vermont on a sales trip, his mother became seriously ill, her battle with rheumatism nearing its end. George rushed home. Sarah Parker clung to life for a few days and then passed away. The blow was a terrible one for all three brothers. George became "ill and broken," as the poor results of his next sales trip to Maine would attest. But with the steady comfort and prodding of Charles, he shook off his listlessness and regained his resolve.

George looked back on the first five years of the George S. Parker Company and took stock of the opportunity he had created with hard work and risk taking. How could he capitalize on this opportunity? How could he avoid a major misstep that might ruin the fruits of his labor? Without the benefit of a college education, where would he find the right principles to steer him through uncharted waters?

Instinctively, he drew a parallel between the rules needed for each game he published and the "rules" of successful commerce. Business was like a game—just as unpredictable in its outcome, but more often not fairly determined by good moves and bad moves. A consummate game player in the best sense of the term, George began to codify a set of guiding principles, one by one, as he discerned them. He came to see a relationship between the *strategies* that guided success in parlor games and the *principles* that enhanced success in the "game" of business. The first principle gleaned was, perhaps, the most important: He needed a goal. Building a business meant more than earning a living. His aim became to build the best game company in the nation.

As his business experience mounted, he came to believe in eleven more principles. He became convinced that, when applied faithfully, these twelve principles led to success in business. And he would instill these tenets in his successors.[9]

1. Know your goal and reach for it.
2. Find "winning moves."
3. Play by the rules but capitalize on them.
4. Learn from failure; build upon success.

5. When faced with a choice, make the move with the most potential benefit versus risk.
6. When luck runs against you, hold emotion in check and set up for your next advance.
7. Never hesitate and give your opponents a second chance.
8. Seek help if the game threatens to overwhelm you.
9. Bet heavily when the odds are long in your favor.
10. If opportunity narrows, focus on your strengths.
11. Be a gracious winner or loser. Don't be petty. Share what you learn.
12. Ignore principles 1 to 11 at your peril!

Parker Brothers Is Born

By this time, 1888, George Parker accepted where his talents lay: inventing, developing, and selling. He also knew his weakness: dealing with the production and financial aspects of his firm, which he regarded as necessary evils. By contrast, his brother Charles had a talent for keeping the wheels of a business turning smoothly. In his spare time, Charles Hanford Parker shored up George's weak points; helped with bookkeeping, account collecting, and the purchase of new inventory; and arranged for shipment of goods (from storage space he provided for George at his business on Derby Wharf). What Charles lacked was a talent for inventing (although he was always willing to test George's latest idea and offer suggestions). A natural harmony existed among the brothers' skills.[10]

In the spring of 1888, George made Charles an offer: Join me full time, we'll form a partnership, and we'll name it Parker Brothers. Charles, a poised and confident man, was now engaged to Abigail Streeter, which furthered George's perception of him as a man whose personal maturity rivaled that of older brother Edward (happily married and a successful newspaper editor in Boston). Charles had also proven his professional mettle. He was now a full partner in the firm of Smith & Parker, located on Derby Wharf in the heart of Salem's southern harbor. Originally just coopers, the company had successfully expanded into coal and oil wholesaling and fueled Salem's commerce. Charles handled the accounting, billing, and shipping. His partner, Winchester Smith, handled the sales and service to their mercantile clientele.[11]

To accept George's offer would mean that Charles would be accepting lower income, a delay in his marriage until 1889, the awkward position of taking orders from his younger brother, and the anguish of undoing the partnership with a close friend. But two emotional factors offset reason. The first was the extraordinary nature of the Parker Brothers firm he would help to build, especially compared to the ordinary nature of Smith & Parker. The second was George's unrelenting, almost mesmerizing power of persuasion. George cleverly reminded his brother of his own advice. Wasn't a man's career satisfaction more important than money?

One other factor convinced Charles that he must say yes. Call it a deep sense of family obligation. Charles knew that, for all of George's creative brilliance, his younger brother could not run a sound business without him. Two Parkers against the world could succeed. One could not. They shook hands. Charles became a minority owner, and the Parker Brothers Company was born.

Publishers of Games

George had invented many games since 1883, but the one he loved best was a game of strategy he named *Chivalry*. A cross between chess and checkers, it pitted two players in a head-to-head battle of pieces representing knights and men placed in rows on a gridlike board. The object was to break through the opponent's battle line and occupy his castle,

FIGURE 1-3
Chivalry

George Parker's favorite creation, 1887.

located several spaces in the rear. George had brought *Chivalry* to market in 1887 but had been disappointed by its anemic sales. He rationalized that the game was "too skillful and scientific for the general public."

Charles encouraged him to look beyond this minor failure to find the key to major success. They needed a credo. Exactly what type of games would succeed? Which games would sell in quantity? What qualities would inspire a customer to buy a Parker Brothers game?

They came to several conclusions. A customer—at any store, in any city—must be attracted by the intriguing name and colorful artwork on the cover of every Parker Brothers product. Each game must each have an exciting, relevant theme and be easy enough for most people to understand. Finally, each game should be so sturdy that it could be played time and time again, without wearing out.

To address these needs, George combined his editorial talent with his knack for designing games. He came to see his role as that of a great editor who molded to perfection the "manuscripts" of other inventors in order to build his line. Henceforth, he would invent on his own only when opportunistic.

Simultaneously, the salesman within George Parker would lure buyers by emphasizing both the durability of his games and the "excellence of their playing qualities" over the competition's, especially McLoughlin Brothers. To support George's claims, Charles sought out vendors who, through proper physical construction, made games that would last and that were satisfying to handle.

"Make it last" became the creed of Parker Brothers. George etched these words into the fabric of his being.[12] Belief in enduring value anchored the simple philosophy by which he approached life as well as business. He wanted his family to endure along with his products; he wanted the business to succeed for the benefit of future generations of Parkers.

It was time to extend this philosophy into the nation's heartland. With Charles minding the store and Harry Phillips gathering regional sales, George packed his trunk and set off on his longest train trip yet—to Chicago and points in between. The great Marshall Field Company placed a sizable order and became a loyal purchaser of Parker Brothers games for decades to come. The revenue gained from this trip convinced the brothers that there were only two barriers in the path of rapid growth: the challenge of finding and selling to every store that stocked games for the nation's 60 million citizens living in its thirty-nine states (six more would be added by 1890), and money for more inventory and better facilities.[13]

They could conquer the former with time; the latter they could not. Neither brother had money to spare. Every hard-earned cent was already invested in the business. With no other reasonable alternative, they agreed to seek out "special partners" to provide capital to fund the growth they were convinced awaited their firm. They persuaded two local businessmen, Andrew W. Rogers and Sidney W. Winslow, to bankroll them. (Winslow, as a boy, had learned shoe making at the hands of his father; by 1888, he was a tycoon in the field of shoe making equipment. His machines had reduced the cost of labor to make a good pair of shoes from $5 to just seventy-five cents and eventually resulted in the huge United Shoe Machinery Company, located in the adjoining town of Beverly, Massachusetts. It was to be his brainchild in the coming decade.[14]) Each special partner initially loaned the partnership $2,000. To secure these loans, George and Charles had to agree to cap their salaries and offer a share of their profits.[15]

Charles immediately set out to improve profitability. He calculated that the firm could save substantial money by buying components and assembling finished games under its own roof. To do so, they would need more space. The Franklin Building held retail stores, not workshops. Parker Brothers would have to relocate. The brothers leased space from the Harris family—grocers to the city of Salem—in an old laundry building on Bridge Street, which abutted Mall Street, where George still lived. The clapboard-encased building was three stories tall and about one hundred feet by sixty feet on each floor. It stood a few hundred feet from the North River and the railroad tracks of the Boston & Maine. Swampy land sloped behind the building. Charles realized that this was actually a blessing because it was likely to remain vacant for a long time, and therefore be available for expansion. The building on Bridge Street had a small loading dock, which was also attractive to Charles because it would speed up shipping and receiving. Soon, four hired laborers were assembling, packaging, and shipping games in the firm's new building.

Occupying the bottom floor in the back was a blacksmith and also a wheelwright who repaired the wheels for the town's countless horse-drawn buggies. The blacksmith made an indelible impression on George that summer. With his second-floor window open, George could hear the smithy's deep, booming voice recite excerpts from the plays of Shakespeare and, as George put it, other "high-flown artists of that time." The employees of Parker Brothers listened while they worked. George later remarked that they had radio at Parker Brothers before there was such a thing.

George and Charles then seized another opportunity. The W. & S. B. Ives Company of Salem was virtually extinct when the final Ives brother died in 1888. The brothers purchased its games, including rights to the *Mansion of Happiness*. Invented in 1830 by a Miss Abbott—a clergyman's daughter and Salem native who had also invented the famous set-forming card game *Authors*—the *Mansion of Happiness* was the progenitor of American board games. In keeping with his view of himself as more publisher than inventor, George wanted the new *Mansion of Happiness* to be faithful to the original in every way, except its packaging. In particular, he insisted its board be hand-colored, as the Ives version had been. George proposed a primitive production line to color the new game boards. Charles purchased game board labels (the paper sheets that depicted the game's track of spaces) with illustrations, printed with just their black outlines. Several women hired for the assignment lined up along a table, each with a small brush and a pot of paint. Following a guide, a painter would add her color to each appropriate illustration on the label and pass it along to the next woman. The result was a complete, multicolored game board. *The Mansion of Happiness* would endure in Parker Brothers' catalog for thirty years.

The new, better-capitalized Parker Brothers published bigger, more impressive games. It frequently mounted a game board's label (printed playing surface) inside a sturdy box bottom to avoid the need for a more expensive folding board. This made some games immense in size. The box for one of these, *The United States Game* (originally called "Across the Continent"), was over three feet long! With the instincts of a newspaper publisher, Parker Brothers exploited the excitement for the country's most important and fastest means of travel—the railroad. In 1840, less than three thousand miles of tracks served the Atlantic seacoast. By the late 1880s, the United States was crisscrossed by tens of thousands of miles of railroad tracks and both coasts were linked.[16] Ordinary people could travel by rail and trolley from small towns in the United States to any other town or city. Railroads allowed George and his assistants to visit every important city in the nation and eventually to complete their own coast-to-coast network of retail stores and wholesaler distributors. George's travels inspired the *United States Game,* which pitted players in a race from coast to coast. The rail lines on the board connected cities nationwide, large and small, enabling a player to span the country by many different routes and thus counter his opponents' itineraries.

Innocence Abroad

With its newfound reach, Parker Brothers needed to publish games with wider appeal. Many of Parker Brothers' early games had only regional appeal—such as *Ye Yankee Peddler,* the Yale-Harvard game, and *Billy Bumps' Visit to Boston.*[17] In 1887, George had noticed that the country was in love with the young heroes found within the pages of juvenile novels written by Unitarian minister Horatio Alger—young men who conquered all in their rise from obscurity. Over 20 million of his books were sold during his lifetime. The *Office Boy Game* transferred Alger's rags-to-riches theme to the game board, using stories of boys who overcome obstacles and rise from the bottom to the top of a big company. In a clever twist on the *Mansion of Happiness,* George designed a honeycomb-patterned board whose outer spaces denoted entry-level positions in a company ("office boy," "porter," "stock boy") and whose large innermost space was "Head of the Firm." Along the way, one hoped his wooden token would avoid being set back by spaces marked "careless," "inattentive," and "dishonest," while steering toward "capable," "earnest," and "ambitious" and the job promotions these qualities brought into range.

The success of the *Office Boy Game* sent a clear signal to George: The right book could be the basis for a game capable of selling tens of thousands of copies. In 1889, it arrived.

A Mrs. Shephard submitted a game to Parker Brothers that George felt had immense appeal. It was named *Innocence Abroad,* a takeoff on Mark Twain's perennial bestseller *The Innocents Abroad* (first published in 1869). Embraced by the masses, the irreverent author's book consisted of humorous letters to the San Francisco newspaper, the *Alta California*, that had sponsored his participation in the nation's first pleasure cruise—a trip to the great cities of Europe and the Holy Land. Six hundred fifty pages long and filled with engravings, it invited Americans aboard the *Quaker City* to "travel" with Twain every league of the way.

Flush with success, in the fall of 1890 George decided to try something never done before in the field of games. He purchased newspaper ads for *Innocence Abroad.* Oldest brother Edward, still ensconced in the newspaper business, helped George place ads in Boston and New York papers. The ads worked. Stores in both cities reported brisk sales well before Christmas and placed several reorders. This promotional victory increased Parker Brothers' retailer loyalty and stores' desire to support next year's advertised hit. (Print advertising would become a mainstay of Parker Brothers' annual plans for decades to come.)

In 1869, *The Innocents Abroad* had made Mark Twain a household name. Twenty years later, *Innocence Abroad* did much the same for the brothers Parker. *Innocence Abroad* is the first game known to be licensed by Parker Brothers for publication. George's editorial skill polished Mrs. Shephard's game into a smooth-playing, episodic experience. Its folding game board beautifully depicted a body of water and a land beyond. Players' tokens journeyed across the water to their distant destination, incurring expenses and mishaps on the way. George wrote in the company catalog, "INNOCENCE ABROAD is, to a certain degree instructive, but its principal ingredient is PURE FUN."[18] It retailed for $1.25, a lot for a game (about $25 today).[19]

Bolstered by their share of the profits, Rogers and Winslow renewed their loans, and would do so annually for many years to come.[20]

Parker Brothers Abroad

With finances solid, the brothers needed more laborers. Among those hired was a young boy who first showed up wearing knee breeches, like most other twelve-year-old boys of his day. He was told to go home, that he was too young for consideration. When hiring day arrived the following week, a short young man showed up wearing trousers, his hair cut and neatly combed, his face brimming with determination. He was accepted and entered the Parker Brothers work force that same day as a picker and packer in the shipping department. Henry Fitzpatrick's makeover had fooled the foreman. No matter; Henry's work ethic and love of his job made the foreman look wise in the light of history. Over fifty-eight years, he would rise in the firm and stay longer than any other employee, save George Parker.[21]

With the work force growing in size and capability, George and Harry Phillips worked the rails and added new cities to the firm's base of distribution, permitting steady expansion of their product line. In 1893, two audacious moves were undertaken, despite a temporary setback to the firm caused by the nation's financial panic that year.

First, the brothers took a chance and rented exhibition space at the magnificent Chicago Columbian Exposition, located in what became Jackson Park on the city's South Side. This was a world's fair of ideas, culture, and products. It celebrated the discovery of America by Columbus four hundred years earlier and would inspire the Columbus Day holiday.[22] To the brothers' pleasure, they won a gold medal for their games, which was proudly touted for years on the cover of their annual catalog.

Second, George sent his "remarkable young salesman," Harry Phillips, to London. Parker knew, from experience, that many popular toys and "standard" games (whist, halma, and reversi, for example) had originated in Europe, especially in England. George also reasoned that if European toys and games enjoyed success in the U.S. market, why wouldn't U.S. games sell equally well over there? Parker Brothers was located close to Boston, with ready access to the cargo ships that plied the seas. No other U.S. game company had capitalized on this export-import opportunity. Harry Phillips's mission became twofold: Make deals with the great merchant stores of London to import Parker Brothers games, and scoop the selling rights for the best of England's new games. Victorian London was the world's largest city. Four million people lived within its boundaries. It was also the richest city in the world, the heart of global commerce. Twenty thousand vessels docked at the port of London each year.[23] One of them carried Harry Phillips. He stayed two weeks and returned with encouraging stories about London's vibrant game market and sophisticated consumers. More important, his briefcase was filled with orders for Parker games and his trunk packed with samples of promising new English games.

With the foundation laid down by Phillips, in 1895 George made the first of many ocean voyages to London. He stayed ten weeks, traveled to several cities, and established distribution in every one. Despite being treated like a lower-class foreign vendor, which class-conscious English protocol required (but which would perpetually infuriate him), Parker formed budding relationships that would strengthen as his business grew, and new games developed on both sides of the Atlantic.

All in the Family

Twenty-nine years old and finally enjoying a sense of financial security, George found himself in love with twenty-one-year old Grace Mann. Born in Salem but raised in Chicago, Mann had recently returned to the small city of her birth. In the early 1890s, she came to work as a secretary at Parker Brothers.[24] A diminutive young lady, Grace was also bright, confident, and stylish. She soon had the boss's complete attention. After a proper courtship—and a sleepless pre-wedding night—George married Grace in Boston on Monday morning, June 15, 1896; the couple then promptly left for the Waldorf Hotel in New York. From there, they sailed on the *Havel* to London. George wrote that his spirits were as high as the gulls gliding in the sky above the waves. Their combined honeymoon/business trip lasted ten weeks.[25] Grace left the firm and gave birth to a son, Bradstreet, ten months later.

In the summer of 1897, when George made another sales trip to the United Kingdom, he found himself holding many a luncheon meeting in a pub named the Cheshire Cheese, located in an alley off of Fleet Street near St. Paul's Cathedral. The publishing center of London was situated in the City district near Fleet Street. Although the emotional side of George Parker was carefully hidden at work, he was often deeply struck by what he felt and saw in his travels. Among the many poems he penned while away from home was a long one about his favorite eatery, which began:

> *There's a cozy old tavern just off the street,*
> *Through an ancient arched alley that runs from the Fleet.*
> *When just as you enter, your eyes you may fill*
> *With a glimpse of St. Paul's over Ludgate Hill.*
> *But ere entering, thoughtfully pause if you please,*
> *For you stand at the sign of the Old Cheshire Cheese.*[26]

The pub framed George's poem and displayed it proudly until the building was bombed during World War II.

While Grace and George were starting their family, Charles and Abigail were experiencing heartache in theirs. Abigail gave birth to a daughter, Lois, in 1891, but the tiny girl died within months. Daughter Mary, born in 1892, was a healthy child, but their son Bradford died shortly after his birth in 1894. Charles and Abigail drew closer through the family hardship to Edward Parker, now forty years old, and his wife Laura.[27]

More and more, Charles began to discuss the games business with Edward and seek his advice. Good-natured, clear-headed, and unpretentious, Edward Hegeman Parker had wed Laura Foster in 1879. Foster, their only child, was born in 1888. Edward had established himself as a competent businessman in his field with a knack for scheduling and production within the brutal deadlines and intricate literary demands of the newspaper business. While not a formal member of the company, the eldest Parker was helping to build a structure atop the solid foundation set by his younger brothers (he had advised George on how to make use of advertising, for example). Agreeing to stretch their finances, George and Charles soon asked Edward to become a partner. In 1898, he gave up his long career in journalism to become an entrepreneur, and purchased a minority share of the firm. It would now be one Parker for all, all for one.[28]

An outsider, upon seeing the three tall brothers walking together on Washington Street in Salem, might assume that either Charles or Edward was the head of the firm. They resembled each other. Each strode with the easy confidence of a born leader, especially Charles, whose sturdy jaw and impassive features evoked immediate respect. Despite his height of six feet, George's face bespoke his youth, and his flared nostrils immediately differentiated him from the straight-nosed countenance of his brothers. He tended to swing his arms as he walked, as if to suggest his importance, but that mannerism further belied his youth.[29]

Charles had grown a mustache and beard. George, acting on a whimsical suggestion by an associate, decided to do likewise. He came to relish the feeling of respect his facial hair engendered and decided his mustache and beard were here to stay. (Charles was to shave his.) In time, George's full beard was to be neatly trimmed into a Vandyke (a short beard that came to a point) which he would wear for the remainder of his life. George also observed and copied the attitude and clothing of the rich, whom he aspired to join. He began to develop a proud manner and to wear expensive wool suits no matter what the occasion, be it work or play. While devoted to his workers and customers, he grew convinced that a leader must stand aloof, above his followers, and maintain a formal bearing.[30]

From $500 in 1883, annual sales grew to $40,000 by 1890 and rose to $110,000 in 1898.[31] In fifteen years, George S. Parker's company had moved from the basement of his mother's home to a storefront in downtown Salem to a three-story industrial building brimming with activity.

Chapter Two

Learning the Game

1898–1910

O NE OF GEORGE PARKER'S FIRST WINNING MOVES
had been the opening of trade with his English counterparts.
Now he began to exploit this gambit, as his second principle
compelled.

Winks and Balloons

When word reached him of the success of a funny little flicking game
being played everywhere in Queen Victoria's country, he grabbed the
U.S. rights. The game was called the *New Round Game of Tiddledy Winks*
and was sold by the firm of J. Jacques and Son. It consisted of a small pot,
made of wood or glass, and circular counters made of bone. The aim was
to flick each smaller "wink" into the pot by pressing on its edge with a
larger counter ("tiddledy" or "shooter"). With a bit of skill and dexterity,
even a child could learn to launch the little winks toward the pot from
several feet away.

The game became one of the first novelty activities to sweep the country. Parker Brothers immediately applied for a U.S. trademark for the
name *Tiddledy Winks*. Fourteen editions appeared in the following year's
Parker Brothers catalog, with prices ranging from twenty-five cents to $1.
George wrote proudly of the "continuous hold" the game had on "little
ones."[1] Protecting his hold on its rights was another matter. The trademark did not clear, being deemed generic. During the next few years,
while Parker Brothers' winks were being flicked everywhere in the nation and "made a considerable sum," Parker Brothers had to share its

rewards with many other makers that honed in on the vogue for *Tiddledy Winks*. Milton Bradley, Selchow & Righter, McLoughlin Brothers, and several smaller firms quickly marketed their own versions of the game that George had purchased in England.[2]

The next game George acquired in London was an exclusive. He returned there in 1897 and met with former acquaintances, the Roberts brothers. They were marketing a lighthearted indoor action game named *Pillow-Dex* that was on the verge of sweeping English society. Parker Brothers purchased the U.S. rights and this time succeeded in securing a U.S. trademark. *Pillow-Dex* was an indoor "ball" game. It consisted of a balloon and a string line that was stretched across the center of any table or laid across the floor. Players attempted to bat the balloon back and forth with the backs of their hands to keep it in the air, not allowing it to touch the surface on their side of the line. The game quickly became a rage. Hundreds of thousands were sold, most at twenty-five cents. (A deluxe version in a wooden box cost $1.)

Americans everywhere invited friends to *Pillow-Dex* parties. This gave the Parker brothers the idea of paying New York socialites to endorse

FIGURE 2-1
Tiddledy Winks

One of Parker Brothers' fourteen Tiddledy Winks *sets, 1890s.*

FIGURE 2-2
Pillow-Dex

Pillow Dex—*an indoor fad that swept the nation in 1897.*

Pillow-Dex in local print advertising. The game also offered an excuse for proper young women (the elegant Gibson girls image was all the rage) and their ever-so-proper gentlemen escorts to let down their hair and flaunt social etiquette by flailing wildly at the airborne balloon. The *Pillow-Dex* trademark proved to be sound and Parker Brothers enjoyed sales success with this novelty for two decades.[3]

The London outreach had provided two winning moves for George, and another was soon to follow. Before this occurred, he exploited a new opportunity at home.

War and Business

In 1898, a series of events occurred that generated such national pride, Parker Brothers felt compelled to feed that pride or risk being called unpatriotic. Fanned by the so-called Yellow Press (named after the non-objective, florid reporting that appealed to reader's emotions), certain New York papers stirred enough passion to force Congress to declare war on Spain on April 25. The Spanish colonial government had ruthlessly dealt with Cuban rebels. The explosion of the U.S. battleship

Maine in Havana harbor was thought to be a treacherous act by the Spaniards, rather than an accident. The country wanted to save the Cubans, and it wanted revenge on the Spaniards. Commodore George Dewey's fleet sank the Spanish fleet in Manila harbor that May. Spanish Guam and unclaimed Wake Island were seized. Congress annexed the Hawaiian Islands. Then, in less than four hours, Commodore Winfield Schley sank the Spanish ships hiding in Santiago harbor, Cuba. Following the heroics of Teddy Roosevelt and his Rough Riders, the Spanish garrisons on the island surrendered on July 17, 1898. The U.S. army conquered the Philippines in August. In December, a peace treaty was signed that ended the "splendid little war." The treaty granted the United States Puerto Rico and all of its conquests except Cuba, which would soon be independent. The mood in the country was ebullient, to say the least.[4]

Parker Brothers published five war games before the war began and four during the conflict, including *War in Cuba*, *The Siege of Havana*, *The Battle of Manila*, and *The Philippine War*. All made money and cemented the identity of Parker Brothers as "America's" game company. Many of these war games were simple target-shooting games. Die-cut soldiers on bases were knocked over with wooden "bullets" fired from spring-loaded, handheld "cannons." This concept would be used time and again over the next two decades. For example, England's trouble with the Boers of South Africa a few years later inspired two more Parker Brothers target-shooting games (but little in the way of sales).[5]

George Parker viewed both war and business as ideal themes for games. He saw the obstacles confronting a military leader or business-man as akin to the challenges faced by a game player. The *Office Boy Game* was still in the company's line in 1896 when a twenty-year-old business school graduate named Albert Richardson joined the firm as a real office boy. He learned the art of selling by accompanying his boss on trips to New York and beyond. (It was typical for George to record among his trip expenses lodging, lunch, dinner, cigars, cars, and "Albert."[6]) Richardson would apply well the lessons he learned at George Parker's side. He was destined to have a forty-two-year career as a traveling company salesman, in the United States and abroad. When not on the road, he helped George in the development of new games. His loyalty, like that of many Parker Brothers employees, was ironclad. As he helped the firm's sales grow to new records, Richardson was quietly rewarded by George (with cash and, eventually, with shares of the firm's preferred stock).[7] Employees like Richardson enjoyed their jobs at Parker Brothers, which provided more satisfaction than making shoes, spinning cotton, or forming electrical filaments—as their friends did at other big employers in the city of Salem, such as the Naumkeag Cotton Mills and Sylvania Electric.

Salem

Salem, Massachusetts, had been the nation's sixth-largest city during the American Revolution and its most important port. George Washington came to Salem after the war to thank its citizens for their vital support. Many merchant sailors from Salem roamed the seas to secure treasures—from both the savage and the civilized—and bring them back to a young and growing nation.[8] On the opposite side of the globe, natives of what is now Malaysia asked traders from other U.S. ports if the United States was anywhere near Salem.[9] Two great museums (the Essex Institute and the Peabody Museum) displayed the artifacts these sailors brought back from China, Africa, and the American West. When these seamen and their captains returned home, they were flush with cash and wanted to enjoy themselves.[10]

Despite its great role in commerce, the city would be forever known as the Witch City because of the trials held in Salem in 1692. But it was also home to great writers and scientists, such as Nathaniel Hawthorne (born "Hathorne")—author of *The House of the Seven Gables*—and Nathaniel Bowditch, who revolutionized celestial navigation for sailors around the world. In 1877, Alexander Graham Bell demonstrated first to the Salem public a new invention called the "telephone."

The merchant shipping industry had disappeared before George Parker graduated from high school. Two wars and the European embargo enforced by Thomas Jefferson from 1807 to 1809 had withered the canvas fleet. When steam power transformed the size and power of ships, it was neighboring Boston that provided the depth of harbor they needed. By the 1890s, Salem was just another small city.[11] But the stories of its maritime glory loomed in George's mind. Salem, to him, was a community built on the backs of the merchant captains whose mansions still lined Chestnut Street (where he hoped to live someday). They had been masters of the sea. He saw himself carrying on their tradition by becoming a master of commerce on land.[12]

While the Parkers were the captains, many other Salem families supplied the "crew" who fabricated, assembled, packed, and shipped the company's games. From the early 1890s onward, a bond developed between Salem and its game company. The success and family atmosphere of the firm gave rise to a feeling of security for its workers. When an opening arose, it was not uncommon for a father to encourage a son, or an uncle, or an aunt to join the company. Even if the pay wasn't exceptional, it became a source of pride to say, "I work for Parker Brothers." Charles and Edward Parker made a practice of touring the factory each morning and greeting each worker by name. George was more distant, but the workers respected his commitment and talent as the unquestioned source of the firm's growth—and their well-being. The men and women of Parker Brothers were inspired by the way the Parkers approached their jobs and came to embrace a code of devotion that would one day be nicknamed "Parkerized." It stood for a commitment to produce quality products, to take pride in working for the firm, and to maintain a good attitude toward fellow workers and management. It furthered the sense of family within the clapboard walls on Bridge Street.

George's own family grew again in 1900 when Grace gave birth to a second son, Richard. George soon purchased a spacious home on Lafayette Street, a streetcar's journey from Bridge Street near the south end of Salem. He also purchased a horse and a surrey and, from time to time, took his family on excursions through the surrounding towns on Boston's North Shore.[13]

By 1900, annual sales had reached $140,000.[14] McLoughlin Brothers was still the country's biggest game company, but Parker Brothers was perceived to be a strong number two, in large part because of the visibility its newspaper advertising afforded in New York.[15] After the turn of the century, the brothers' only obstacle seemed to be their dependence on funding from their "special partners," and there were more of them now than just Rogers and Winslow. So voracious was their appetite for profit sharing that pressure was brought to bear on George to dismiss Edward to save his $1,500 annual salary. (Edward's pleasant personality made him an easier target than the more assertive Charles.) In February

1901, George took a stand. He argued that Edward was "the safeguard and watchdog of the business." George felt that he was reliable to a fault; the firm, and its profits, would suffer mightily if he were cut. George won this battle, but only after agreeing to roll back Edward's salary. Resentment grew among the brothers because of the limits placed on their salaries to bolster the profit share pledged to their financiers. The brothers vowed to find the means to pay off their creditors and eliminate them from the business as soon as possible. The means would have to be another national hit, and the careful mothering of the cash this game would generate.

Incorporation and a New Hit

On December 12, 1901, Parker Brothers incorporated. Papers were filed in Maine because this state had more benign regulations than did Massachusetts. George became president. Charles was confirmed as vice president and Edward as treasurer. Their capital stock consisted of two thousand shares at $100 each. Half of the shares were common—which the brothers owned among them (mostly by George). The other one thousand were nonvoting preferred shares—mainly for future investors and for gifts to worthy employees.

Around the time of the firm's incorporation, a national event was hurting sales and weakening the company's finances. President William McKinley's assassination on September 6, 1901, sobered the country and shook its sense of prosperity. The markets went down and consumer spending nose-dived. Sales of Parker Brothers games dipped for the first time in its young history, then recovered after newly appointed President Theodore Roosevelt demonstrated continuity of McKinley's policies and retained his key advisers.[16] Following the recovery of consumer confidence, opportunity existed for Parker Brothers to market a game that would put smiles back on the faces of the nation's 78 million citizens.[17]

Ping-Pong

Principle had guided George Parker well in the past, and the experiences of recent years honed another for him. Principle 3 became "Play by the rules, but capitalize on them." He first learned this principle by watching the way his competitors capitalized on the *Tiddledy Winks* fad after he was unable to secure its trademark. Following that, they had ridden his coattails during the Spanish-American War frenzy, publishing games similar to his own. In contrast, *Pillow-Dex* was a Parker-only success, and it whetted his appetite for another scoop of the competition.

George sailed to London again in the spring of 1902. Accompanying him was a new assistant, Ellery Brown. Together they played, and fell in love with, an indoor ball-bouncing game. It was called *Ping-Pong*.

One of the most important trading partners for George in London was the firm of Hamley Brothers, England's largest dealer in sporting goods. Hamley had acquired an inventor's rights to the idea for an indoor table tennis game that employed a hollow ball made out of the world's first plastic resin, Celluloid, to be hit by small wooden paddles across a net stretched over a table. The English public took to it immediately and it was given a name based on the sounds made by the ball as it was struck back and forth: "ping" and "pong."[18]

Celluloid was a mixture of cellulose nitrate and camphor. It was invented by an American named John Hyatt as a possible substitute for ivory billiard balls, to help reduce the wanton killing of elephants. The first billiard balls were made with a hardened solution known as collodion, but they exploded when they hit each other. Hyatt solved this problem when he added camphor to the solution. The resulting material was still highly flammable and therefore had limited practical uses.[19] The manufacture of combs and piano keys were two. Thomas Edison capitalized on another application of Celluloid. With it, he made flexible reels of motion picture stock. Parker Brothers benefited from another use.

George Parker dutifully submitted the name *Ping-Pong* to the U.S. Trademark Office and Edward Parker established a woodworking department inside the factory to fabricate wooden paddles. Charles Parker found sources to supply the hollow plastic spheres. The standard edition of their game would cost consumers $1. By late 1902, the pleasant bouncing sound of the little Celluloid ball was heard daily in countless homes across the country. People played on their dining room tables, caring less about the rules George Parker so carefully codified and more about just having fun, whacking the ball off of mirrors and vases and pets, causing no injury, just startled surprise. For "naughty fun," one could strike a match and hold it to the ball and watch it disappear in a flash. George worked tirelessly to make *Ping-Pong* a legitimate sport. He helped organize the American Ping-Pong Association and sponsored tournaments using the standardized five-by-nine-foot table. The prize at these tournaments became known as the Parker Cup.[20]

Ping-Pong was a significant moneymaker for the company. In fact, the profits from this ball-bouncing indoor sport gave the brothers the leverage needed to make two crucial moves. First, they repurchased the debt owed their special partners, including Rogers and Winslow, and unlocked the shackles that bound their compensation and decision making. Next, they bought from the Harris family their building, the swampy ground behind it, and an adjacent building. The brothers hired carpenters to connect the two wooden buildings, forming a U.[21] At the base of the U a loading dock was constructed where the blacksmith had once maintained his shop (the massive wooden support columns inside had been polished smooth by the rubbing of countless horses over the years).[22] The activity on the docks, wafting through the open windows on hot summer days, was an unavoidable distraction for the office workers on the upper floors. And there was one other drawback—the floors of the two buildings, joined at the hip, did not align. Small steps and ramps had to be built at their junction on each floor.[23] However, within its 37,000 square feet of floor space, the thriving business had room to grow.

At home, George upgraded to a handsome new carriage and hired a devoted Parker Brothers employee, Mr. Getchell, to take him to and from work and to drive Grace and the boys around Salem. When George subsequently learned that Mr. Getchell had never seen New York City, he surprised him with an all-expense-paid vacation to the nation's largest city during his next business trip there. George took great delight in showing him a fine time. A few years later, when his service as a carriage driver was no longer needed, George rehired Getchell at Parker Brothers as a watchman.[24]

Toy Fair and the Flatiron

Two events coincided to expand Parker Brothers beyond Salem: the growing national reputation of the company and the construction of the country's first steel-beam skyscraper—the Flatiron Building in New York City. Parker Brothers opened a permanent sales office on its twelfth floor in 1903 and George sent Harry Phillips to manage it.[25] Located at

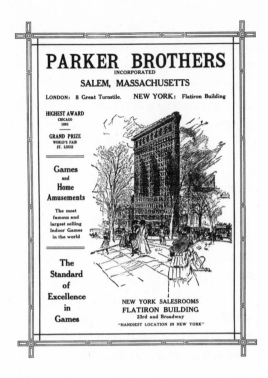

FIGURE 2-3

Parker Brothers, Inc.

Catalog inner cover, 1914.

the intersection of Twenty-third Street, Broadway, and Fifth Avenue, the Flatiron had opened in 1902. It was immensely tall for its day, 307 feet from top to sidewalk. New Yorkers nicknamed it "the Flatiron Building" because of its wedge shape and overhanging flat roof. The name stuck. The twenty-one-story building was the tallest skyscraper north of Wall Street for many years.[26] By opening their first New York sales office in the Flatiron, Parker Brothers gained a presence in the heart of the nation's emerging toy district. Toy companies were congregating here, opportunistically, to attract toy store buyers who passed through New York on their way to Europe to purchase European toys. Like Parker Brothers, many of the nation's leading toy and game manufacturers established a showroom, office, or even a small factory in this neighborhood. Proud of its strategic location, Parker Brothers featured the image of the Flatiron Building on the cover of several catalogs.

Also in 1903, the first New York Toy Fair was held in this district. The nation was beginning to accept the idea that play could be healthy, not merely a reflection of indolence. The toy industry had taken its first step toward permanence and respectability. Over a three-week period in the spring, buyers from many parts of the country came to visit each firm's showroom and make their purchases for the fall holiday season.[27] Similar fairs were soon organized in Chicago and San Francisco. These regional fairs were to lose importance in later years and the New York exhibition would become synonymous with "Toy Fair." Eventually, thousands of buyers would attend the annual event.[28]

Competition and Growth

Twenty years after his first sale of *Banking*, George Parker and his two brothers had firmly established the base of their business. Thanks to *Ping-Pong*, sales soared in 1902, reaching $346,000.[29] The brothers owned their factory, had repaid all their creditors, and had earned the loyalty of dozens of devoted workers plus hundreds of dealers across the country. They had gained sound experience to guide future decisions.

However, some of this experience had a bitter taste. By 1903, competitors rushed to market the generic product called table tennis.[30] The Table Tennis Association sprang up to rival the Ping-Pong Association, and George was frustrated once more in his effort to control a game fad he had sparked. He came to appreciate the difficulty of blunting competition in a free enterprise system.[31] Still, Parker Brothers was a remarkably competitive firm.

The firm's aggressiveness had markedly altered the playing field since George Parker started this business twenty years earlier. At the time, the dominant game makers included the powerful McLoughlin Brothers of New York; their pesky rival J. H. Singer; Selchow & Righter (the maker of *Parcheesi*); the educational supply company named after its founder, Milton Bradley; upstarts like the Embossing Company, makers of dominos and checkers; and the venerable Salem printing firm of W. & S. B. Ives. Powerful jobbers included Selchow & Righter, E. I. Horsman, and Bliss Manufacturing.[32]

George Parker advanced his firm's early growth by joining forces with two of these firms, Horsman and Singer. Then he outflanked his competitors by forming strong partnerships in England. When Ives was about to shut down, he acquired the rights to their games before his competitors could move in. Although statistics were unavailable to help him quantify exactly how big his new market share was, its effect was clearly visible. Parker Brothers had become a force in the games business.

Change continued to benefit the brothers. Singer exited the games business in 1895. Horsman gave up games to concentrate on dolls. McLoughlin Brothers began to waver, unable to match Parker Brothers' record of hit games. With Parker Brothers the second best known game company in the United States, George determined to make it number one. He printed with pride a quote that appeared in the pages of *Success* magazine, which said in reference to his firm, "Practically every Game which in recent years has taken the country by storm has been controlled by this company."[33]

Based on growing export revenue, the brothers decided to open a permanent office in London to exploit sales throughout the United Kingdom and France. In 1903, Ellery Brown was sent to run it. His goals were to solicit orders from U.K. merchants and cable them back to Salem, to be on the lookout for new games in the English market, and from time to time to go to Paris and find hits on the continent. Number 11 Lovell's Court, London—in the shadow of St. Paul's Cathedral—was the first address of Parker Brothers outside of the United States. It was chosen because of its proximity to the giant Royal Mail post offices on Cheapside, the many shipping firms whose docks were only a few hundred feet away on the Thames River, and its proximity to the city's publishing industry.[34]

The initial English game Brown signed up was a lively card game based on the fictional detective Sherlock Holmes. While only a modest success, the game's small package and deck of custom cards, purchased from outside vendors, enabled its inventory to be stored in less space than larger board games. This gave George an idea. If he could find the next great card game, it would put far less stress on his resources than traditional board games and would also provide an excellent profit margin.

With Brown on station in London, George turned his full attention toward finding such a game among promising "manuscripts" from U.S. game inventors.

Pit, Flinch, and Rook

In December 1903, Wilbur and Orville Wright achieved the world's first powered flight. That fall, their latest hit powered Parker Brothers' sales to new heights. In late spring, George Parker sat down with a man who had an idea for a most unusual card game. The man was a self-proclaimed psychic; his name was Edgar Cayce. A twenty-six-year old Kentuckian, Cayce believed that he possessed a gift for "readings" and had made a living doing so for the past two years. People began to report that they had been helped by his advice; many of these felt that Cayce had genuinely transformed their lives through his psychic powers.[35]

On the day when Cayce came calling, George suspected he would be shown some type of spiritual or fortune-telling game. But he was very wrong. What Cayce presented was a boisterous trading card game entitled *Pit.* The object was simple: Trade your cards until your hand held all the cards of one suit. The suits represented commodities traded on the Mercantile Exchange in Chicago, such as wheat, corn, oats, and barley. Parker had never seen a game quite like *Pit.* It broke the rules. Players did not take turns; they all shouted at once ("Two, two, I'll trade two!" or "I want three, three. Who'll trade me three?"). Within a minute or so, a player won the hand. It was fast, maybe too fast, and it was chaotic. But George sensed it would go over big if a few improvements could be made. He made a deal to buy out Cayce's rights and never saw the man again.[36]

George added to the game's roller-coaster ride of excitement by injecting a Bull and a Bear card (the Bear was always bad while the Bull was sometimes bad, sometimes very good).[37] George had a hunch about the universal appeal of *Pit,* so he rushed it into production in late 1903. Spectacular sales poured in immediately. For the first time, George was so excited about the popularity of one of his games, that he frequently recorded its mounting sales in his diary. By October 31, 38,000 had been shipped. Twenty-six thousand more were sold the next week. By January 16, 1904, 390,000 had been shipped, and by March 21, the total had grown to 750,000![38] In the 1904 catalog, he called *Pit* "The Latest Craze," adding, "As a pure, fun-making game FOR LAUGHTER, EXCITEMENT and a general good time, PIT has no rival. Price: 50 cents."

Sales of *Pit* continued without letup. Charles and Edward had to hire three makers of cards in 1904 to keep up with demand, including the United States Playing Card Company, which somehow made up shortfalls from the other two hard-pressed vendors. As a consequence, most of the card decks made for Parker Brothers games over the next half century would be made by this Cincinnati-based firm. Within one year, *Pit* had become the biggest moneymaker in the firm's twenty-year history.[39]

Given *Pit*'s success, the brothers invested in an exhibit at the great Louisiana Purchase Centennial—the World's Fair in St. Louis—which opened in April 1904. There, they displayed their games in a stylish booth in the Palace of Manufacturers, which featured makers of foods, furnishings, and household articles—many previously unknown to most Americans. The crowds were enormous (more than 19 million people were drawn to the fair during its seven months of operation).[40] As in 1893 at the Chicago Columbian Exposition, they were awarded a grand prize and a gold medal. *Pit* and *Ping-Pong* were the featured games at the fair and now millions more potential consumers knew about them.

After the fair opened, George took his family on vacation to Washington, D.C. On May 3, he shook hands and talked with the president of

FIGURE 2-4
World's Fair

Parker Brothers' booth at the World's Fair held in St. Louis, 1904.

the United States, Theodore Roosevelt. To George Parker's pleasant surprise, he discovered that the nation's leader enjoyed playing *Pit* and other Parker Brothers games with family and friends. This incident galvanized George. It made him realize that, despite the relatively small size of his enterprise, his products could touch the lives of all Americans. He was not Andrew Carnegie or Thomas Edison or Alexander Bell, but he was not without broad influence. This cemented his belief that what he did for a living wasn't trivial. It mattered. It was honorable for his work to endure.[41]

After George returned to Salem, Charles and Edward reported that *Pit* would be the company's first million-unit seller during a calendar year (and, via the London office, was on its way to fad status in England as well). They pressed George to focus his efforts on finding another game to build upon the success of *Pit*. They discouraged him from looking for more board games, as the popularity of even the best Parker Brothers board game was a fraction of *Pit*'s. George came to accept Principle 4—Learn from failure; build upon success. While his firm had suffered no failure in absolute terms, the overwhelming success of *Pit* made the sales of other board games look disappointing in comparison. George aimed to find another game with the same attributes of success as *Pit*: low cost, compact size, a handsome profit margin, ease of play, and great word-of-mouth potential to spread its popularity. Edward and Charles believed the retail trade would support whatever card game followed in the mighty footsteps of *Pit*, no matter if it were good, bad, or mediocre. George agreed that the extraordinary success of *Pit* could be used to rapidly launch another card game, but given his many sales trips during the firm's early years, he appreciated how fast this hunger would dissipate if his next game failed. He became determined not to squander this opportunity. He needed a sure thing, and he found it.[42]

Flinch was a simple numerical card game, first published in 1903 by a Kalamazoo, Michigan, company known, not surprisingly, as the Flinch Card Company.[43] Where *Pit* was boisterous, *Flinch* was thoughtful. There were ten each of cards numbered 1 to 15. The object for each player was to get rid of the ten cards received in the deal by playing them on piles that grew from a number 1 card to a number 15. The game was easy to understand but surprisingly challenging. And the Flinch Card Company was already selling big quantities of it. George used the success of *Pit* for dual advantage. Armed with it, he convinced the Flinch Card Company to allow him to sell a test quantity of its game. After the successful test, he wrote, "Parker Brothers are anxious to sell Flinch, and all we can of it." Bolstered by the profits of *Pit*, Parker Brothers bought the Flinch Card Company outright in 1905. *Flinch* outsold *Pit* that year. The firm now owned two high-volume card games.[44]

Around that time, George Parker organized an archive inside Parker Brothers. He set aside a room on the third floor to maintain a collection of Parker Brothers games made since 1883. He added scores of competitive games for reference. Scrapbooks were compiled of the firm's ads, and publicity photographs of life within his factory were neatly filed. One of these photos captured a play session. George is seen playing cards with three similarly attired women from his office—their blouses white and puffy, their skirts long and pinched at the waist, their hair piled neatly atop their heads. These ladies exemplified the "Gibson girl" style, which remained in vogue for three decades. There was no real model by the name of Gibson. Rather, this Victorian Age glamour gal emerged from the pen of New England–born illustrator Charles Dana Gibson. There was a "Gibson man" as well. He was always competent, assured, and sensible, not given to whim or extravagance or show of undue emotion in public. Consciously or not, George molded his appearance in the image of the Gibson male as surely as the Gibson girl influenced the manner and appearance of his female employees.[45]

The game being tested in the photo was the firm's next great card game. George invented it, with the help of wife Grace. It came about because standard playing cards, with their kings, queens, and jacks, were frowned upon in many parts of the country. The Puritan ethic denounced them as especially unfit for children. This was because playing cards had evolved from the tarot, whose cards were considered by many religions to be works of the devil.[46] Religious consideration aside, many enjoyable games were played with cards, independent of their pictures—for example, whist, a very popular trick-taking game (the ancestor of bridge). George saw an opportunity to capitalize on these play principles by publishing a game worthy of religious endorsement, rather than denouncement.

To accomplish this, George and Grace recast the standard deck of playing cards. They replaced the Ace with a "1" and the jack, queen, and king with "11," "12," and "13" cards, and added a "14" card as well. The hearts, spades, clubs, and diamonds were replaced with "suits" of colors: red, yellow, green, and black. With this new fifty-six-card deck, whist and most other common card games could be faithfully played. The game now lacked only a title. Grace suggested naming it, for reasons unknown, *Rook*, after a type of crow. George commissioned an illustration that pictured a rook holding a fan of five cards in its right claw while perched on a branch. Husband and wife hosted parties to play *Rook* and decide on the ten games to include in its rules.[47] "Most of these games are light, bright and spirited," wrote George in the 1906 catalog. "One or two of them are very easy, simple games; others are equivalents to Hearts and Whist." *Rook* also sold for fifty cents. Unlike *Pit*, which was an instant success, and *Flinch*, which had a following before Parker Brothers acquired it, sales of *Rook* were slow at first. Because Grace was such a believer in the merits of the game, George stuck with it doggedly, advertised it carefully, and gradually built it into a game whose life would outlast his own.

By 1906, George Parker was spending more time developing games and less time on the road. (Albert Richardson had become known to accounts across the country as the man who sold Parker Brothers games and faced the "perils" of the road He was in San Francisco on April 18, 1906, when a devastating earthquake struck the city. Fortunately, he emerged unscathed.)

Not every card game found favor with consumers as had *Pit*, *Flinch*, and *Rook*. George had patented another one in 1905, called *Block*. Intended for young and old players alike, it consisted of five suits each bearing a number and a letter. As in the common card game crazy eights, each player tried to play a card of the same suit as the prior card, but of the next higher rank. "Block" cards changed the suit and "count" cards added to one's score. George felt so strongly about this game that in the 1906 catalog he wrote, in his own script: "Block is the best card game we have ever published." Two editions were published to satisfy the range of expected demand. It never materialized. *Block,* a distant ancestor of today's immensely popular *Uno* game, disappeared from the line a few years later. Nevertheless, by 1907, sales of *Pit*, *Flinch*, and *Rook* enabled Parker Brothers to approach those of the once-mighty McLoughlin Brothers. George Parker's goal of becoming the nation's largest game company was within his grasp.[48] George's satisfaction with his business was matched only by the pride felt for his growing family. The Parker household was a merry, lively place in March of that year when George purchased, for $2,800, his first automobile (a Knox "Waterless").[49] In April, Bradstreet turned ten and Richard reached seven years of age. Both were active, bright children—Bradstreet being the more inquisitive and bossy, while Richard was the more dutiful and reasoned of the two. In September, Grace gave birth to a "beautiful little girl," named Sally.[50] As George entered his fifth decade, his happiness seemed complete. But within, he worried about what would become of his family if an accident befell him. Prior to his next trip to Europe, he left Grace a letter with instructions on what to do should he die. He recorded the names of banks where $47,000 of savings had been tucked away and reminded her of his $40,000 life insurance policy. He advised her, in the event of his untimely death, to invest everything in blue chip stocks and AAA bonds to maximize her annual income. He urged her to retain his Parker Brothers stock and get herself elected to the board with the help of brother Edward. And he admonished her to never sign anything unless she fully understood the request.

The sum of $87,000 was a small fortune after the turn of the twentieth century, but it was insufficient in George's eyes to provide all the advantages he hoped to bestow upon his family. He did not slacken the pace in his quest to maximize profits, which determined his annual dividend income. (George not only held a significant majority of the firm's common stock, but he had acquired a plurality of its preferred stock, in lieu of part of his salary.)

Pastime Puzzles

The Parker Brothers line grew broader with each year because slow-selling games were backlisted rather than discontinued. To expand distribution in variety and low-priced stores, Parker Brothers began to offer "standard" games. These included Parker Brothers editions of checkers, dominos, and whist sets. And for twenty-five cents, a game enthusiast could buy custom versions of card games like snap (take all the cards when a pair shows up on the table), authors (collect the most four-of-a kinds), and old maid (avoid holding the final card).[51]

Like its competitors, Parker Brothers also sold "sliced goods." At first, these consisted of dissected maps, mounted on thin wood, of the United States or the world. Later, many types of pictures were used. Regardless

FIGURE 2-5
Typical *Pastime Puzzle* Package

of subject matter, sales of sliced goods remained too low for them to be considered other than a sideline for Parker Brothers. This soon changed.

Technology had played a small but important role in the first quarter century of Parker Brothers. Certainly the mere existence of a hollow plastic *Ping-Pong* ball was a marvel to anyone who saw and heard it bounce for the first time. In 1908, another new technology offered a chance to revolutionize the Parker Brothers product line. Thanks to precision engineering and fabrication, the French had developed an extremely fine blade for electric jigsaws, only .007 inch thick. Mounted between a spindle at the end of a long sweeping arm and another under its base, it was possible to intricately and smoothly cut a large piece of thin wood into many pieces.

In 1876, at the Philadelphia Centennial Exposition, the power scroll saw had been introduced to the public. It became known as the "jigsaw" and a foot-powered treadle version began to sell well, at a cost of only $3. Rev. Charles Jeffreys of Philadelphia is the earliest documented maker of puzzles made by cutting pictures mounted on wood into many pieces with a jigsaw. Eventually, craftsmen began to make picture puzzles with interlocking pieces. By 1908, some of these picture puzzles were being sold commercially in Boston, and they sold well.

Although George had not been enamored with sliced goods, the marketplace was buying them, and principle dictated that he capitalize. Charles and Edward quickly figured out how to mass-produce these "one of a kind" products. They were accustomed to making games in quantity; each copy identical to the one made before it. Jigsaw puzzles would have to be cut by hand, one piece at a time. Of necessity, every puzzle would be cut uniquely, even if the mounted picture were the same for many of them. There was no set pattern or "die" to make endless copies. It took the artistic skill of a single operator to make the cuts, following the impulses that caused a pair of hands to maneuver plywood creatively against a rapidly moving French-made blade. To enter the jigsaw marketplace, the brothers needed operators who had the right touch to attractively and precisely cut such puzzles. Fortunately, a local industry held an abundance of the needed talent. Skill at stitching seemed to mark the skill needed to cut out a jigsaw puzzle. The New England region was known for its shoe making, and shoe making required an abundance of stitchers (who were mainly women). Several were soon hired to work in Parker Brothers' Salem factory.

George applied his claim regarding "excellence of their playing qualities" to his newly christened *Pastime Puzzles*. He insisted on attractive subject matter for his puzzle labels and top-quality plywood because he assumed that these puzzles would appeal exclusively to women of society. Each piece must feel pleasant to the touch, with no rough edges. Each piece must be durable and survive several assemblies.

The Friend Box Company of Salem mounted printed pictures on plywood and cut them roughly to size. The mounted sheets could then be

FIGURE 2-6
Pastime Girls Cutting Puzzles

bundled and carted to the Parker Brothers loading dock, where laborers would take them up to the prep room to cleanly cut and sand their edges. Wheeled carts would roll stacks of uncut puzzles to the heart of the operation—the jigsaw room—where the "Pastime Girls," as they became known, awaited. Each sat on a backed stool in a long row. Before each was a jigsaw below a hanging electric light. The Pastime Girl would place an uncut puzzle on the base of her saw and start its blade. The result was a one-of-a-kind puzzle cut into uniquely shaped pieces.[52]

Each Pastime Girl was expected to cut 1,400 pieces per day. Initially, the puzzles offered for sale ranged from 150 pieces to 400 pieces. Later, the range was expanded from 60 pieces to 1,250 (and sometimes, for custom purchase, even more). As a Pastime Girl became more experienced, it was less exciting to cut pieces at random, and became a matter of honor to cut some pieces with recognizable shapes. These became known as *figurals*—pieces resembling letters, numbers, animals, common objects, and symbols. It was not unusual to find a puzzle with an "H," a "5," a fox, a wheelbarrow, and a heart among its pieces. The novelty of these figurals was deemed sufficient to apply for a patent (taken out in the name of the department foreman).[53]

The next innovation was the "intricate design" piece. In the evening, at home, a Pastime Girl would create each such pattern by folding a piece of paper in half or in quarters. Using fine scissors, she would cut out a curvy shape, then flatten the paper. The next day at work, she would incorporate some of these decorative figures into each of her puzzles. She did so by carefully holding each paper design, one by one, atop an area of a puzzle and cutting around its borders. A standard requirement was soon established—each puzzle must have twelve figural and intricately designed pieces per hundred. Thus, a three-hundred-piece puzzle would include thirty-six such pieces. Cutting along color lines of the puzzle's picture became desired, to increase the challenge of reassembling it.[54]

After a girl cut out a puzzle, its pieces were placed in an appropriately sized box. The boxes were plain, with only the *Pastime Puzzle* and Parker Brothers logos printed on top. On one side, a small label was adhered that identified the name of the puzzle and a rough count of its pieces. Stacks of these loaded boxes next went to the finishing department. There, a "polisher"—usually a boy or man with taped fingertips—would open the box and sand any rough underside edges on the pieces found inside. No matter how fine the French blades, the sawing process occasionally left burrs, which had to be sanded smooth.[55]

An inspector examined each puzzle once the polisher had done his job. A small printed label was adhered to the inside of the box lid, and the inspector filled in its blank lines—the number of pieces counted at the factory, the number of the Pastime Girl who had cut the puzzle, the name of the polisher, his own initials as inspector, and the date. In all, the label was a sort of "birth certificate" that named the parents and attending physician for the newly born puzzle, now up for "adoption."

George Parker billed the *Pastime Puzzles* in his 1908 catalog as "The Latest Fad of Society . . . For Adults." He expected to sell them to department stores and nowhere else, so he added the line, "Send for sample. You will have calls for them," to arouse interest from his other accounts.

It wasn't necessary.

Shortly after *Pastime Puzzles* reached the department store shelves, word of them spread faster than a flame engulfing a *Ping-Pong* ball. Orders poured in from every type of account.

Parker Brothers faced its first "demand" crisis. It could make puzzles only as fast as the girls could cut them; it wasn't prudent to push them to work beyond the "scientifically" established norm of 1,400 pieces per nine-hour day. The only solution was to hire more girls and buy more jigsaws.

The game player in George helped him to realize another key principle (number 5). When faced with a choice, a good player always makes the move with the most potential. George convened a meeting with Charles and Edward in early 1909, and together they made an extraordinary decision based on this new principle. Faced with a choice of either satisfying demand for *Pastime Puzzles* or letting the competition benefit, they made a dramatic move. All game assembly would be suspended inside their factory. Parker Brothers games, George's first love, would take a back seat to Parker Brothers puzzles. All assembly space would be given over to jigsaws atop tables manned by Pastime Girls. Room was carved out for 225 machines and operators and production eventually exceeded 15,000 puzzles per week.[56]

Finding subject matter for the puzzles became a priority. The scenes were mainly pastoral, several from around Salem itself. Artists had to be commissioned to paint pictures of equestrians jumping over hurdles and sailing vessels plowing the seas. Imaginative subjects—one favorite was a picture of a little boy using his family's wood basket as if it were a boat—were in high demand. Others were mounted with reproductions by the old masters. At times, the firm mounted a custom photo sent in by a customer and turned it into a one-of-a-kind *Pastime Puzzle.*

Naming each picture imaginatively was quite important because no photograph of the assembled puzzle was provided. The consumer who accepted the challenge to put the puzzle together had only the name as a guide. George Parker took it upon himself to do the naming in conjunction with a Pastime Girl he felt was especially imaginative—Mrs. Arthur Manning, who had come to work for his firm in 1905 after her husband, himself a Parker Brothers employee, died. More often than not, her recommendation was superior to George's, such as "The Sea-Going Wood Basket" for the puzzle of the little boy's imagined boat.[57]

Mrs. Manning's fourteen-year-old son found work at Parker Brothers as well. He became one of the polishers and learned early the importance of taping his fingertips to prevent them from becoming raw and bloody by day's end.[58] Child labor was considered one of the scandals of the nineteenth century, yet no national, and few state, laws had been enacted to prevent it. In Massachusetts, the great mills depended on boys and girls for menial jobs. Many of them worked sixty hours a week or more. It was not uncommon, in this era lacking in social welfare, for an eighth-grade graduate like Harry Manning to forego high school to earn a living—especially if a family had lost a father, as his had.

The packing and shipping of *Pastime Puzzles* were also labor intensive. Each puzzle was wrapped with custom Parker Brothers paper and then stacked on the second floor above the shipping department. When an order arrived, men in the shipping department would "pick" the puzzles required. Sometimes the order was small and could be mailed or taken to the Railway Express office in town. But for a large order, workers in the shipping department had to construct a wooden crate, made of sections called *shooks.* Knocked down shooks were purchased from regional packing material firms. They were nailed together, loaded with puzzles, and stuffed with excelsior to cushion them during transit. Then the crate would be stenciled and taken to the loading dock for transport to the main railway station in downtown Salem, a few blocks away.[59]

All of this effort yielded a product that sold for a penny a piece. A three-hundred-piece puzzle cost the consumer a tidy $3 (about $55 today!). Yet demand for the bigger puzzles exceeded all expectations. In many cities, this was due to puzzle-renting libraries. Consumers would pick out a puzzle and take it home, then pay for how many days it was borrowed. Bigger puzzles took longer to assemble and were therefore more attractive to these libraries. Among the best-known fans of *Pastime Puzzles* were President Teddy Roosevelt (he had a knack for fitting the pieces together with little deliberation), the Royal Family in Buckingham Palace, and Czar Nicholas of St. Petersburg, Russia.[60]

Diabolo

While *Pastime Puzzles* were captivating people hunched over tabletops, another novelty was occupying their attention outdoors—*Diabolo*. A French engineer named Gustave Phillipart claimed *Diabolo* to be his invention. In reality, he had improved a Napoleonic toy, which in turn had originated long ago in China. *Diabolo* was a double-coned bobbin that was twirled, tossed, and caught on a string secured to two wands, one held in each hand. A skilled person could catch it, hurl it fifty or sixty feet into the air, then catch it again with little effort. Charles Parker beat his U.S. competition to Phillipart's door and grabbed the U.S. license for *Diabolo*.[61] A U.S. patent was received in 1906. By 1908, this toss-and-catch game was sweeping the states. Harry Manning, like so many of the boys who worked in the puzzle department, would demonstrate it outside the factory during his lunch break. Workers on the second or third

FIGURE 2-7
Diabolo Ad

floor would see the spinning bobbins levitate outside their windows before dropping below their view, only to return again.[62]

The *Diabolo* fad became so widespread that it was ridiculed in the press. Lampoons of politicians and proper society people, seen clumsily holding *Diabolo* wands in hand, sparked even more demand. The Venus de Milo was the subject of a cartoon wherein she was seen playing with *Diabolo*—with arms restored. Another depicted a burglar caught in the act because he had come across a *Diabolo* set and could not resist toying with it. The cover of the 1908–1909 Parker Brothers catalog featured a series of photographs of a Gibson girl, wearing a long white dress and sunhat, playing with a *Diabolo*. The first three pages were entirely devoted to the novelty. In all, eight different models were available for sale. Consumers paid from $1 to $8 for a set. Parker offered a luxurious set that included a felt-lined wood case and silver mounted rods. It was described as being "a gift set for experts or those desiring the best obtainable."

But once more, to George Parker's chagrin, competitors clung to his coattails. Although their *Diabolo*-like devices bore different names, their poor quality stopped the fad dead in its tracks. Parker Brothers used steel for the bobbins, with molded rubber ends, and also made some versions out of hollow Celluloid—which, because of its "frictionless" properties, spun even faster than steel. Most competitors used lathed wood, sold at cut-rate prices, which did not spin as fast or toss as high.[63] Parker Brothers countered with a small line of wooden *Whirling Wizard* bobbins, but by so doing only hastened the fad's extinction.

Diabolo and its competitors spun out of sight by 1910. Retailers reported loads of unsold inventory. They were immune to the promise of new models. They only wanted to return those that clogged their shelves. Its disappearance from the Parker Brothers line was notable considering George's custom of backlisting all inventory. If inventory of a boxed game remained in the warehouse, George insisted it be listed in the annual catalog. The Parker Brothers catalog now had more than 250 items for sale within its pages. In 1910, for example, *Tiddledy Winks*, *Pillow-Dex*, and especially *Ping-Pong* were still available in multiple editions. *Diabolo* was conspicuous by its absence, so sudden did its fascination end (a harbinger of countless fads to follow in the toy and game industry).

By the end of the decade, sales of Parker Brothers games, puzzles, and novelties exceeded $700,000 per year.[64] In the seventeenth year of its existence, the firm surpassed McLoughlin Brothers and became the country's largest game company. It had published three immensely popular card games, sparked the jigsaw puzzle phenomenon, and marketed a novelty action craze that many of the country's 92 million citizens had heard of or experienced.

While Parker Brothers seemed incapable of making a losing move, it is often said that character is tempered less by success than by adversity. George Parker and his principles were now about to be shaped by the latter.[65]

Chapter Three

Dealing with Setbacks

1911–1933

IN THE GAME OF BACKGAMMON, WHICH GEORGE PARKER (and daughter Sally) greatly enjoyed playing, luck is often a bigger enemy than the opponent. If bad luck leads to early setbacks, an experienced player will switch from trying to outrace his opponent and instead bolster his defensive position. He'll lie in wait and hope to knock out of play an unprotected piece of the opponent's and then sprint for victory. It takes added skill, and self-restraint, to play a "back game." In each year of the new decade, George would find himself playing a back game in real life. He was to battle a series of setbacks, during which he laid down Principle 6: When luck runs against you, hold emotion in check and set up for your next advance.

Back Game

During President William H. Taft's term in office, a unique American culture began to emerge—one no longer controlled by European influence. Consumer expectations changed with the culture. The country became wild about baseball, tennis, and college football. Mystery writer Mary Roberts Rinehart became popular; Zane Grey's westerns were bestsellers. Slow dancing gave way to the waltz, two-step, and then ragtime.[1] "Pep" was a key ingredient of toys that were "in," like American-bred Erector sets and Tinkertoys.[2] What fell "out" were quiet, mental diversions—like board games and *Pastime Puzzles*.

Nonetheless, those quiet diversions were acclaimed hit makers. They had made the Parker Brothers firm number one: No other game company had sold as many games and puzzles as Parker Brothers had in the prior five years. But the trade now reported slowing sales of board games and encouraged Parker Brothers to come up with the next great thing. The emotional cheer from years of success can easily cause a business-man to ignore the voice emanating from the marketplace, especially when it urges caution or change. George Parker was slow to listen and, for a while, he continued to publish the kind of board and card games America once wanted.

Other problems delayed his attention to the change in consumer ex-pectations. The London office wasn't making money. Material prices had been rising steadily. The high cost of packing and shipping games across the Atlantic translated to stiff retail prices in Great Britain and Europe. Furthermore, Ellery Brown was homesick. Charles Parker and his family enjoyed Europe, so he volunteered to take over and relocate his wife and daughter to London. Once settled, he would establish a small factory. The brothers decided it would be far cheaper to send unassembled com-ponents and printed sheets to London so that boxes and boards could be made locally. Harry Manning, now working in the shipping depart-ment in Salem, packed the shooks bound for the port of London. Where once he had sent finished games, he now packed reams of printed sheets, sacks of tokens and dice, and bundles of card decks.[3] The savings on custom duties and transportation would allow lower prices of Parker Brothers games in Europe. Charles soon moved the office to 19 Ivy Lane (even closer to the Cheshire Cheese pub) from nearby Lovell's Court. He could be reached by cable at "Parkergame."[4]

The Foibles of George Parker

George Parker's character was forever shaped by the problems besetting his business and determination to emulate the behavior of other cap-tains of industry. Without Charles to consult, forty-six-year-old George often became lost in thought as he wrestled with key decisions. Edward remained devoted and ran both the plant and the treasury, but he did not have Charles's mentoring quality and tended to agree with George without challenge. George responded by weaving the tapestry of deci-sion making within his mind, relying on his principles, before sharing his thinking with Edward—or anyone else for that matter. To increase his efficiency, he installed a buzzer on his desk. With so many presses of its button, he could summon a specific employee in the factory whenever he had a question or needed information. Young Harry Manning was one of the chosen few—not because of his counsel, but because of George's absentmindedness. With a self-effacing grin, George would say, "I've forgotten my glasses again this morning, Harry. Here's carfare. Could you take a [trolley] down to my home? My wife will help you find them." As this happened regularly, Manning came to keep the coins, eschew the streetcar, and run like the wind to the Parker household. Grace Parker's search for the missing glasses then ensued, as she would have no idea where her husband had last left them.[5]

Grace Parker had learned to play the role of a Yankee Gentleman's wife. She stood at George's side when her husband needed her assistance, but was required to walk behind him with the children whenever they strolled the sidewalks of downtown Salem. However, she had become a strong, talented woman who, despite her diminutive height, always stood her ground in arguments with him. She pursued her ambitions of tracing her family's roots through England and Scotland. Eventually, she would succeed in following them back to distant knights in the twelfth century. One ancestor, James Tytler, was the first Englishman to ascend in a hot-air balloon (1784). Tytler was also a founding editor of the *Encyclopaedia Britannica*.[6] George trusted Grace's judgment and was very proud of the taste and beauty with which she had decorated their home. She helped develop his taste in Scottish tweeds. His finely tailored three-piece suits furthered his air of dignity. But many in the firm did not see his softer side, as did Harry Manning. Some considered him an insufferable snob who acted like a lord over his vassals. However, his insistence on proper etiquette led to decorous respect among men and women throughout the factory—from the floor sweeper to the collating girl to the foreman. And his sense of decorum would set the dress code for executives and demeanor inside Parker Brothers for decades to come.[7]

His brothers did not share his stuffiness. Charles and Edward, while always well dressed, lived life with a more casual air. They didn't hesitate to try to deflate George's balloon. Charles, in particular, when he was not in England, would bring his younger brother down to earth with a joke or a "Hey Georgie!" This usually rattled George, as intended.[8]

George's future secretary, Helen Mitchell, would note that "George enjoyed humor, but he did not create it."[9] Ironically, his business was to create fun. And whenever he played games, he seemed to transform into a kid once more—carefree, lost in the enjoyment of pleasure, not a trace of stuffiness to be seen.

The employees were often amused by this about-face and by the interplay between the Parkers. And they had ample time to observe it. The Parker Brothers workweek was typical for the era: five and a half days. As the office was about to close at noon on Saturday, young Harry Manning was sometimes summoned to George Parker's office. With a kindly smile on his face, George would ask Manning what he planned to do for the rest of the day. Manning usually said that he had no plans. George would smile and hand him a dollar or two and tell him to "go have a good time."[10] Given Manning's eight-dollar-a-week salary, this was a bonanza.

Taxes and benefits were nonexistent for most U.S. workers, but George Parker often took an interest in the well-being of his employees: *noblesse oblige*, as he would later write when acknowledging his sense of obligation to those who depended on him. With ample cash to back him, he began to quietly help veteran employees in need. It did not take long for him to learn of an employee who was having trouble making the mortgage payment or repaying a debt, or who was suffering from an illness. His aid usually took the form of a loan that more often than not was forgiven. Or for favored employees like Henry Fitzpatrick, Albert Richardson, or Harry Manning, a little something extra placed in hand without warning, and a quiet "Thank you." These favors were never publicized. George's reward seemed to be the act itself.[11] He was cautioned by the realization that if he were to tout his generosity, it would lead to abuses by his employees.

With Charles across the Atlantic, Edward continued the practice of a morning walk through the factory. George also felt compelled to walk through the plant on occasion, in place of Charles. While he too knew every worker, he would only nod occasionally without turning his head. The workers so recognized would respond with a "Good morning, Mr. Parker," in keeping with protocol. All of the men, regardless of rank, addressed each other as "Mr." and all women as "Mrs." or "Miss." But when he was out of earshot, workers tended to refer to George Parker by his initials—either "GS" or, more commonly, "GSP."[12]

One of George's most unpleasant tasks was to approve a reduction of the workforce as demand for *Pastime Puzzles* came back to earth. The firm's department foremen had responsibility for hiring and firing. (The idea of a separate personnel department was not even a gleam in management's eye then.) Edward instructed them to downscale by letting go "the weakest" at the slightest provocation.

One afternoon in 1911, when young Harry Manning had no games to ship, he stared out of a third-floor window at the turrets of Salem jail across the street. His foreman was outside directing a team to the loading dock and happened to look up at the idle youth. The next time this happened in front of the foreman's watchful eyes, Manning was fired.

Given his mother's esteem in the eyes of George Parker, Manning could have protested. Instead, he shrugged his shoulders and eventually made a career working for the telephone company.[13]

One bright spot in this difficult time was *Rook*. Five years had passed since Grace and George's card game had been published. Its sales had increased annually as word spread that it was "safe" to play whist and auction bridge with its numerical colored cards (not that George didn't hedge—by 1912, pages of bridge-related items were for sale in his catalog). Steady print advertising continued to back *Rook*, and it worked. *Rook* sales now surpassed two hundred thousand copies a year, at fifty cents apiece.[14]

Edward had to contend with the steady rise in wholesale material prices that had begun in the late 1890s. After the Civil War, material prices had fallen steadily for thirty years. When Parker Brothers was founded, prices were nearly three-quarters lower than they had been in 1864. But by 1912, material costs were 30 percent higher than at the turn of the century.[15] The retail price of many Parker Brothers games had to go up. Consumers become accustomed to what things "should" cost, so the price increases dampened Parker Brothers' sales.

Looking for "Pep"

George now accepted that times and tastes were changing. Principle dictated that he hold his emotions in check and look for the next competitive advantage. He began a search for items with "pep." For a while, the firm's best new items weren't even games. They were play sets from a line entitled *Toy Town*. The *Toy Town Grocery Store* was a miniature grocery store with counters and shelves, a nonworking cash register, toy money, and more than forty little packages, including replicas of Gold Medal flour and Franco-American soup (whose makers permitted their use, seeing this as a beneficial form of advertising). There were also little train stations, complete with tracks and switches, and, of course, a *Toy Town Toy Store*. Other attempts at diversification—such as kindergarten supplies, an indoor bowling set, and a toy gun that shot paper discs "with the accuracy of bullets"—failed.[16]

The *Electric Book of Wonders* was aptly named, although not terribly successful. George believed he might successfully publish books, as long as each had an added feature, a Parker Brothers "twist." For this one, the clever use of hidden magnets enabled the pivoting arm of a student pictured on the last page to point to the correct answer for each question. The pages each had a big circular cutout with a ring of questions printed on one side and a ring of answers on the flip side. A former Bell Telephone engineer invented it. It worked flawlessly but failed to capture the public's imagination.[17]

An Optimist in the Face of Changing Times

Edward's son Foster married in 1911. Late the following year, Foster's wife Anna gave birth to Edward P. Parker, named in honor of his grandfather (whose health was suddenly on the decline). Charles's daughter Mary was then twenty years old; George's sons were fifteen and twelve. They were active boys who loved sports and the outdoors. Remembering how his friends had influenced him to create *Banking*, George tried to learn from his sons and their friends to help guide his product selection, but without success because, ultimately, he found it difficult to accept their criticisms.[18]

In 1913, the Sixteenth Amendment, which permitted the levying of taxes on individuals and businesses, became law. Most Parker Brothers employees would pay no tax but the brothers would have to, and so would their business. This lowered their personal income and the firm's net profits. President Taft's popularity declined in response. Woodrow

Wilson won the presidency in the next election. Parker Brothers also lost the honor of having an office in the most prestigious office building in New York City. Parker Brothers' most important retailer, the F. W. Woolworth Company, now held that claim. To the wonder of visitors to Manhattan, its new building rose 792 feet high.[19]

Charles, Abigail, and Mary enjoyed life in London. The Parker Brothers office was again relocated, this time to 8 Great Turnstile Street, a mile to the west of the former Ivy Street address.[20] From here, Charles could walk in seconds into lovely Lincoln Fields. The British Museum lay a few minutes to the north. By angling south of Oxford Street, Charles and Abigail could visit the many bookstores on Charing Cross Road. Heading further south, they could frequent one of the countless theaters in the West End, absorbing the sounds and aromas heavy in the air amid the gaslit world of London's nightlife.[21]

Art appreciation came into vogue with the International Exhibition of Modern Art in New York. People began to read more, thanks to advances in book production (most hardbound books cost a dollar). Popular titles included *Rolling Stones* by O. Henry and *Pollyanna* by Eleanor Hogman Porter, a juvenile novel that sold over a million copies.[22] Remembering his success with *Innocence Abroad*, George decided to license the game rights for *Pollyanna*, with its eternally optimistic character. George's new game played much like *Parcheesi*. The object was the same—to move all four of one's pawns, by a roll of two dice, along a path from Start to Home. But the pathway of *Pollyanna* featured turnouts along the way, giving players a chance to play it safe by taking a longer route home. Its familiar game play and theme appealed strongly to girls and women. It clearly had pep as sales mounted month by month. *Pollyanna* was destined to endure in Parker Brothers' line for over forty years. This inspired George to introduce a similar game called *Broadway*, aimed at boys and men, that pictured scenes from New York's Broadway around its perimeter.

The Great Salem Fire

On the afternoon of June 25, 1914, as workers in the collating department were stuffing *Broadway* utensil boxes, they noticed a thick plume of smoke about a mile away along the North River. Soon the sounds of fire vehicles and teams were heard responding to the fire, which was intensifying by the minute judging from the flames dancing snakelike in the clear blue sky. Word reached the Parker Brothers factory that the fire had started in one of the leather firms in "Blubber Hollow," whose nickname probably came from the whale blubber from which tanning oil was extracted. Large shoe factories had sprung up near the tanning companies, and so had tenements housing immigrant workers.[23]

The blaze became an inferno as the afternoon wore on. It began to move eastward, creeping closer to the Parker Brothers factory where the reverberation of exploding Celluloid and the smell of burnt wood, oil, and fabric wafted into the open windows. Fire companies from many surrounding communities began to rush into town, but many of them stood by helplessly because Salem's fire hydrants were not standardized and therefore their hoses could not be connected.[24] Some Parker Brothers workers bolted home to rescue their families. Others joined the volunteers trying to halt the blaze. The rest prepared to defend the factory if the flames leapt the ground between the intervening HP Hood dairy barn and their building. But in late evening, the fire curved toward the south; the Parker Brothers plant was spared.[25]

Much of Salem was less fortunate. While the lovely mansions and stately homes on Chestnut and Essex Streets were also spared, South Salem was gutted. The fire was stopped just two houses north of George and Grace's home on Lafayette Street. The biggest employer in town, the Naumkeag Cotton Mills, saw its massive building on Salem harbor reduced to charred rubble. And the nearby National Fireworks building on New Derby Street lit up the sky with a spectacular display, sending people on adjoining blocks running for cover. In all, 1,800 buildings were destroyed—including a fire station, orphanage, and church—before the fire was beaten down the next day. Miraculously, only six people died.[26]

George and Edward Parker provided comfort and financial aid and did what they could to find housing for the workers who had lost their apartments. Output at the factory limped along as workers were given time off to handle personal calamities and suppliers struggled to deliver basic materials to the plant.

World War I and Bradstreet Parker

Across the Atlantic that summer, tensions among Europe's governments began to mount. President Woodrow Wilson announced that the United States would stay out of any conflict. His fellow citizens—among them, George Parker, a newly avowed pacifist—overwhelmingly supported his position. War in Europe broke out in August 1914 and the resultant embargo on nonessential goods closed the game trade. George and Edward summoned Charles, who increasingly was conducting business in Paris, to come home. An underling was placed in charge at 8 Great Turnstile. The London office would remain open, getting by as it could during the war because George felt that it was vital that the firm be ready there as soon as hostilities ended.[27]

Then, in 1915, at age sixty, Edward H. Parker succumbed to a sudden respiratory illness and died, likely due to his years of heavy smoking. Edward's steady hand on the company's treasury and pulse of the business had long kept the company on track. His grandson and namesake, Edward P. Parker, was but two years old, in the arms of his father Foster, when his grandfather was honored and laid to rest. Charles and George mourned the loss of their closest friend, their brother. The firm closed for a day in respect.

With the conflict came a slew of war-related games. Many were updates of Parker Brothers' popgun games that had been so popular during the Spanish-American War. Acclaimed artist Maxfield Parrish, an acquaintance of George's from New Hampshire, rendered a beautiful painting of a nineteenth-century soldier, for use on one particularly large target. This was the first time an artist of renown had created a painting exclusively for a game, which George proudly proclaimed in his catalogs of this era.[28] But the European war had not yet gripped the U.S. public. It was somebody else's battle and the consumer passion for these games was lukewarm at best.

Despite President Wilson's desires, the United States edged closer and closer to siding with Great Britain and France. German submarines sank several ships that happened to have U.S. citizens and interests onboard. Pressure mounted. Undeterred, Charles Parker made an ocean voyage to France in 1916 to prop up a business deal with a French licensee. George began to keep a scrapbook of cartoons about the war, carefully clipped from newspapers and magazines. He did not reveal his motivation for doing this, but he was vocal regarding his strong pacifist beliefs. He wanted the United States to remain neutral, and he didn't want to read in the papers about the death or wounding of any member of his family of workers.

Yet, even before the United States entered this deadliest of conflicts, Bradstreet Parker ran away from college to Canada, determined to join the Escadrille and fly in the skies above France along with many other young volunteers from the United States. When George realized his son's intentions, he raced to Canada with associates and brought him home. Bradstreet had been sent to fine private schools and was now enrolled in Harvard, class of 1919. George hoped fervently that he would willingly join the family business and be groomed as his successor. But as 1915 became 1916, the gulf between father and son widened. Bradstreet resented his father's attempts to regiment him and set his life's goals. George came to view Bradstreet as "a lost cause" who wouldn't listen to reason, especially when Bradstreet married a woman named Ruth Mansfield without informing his parents in advance.[29]

In 1917, President Wilson acted on the will of Congress and the nation was soon at war with the Central Powers: Germany and the Austro-Hungarian Empire. Once war was declared, several of Parker Brothers' workers joined the navy and the army, and like many a mother's son, each became a "doughboy"—the affectionate nickname given to the U.S. soldiers in World War I.[30] Their exploits sparked a strong patriotic mood in the country, which encouraged Parker Brothers to publish even more games based on the Great European War (as it was then called). When it came to business, George did not believe in fighting trends in the marketplace, even if they ran counter to his personal beliefs or tastes.

While balancing his pacifism with a desire to capitalize on the war fever, George could not imagine his older son joining the ranks of the doughboys. In early 1918, Bradstreet Parker did just that. He took a leave from Harvard and told his parents that he was enlisting as a naval aviation cadet. Twenty-one years old, he would determine his own fate. George and Grace waved good-bye, with their two younger children at their side, as Bradstreet departed for Fort Devens, Massachusetts, and air cadet training. His parents knew of the lethal air battles above

Europe from letters written by friends in both England and France.[31] They feared for the life of their son, well before his departure to Europe. While Bradstreet was in training, the great flu epidemic of 1918 began to sweep the nation. Bradstreet contracted pneumonia and was rushed to a hospital in Boston. With his parents at his side, he died. Like so many others, his death could not be averted in this era before the discovery of penicillin.[32]

Nineteen years earlier, while returning home by train from a sales trip, George had written a poem dedicated to Bradstreet for the occasion of his second birthday on April 13, 1899. Grace had it read at his service. It ended with:

> *Dear little boy with the light-brown hair*
> *Dear little boy with the bright blue eyes*
> *For love of you the day is fair.*
> *Soft the blue of the April skies,*
> *All the honor and joy I know*
> *For the dear little boy who loves us so.*[33]

George and Grace shouldered their grief, supported by the outpouring of sympathy from the employees of Parker Brothers and the countless friends they had made over the years. Ruth Mansfield, Bradstreet's wife, left the area, never to be seen again by the Parker family.[34]

Le Bourget and Richard Parker

George now turned to son Richard as his successor. Richard was accepted at Harvard, class of 1922. To show his pride, George took out a full-page ad in the *Freshman Red Book*.[35] Where Bradstreet was rebellious, Richard was obedient. He respected his parents and shouldered responsibility without complaint. He excelled at whatever he tackled. He was a natural athlete, gifted in social settings, and became a brilliant academic student at Harvard. He was elected secretary-treasurer of his class and business editor of the *Lampoon*; he took part in the annual Hasty Pudding play.[36] To his parents, he was a source of constant pride, and Richard was genuinely enthusiastic about joining Parker Brothers after graduation and accepting the reins of command when his father chose to retire.

On June 25, after completing his junior year, Richard accompanied his parents and fourteen-year-old sister Sally on a grand tour of Europe. Sally and Grace shared one cabin on the *Olympia* while Richard and George shared a second. This gave George a perfect opportunity to discuss, in earnest, the current status of Parker Brothers and settle the plans for Richard to join the firm. Father began to impart to son the business lessons and principles learned during more than a quarter-century's entrepreneurship. The *Olympia* arrived in Southampton a week later and the Parkers took the train to London to begin three weeks of touring the British Isles and introduce Richard to his father's longtime business associates. Next, they toured Paris and several other cities in France. Then on to Genoa, Milan, Venice, Rome, and smaller cities in Italy. Finally, as August turned to September, the family returned to Paris where, on September 3, Grace, George, and Sally bid Richard farewell. As they crossed the Atlantic on the *S. S. Paris*, he would head in the opposite direction.[37] Richard would begin a round-the-world trip, accompanied by Harvard alumnus Herman Smith, who bore letters of introduction, including one to the viceroy of India written by former president William Taft. Their trip would be for educational purposes and would qualify Richard for graduation the following spring when he returned to Boston. Before their journey began, Richard planned to make a brief excursion to Strasbourg, then return to Paris by air.[38]

On the morning of September 7, the captain of the *S. S. Paris* received an urgent telegram from Mr. W. Fish, an American executive with the International General Electric Company of Paris. The telegram read:

Find Mr. G. S. Parker alone. Tell him his son killed aeroplane accident. Body in Paris. Fish returns Wednesday next and will bring body if authorized. Talk with Parker and not with his wife. Wire his desires quick to Directeur Franco-Romanine, 22 Rue des Pyramides, Paris.

Richard Parker and four others had died in the first airplane crash at Le Bourget Airport in Paris (where Charles Lindbergh would land, after crossing the Atlantic, six years later). As their craft made its approach, it suddenly wavered and dropped short of the runway. There was only a hotel bill on Richard's body to identify him. The Harvard-sponsored journey was over before it began. In respect, the university would dedicate its 1922 yearbook to Richard's memory and award his degree, posthumously.[39]

George somehow kept the news from Grace for a day and then broke down and told her of the second tragic death of a child she had lovingly raised. Like Bradstreet, Richard was twenty-one years old when he perished. (When daughter Sally turned twenty-one several years later, Grace and George would live in fear for the entire ensuing twelve months.[40])

At Parker Brothers, the employees again expressed sorrow with flowers and tears upon their founder's return. They knew the magnitude of this loss and its likely impact on their trusted leader. He was now without a male heir, and the long-term future of the company, and their security, was in jeopardy.

George began to lean on Charles more than ever. He shared his concern that they would have to give up the firm when both reached an age of feebleness. Who was there to turn to? Charles had lost two of his three children when they were infants. Only his daughter Mary remained. Edward's son, Foster Hegeman Parker, had belatedly joined Parker Brothers in 1919. Like George's sons, Foster had attended Harvard, but after graduating had chosen to move to Baltimore. There, he purchased and ran a great farm until, satisfied with the experience, he moved his family back to New England and became Parker Brothers' corporate secretary. Light-haired and athletic, Foster had an engaging, considerate manner that won the admiration of a work force that had revered his father.[41] But while he proved invaluable to George and Charles, and eventually would be promoted to treasurer—the position his father had occupied—it was uncertain if he could become the forceful leader needed to preside over the firm in the coming decades.[42]

At the same time, conditions in the original building were deteriorating. The structure was nearly a half-century old. It housed well over a hundred workers, lacked storage space, and needed general repairs. Its layout was glaringly inefficient for a modern factory whose annual output exceeded a million dollars of revenue. Despite initial hesitancy, George agreed with Charles that to be the country's number one maker of games, they needed to control more of the manufacturing process—most significantly, they needed to make their own boxes and game boards. The facility needed better ventilation and better lighting in the collating department. They needed more storage space. A large addition was planned and soon erected on the rear of the original building. It provided three floors with spacious rooms with windows on all sides. At last, all assembly could be done in one common area on the third floor. On the second floor, new box and board making machines were installed, while a new warehousing area made its home on the first floor. The original building was refurbished, cleaned, and reorganized and given more office space.[43]

George hired two friends of Richard's from his Harvard days. Paul Haskell was given the responsibility of handling purchasing—which enabled Foster Parker to concentrate on production—while Benjamin Hunneman became manager of the sales department. Charles returned to Europe for long stretches once these positions were filled.

Despite the recent years of turmoil, no game maker of this era threatened Parker Brothers' dominance. Milton Bradley replaced McLoughlin Brothers as Parker Brothers' chief rival. Milton Bradley had swallowed up McLoughlin Brothers in a 1920 takeover because it coveted McLoughlin's educational book business. By now, the big McLoughlin factory in Brooklyn was a memory; all production had been moved to Milton Bradley's Springfield plant in western Massachusetts. But after the deal was made, retail prices—which had skyrocketed after World War I—abruptly declined. Milton Bradley's newly acquired inventory clogged its warehouse. Weakened financially, the firm could not capitalize on the McLoughlin Brothers acquisition.[44]

Once the effects of the war subsided, a great boom gathered strength throughout the nation. The American people, led by President Warren Harding, enjoyed the postwar expansion, and a renewed feeling of optimism spread across the land. An exciting invention called radio was broadcasting music and the human voice into homes across the country. The doughboys had returned from Europe with a broadminded attitude and a desire for entertainment. Marathon dancing became a fad. The Gibson girl was yesterday's ideal; she would be replaced by the flapper with her short skirt and bobbed hair. People felt more liberated than at any time in modern history. They were again ready to have fun.

Bamboo and Ivory

Distant events began to work in George Parker's favor and end his drought of hit games. Ironically, the first such event had occurred long ago, at the 1893 Columbian Exhibition in Chicago—where George had exhibited his games.

At that exhibition, William Wilkinson, British consul at Seoul, Korea, sent a Chinese game for display. The game, which included decorated tiles, drew little notice. It was subsequently given to the University of Pennsylvania for its museum. That same year, Stewart Culin of the *Smithsonian Institute Report* described a game he called Chinese dominos, played with dice and domino-like tiles. Eventually he would find a set of Chinese dominos while on an expedition and present them to his new employer—the Brooklyn Academy of Arts and Science. But he was alone in his enthusiasm for the game, and it was relegated to a display case.

Also in 1893, a man named Joseph Park Babcock was born in Lafayette, Indiana. He graduated from Purdue University in 1911 and went to work for the Standard Oil Company the next year. The firm dispatched its young civil engineer to Soochow, China, as its representative. Babcock took a liking to China, learned to speak the local dialect,

FIGURE 3-1

Mah-Jongg

Mah-Jongg *purchase announcement, 1924.*

and stayed there for many years. He also began to observe and play a game he came to call "mah jong."[45] It was played with tiles, dice, and scoring sticks and oozed with romantic imagery of the "Forbidden Kingdom." Its objective was much like that of the card game rummy—to lay down one's hand of fourteen tiles. Pairs and sets of three or four tiles had to be gathered to accomplish this. Special tiles (winds, seasons, and dragons) offered amazing scoring opportunities.[46] Babcock heard tales of Chinese warlords who lost entire provinces over a game. While an earlier tile game, dominos, had been standardized in China as early as 1120 A.D., the origin of mah jong was murky. It was rumored to be hundreds of years old; it was also rumored to be less than a century old. This game fascinated Babcock so much that in 1919 he tried to persuade a friend at the International Correspondence School of Shanghai to export sets to the United States. He declined. The game had no English rules and the tiles pictured Chinese characters, which were incomprehensible to most Westerners.[47]

Undeterred, and with free time on his hands, Babcock simplified the game, meticulously recorded its rules in English, and added numerals to the tiles. Other friends of his introduced the game and its English rules to Occidentals living in Shanghai during the early months of 1920. They took to it like ducks to water. Soon the entire Western community in the city was crazy for "mah jong."[48]

Given this new popularity, *Babcock's Rules for Mah-Jongg—The Red Book of Rules*, was published in Shanghai that fall. Babcock added the dash and second "g" in *Jongg* to gain a United States trademark for his game, as *mah jong* was considered to be a generic name.[49] The *Red Book* was adopted as gospel by all the clubs in Shanghai. Emboldened, Babcock convinced a lumber importer named W. A. Hammond to purchase a large quantity of the anglicized sets and begin selling them in San Francisco. The game was only a modest success at first, so Babcock hired an American whose surname was Dyas to try and find a major U.S. company to market the game. Dyas was a believer in starting at the top. He went to Parker Brothers.[50]

George Parker admired the elaborate game but was newly cautious. The limited success of products introduced during his long, self-proclaimed retrenchment caused him to doubt his instincts. He did not recall seeing such a game among the splendid exhibits of Chinese artifacts

FIGURE 3-2
Rules? What Rules?

*Cartoon lamenting lack of
standardized rules for the game.*

I have took part in about 50 games of mah jongg and ain't
never seen 2 people yet that played the same rules.

from the late eighteenth and early nineteenth centuries that were on
display in Salem's Peabody Museum. He speculated that this game could
not be popular in China if it had escaped the appetite for Oriental novelties by Salem's great merchant traders.[51] He overlooked the likelihood
that the game did not exist then.

Still, he admired the feel of its tiles, the sound of them "clacking" together, the sight of exotic symbols, and the easy rummy-like method of
combining them into sets, some of which earned gigantic scores. Ultimately, he decided to try a test market, much as he had done with *Flinch*
two decades earlier. Several department stores in New York City obliged
him, but the results were disappointing. George cabled Dyas telling him
that there was no further interest at Parker Brothers. George turned his
attention back to the production of new ball- and ring-tossing games.
Most of the other games featured in the 1922 catalog were quite old;
their inventory clogged the warehouse. But one was different. It was a
beautifully illustrated children's board game based on a Frank Baum
story that had a following, albeit not yet a huge one—and eighteen years
before it was to become the basis for a legendary motion picture. It was
called the *Wonderful Game of Oz*.[52]

Meanwhile, after his return to California, Hammond began to sell his
inventory of imported *Mah-Jongg* sets to local distributors. To facilitate

this, he set up the Mah-Jongg Sales Company of San Francisco. His aim was to get "a story" going (strong word-of-mouth advertising and local newspaper articles) on the West Coast. And what a story he delivered. Sales took off. People throughout California began to buzz about this new, exotic game. Suddenly other firms were publishing books of rules and importing sets of tiles. Hammond and his general manager, a man named J. M. Tess, organized a sales campaign in principal cities and provided free lessons in large department stores. Interest in the game spread so fast that the *Literary Digest* published a story in December 1922 entitled, "Mah Jung, Game of Chinese Mandarins, Displacing Bridge and Poker."[53]

George Parker witnessed the growing wildfire in the spring of 1923. He remembered its predecessors—*Ping-Pong, Pastime Puzzles,* and *Diabolo*—and immediately contacted Dyas, who informed him that Joseph Babcock himself had just arrived in San Francisco, along with 170 tons of *Mah-Jongg* games. George quickly negotiated a deal to acquire rights for Babcock's *Mah-Jongg* trademark and copyright of the official rules. Babcock soon visited Salem. Ultimately, Parker Brothers would import a range of sets that would sell for as little as $2.50, with cheap wooden tiles—and for as much as $25.00, with bamboo-backed ivory tiles packed neatly inside a multidrawer rosewood box.[54] Some of Parker Brothers' components made use of a revolutionary synthetic resin. This new moldable plastic was called *Bakelite*, named after its inventor, Leo Baekeland.[55]

However, thousands of unauthorized sets were pouring into the country and the deluge was out of Parker Brothers' control. To try to gain injunctions to stop them would cost a fortune and take years. In a largely symbolic defense, Babcock and George Parker did adopt the phrase, "If it isn't marked '*Mah-Jongg*' it isn't genuine."[56] Meanwhile, magazines like *Vanity Fair* were running feature stories on the game. Demand was so great that its makers in Shanghai could barely keep up. Young children were employed in the manufacture of new sets. Animal bones had to be shipped from the United States to China to satisfy the need for tile faces and scoring sticks.[57]

The game became so popular that it sparked sales in all manner of Chinese accessories. A good host or hostess was expected to hold a *Mah-Jongg* party in a setting befitting the game. Robes, screens, rugs, lamps, and Chinese food were all essentials for a proper evening of play. Department stores decorated themselves in Chinese style. Upscale stores built temple-shaped enclosures where free lessons were offered to prospective purchasers of luxurious sets, whose prices began at a staggering $150![58]

Parker Brothers benefited enormously from the fad, but George imagined what might have been if he could have locked up ownership of the game before the floodgates opened. Principle 7 etched itself in his brain: Never hesitate and give your opponents a second chance. He vowed never to let this mistake reoccur.

Amid the success and second-guessing, confusion was mounting about how to properly play the game. It seemed that every new maker had issued rules with nuances to make them proprietary. With seemingly everyone playing the game, standardization was essential before the public became aggravated.

A leading authority on the game of bridge, Robert F. Foster, studied the game and proposed laws to govern its play; *Mah-Jongg* associations were soon formed. *Vanity Fair* helped by printing a questionnaire in November 1923 to identify aspects of the game where confusion lay. Robert Foster issued his final "Laws" in early 1924. During this time, Babcock also got his *Red Book* published in the United States with the aim of straightening out the mess. But others entered the fray with different ideas of standardized play.

The export value of *Mah-Jongg* sets from Shanghai now ranked sixth among all Chinese goods. (Only silk, lace, skins, eggs, and tea exceeded it.[59]) In April, *Life* magazine's cover featured, playing at a table, "Pa and Ma Jongg."

Throughout 1924, the battle raged over the correct way to play the game. While the debate continued, the fad began to cool, slowly but surely, until 1929, when it faded from public view. But it did not disappear entirely. The laws of *Mah-Jongg* were ultimately agreed upon and dedicated players continued to enjoy the game. But the man and woman on the street had lost interest. Chinese robes went into storage along with countless boxes of bamboo and ivory tiles.

The demise of *Mah-Jongg* did not disrupt the Parker Brothers factory as had *Pastime Puzzles* at their peak because the Parker Brothers sets were either imported from China or made elsewhere in the United States. Some were shipped directly from China to the stores that purchased them. Those that came to the factory went into the storeroom. Only the shipping and accounting departments actually "touched" the business. The exception was a clever card game version, which George devised and offered for sale.

The hundreds of thousands of dollars flowing in from *Mah-Jongg* both necessitated and permitted Parker Brothers to fulfill a long-expressed desire. In March 1924, the firm successfully petitioned the city of Salem to sell approximately an acre of ground along the North River adjoining the rail line behind their plant in order to erect a 25,000-square-foot warehouse.[60] By 1925, economical freight car loads of raw material were being received there to feed the box making and board making machines. Entire consignments of *Mah-Jongg* games were arriving by rail from West Coast ports along with components of all types made throughout the United States. Although the warehouse was only two hundred feet behind the plant, a private rail line was built along the extension of St. Peter's Street (which ran adjacent to the buildings) to make transfers more efficient. On it, Parker Brothers placed a hand-powered "trolley" that carried materials to the factory and finished games back to the warehouse.

Celebrity Games

Investment in new games was another application for the *Mah-Jongg* windfall. George now became serious about acquiring endorsements. One of the first was with versatile performer Eddie Cantor. Eddie was a talented star of stage, movies, and radio. The goggle-eyed comedic singer, born in 1892, began his career on the Broadway stage in the 1920s with the Ziegfeld Follies and soon was a fixture on the radio. He would make his mark in Hollywood during the 1930s (and remain popular into the 1950s, thanks to the advent of television). He also had a gift for songwriting. Among his most famous were the *Looney Tunes* theme song, "Makin' Whoopee!," and "Merrily We Roll Along."[61] George Parker licensed Eddie's name and likeness for a highway safety game called *Tell It to the Judge* (the idea of the game was to "motor" along the roads depicted

FIGURE 3-3
Tell It to the Judge

1925 ad for Eddie Cantor's game.

on the game board to reach the club space while spending the least money on tickets, fines, and summons.) *Tell It to the Judge* remained in the Parker Brothers line for more than three decades.

The country under President Calvin Coolidge enjoyed a boom like no other. Elected in 1924, Coolidge had a wry wit and a calm manner, which millions of Americans came to appreciate thanks to the advent of radio. "The business of America is business," he said. Advertisers agreed, lifting their spending to over $1 billion in 1925. Deodorants, mouthwash, and Lucky Strike cigarettes were heavily touted. Hemlines inched higher and jazz filled big city nightclubs, where the dancers lifted syncopated arms and flying legs while doing the Charleston. Ernest Hemingway's first novel *The Sun Also Rises* was published in 1926. Then a young aviator named Charles Lindbergh thrilled the nation by flying solo across the Atlantic on May 20–21, 1927.[62]

Sensing opportunity, George Parker negotiated the rights to do a series of games based on Lindbergh's exploits, enabling fans of the aviator to vicariously recreate "Lucky Lindy's" exploits. *Lindy's Hop-Off Game, Lindy,* and *We* were soon selling tens of thousands of copies in stores across the land, bolstered by print advertising, especially in the newly published *New Yorker* magazine.[63]

President Coolidge's optimism drove the stock market ever higher, creating wealth for nearly all investors. It was possible for many Americans to afford cars for the first time. Fifteen million Model T Fords alone had been built by 1928 before Henry Ford switched over to the Model A.[64] But most of the nation's two and a half million miles of roads were just dirt, which turned to mud in wet weather. Most didn't lead anywhere. To get from one town to another, one was still better off taking the train. A man named Carl Fisher recognized the problem. He was the builder of the Indianapolis Motor Speedway and dreamed of building a paved highway that would span the continent. Henry Joy, president of the Packard Motor Car Company, thought of naming the highway after Abraham Lincoln. The federal government soon provided $75 million of matching funds for interstate highway construction. (To avoid confusion, Congress eventually sponsored a numbering system for these highways, rather than a naming system.[65])

The steady publicity and controversy over the Lincoln Highway prompted Parker Brothers in 1926 to market a new board game called the *Lincoln Highway*. Players moved colored pins along "motor trails" on a map game board of the United States, racing from coast to coast. The Automobile Club of America, looking to further its own publicity, endorsed it without charge. Roads on the map were so accurate that a motorist could actually use it to drive across the nation.[66]

FIGURE 3-4
Touring
A 1920s acquisition.

While the *Lincoln Highway* game was a moderate seller, another Parker Brothers acquisition was an even bigger highway game success. A pool table maker, Wallie Dorr of New York, had since 1906 published a card game entitled *Touring*, which had started to sell in substantial quantities. George Parker went to New York and persuaded the firm to sell him the rights. He improved the game by adding a few more types of cards and decided to advertise it nationally. By 1928, it was hailed as "one of the largest-selling games ever published."[67] It was, by and large, a new kind of card game. Players attempted to complete a trip by laying down cards that depicted miles traveled by automobile. The opponents were ready to pounce and cause mishaps with the play of cards like "flat tire" and "out of gas." Remedy cards canceled these and permitted resumption of the "tour."

Like the car pictured on the cover of *Touring*, Parker Brothers was on a roll again. Sales for 1928 were $1,300,000. Another million-dollar-plus year seemed assured for 1929 when newly elected president Herbert Hoover would take office, armed with his belief that the United States was close to "triumph over poverty" and his promise of "a car in every garage."[68]

Brookwood and Camelot

These were also good times for Parker Brothers' employees. Pay was up and the growing work force (nearly two hundred strong) looked forward to the annual summer outing and the latest issue of the *Gamester*—the employee-run house organ. It included articles about past Parker Brothers games, memories of veteran employees, poems by closet poets, and juicy "gossip" such as "A little bird has just informed me that the owner of a certain Ice Company offered [Pastime Girl] Mary Cahill his hand in marriage the other day. What will [Mary's] answer be?"

The prosperity that began in 1922 seemed destined to continue, thanks to the "scientific" management of the economy by the Federal Reserve and the sound vision of Big Business. George Parker turned sixty-two in December 1928. His hair and beard had long since turned white. He was a prosperous man and his form began to reflect his growing prosperity. Several commented that if his beard were longer, he would be confused for the real Santa Claus. Quietly, George bore his sorrows. He missed Edward, he lamented the death of his sons, and he began to think seriously of what to do with Parker Brothers as the sensible age for his retirement approached. He had relaxed his pace a bit and had purchased a country home in Peterborough, New Hampshire—a three-hundred-acre property that contained a small mountain, a forest, and fields enough to plant many idyllic gardens. It was called Brookwood. There, Grace and George dedicated a memorial to their lost sons—a plaque mounted on a large granite boulder that George named "the Rock." And when George heard that his childhood home in Salem, the Watson-Parker house on Essex Street, was going to be demolished to make room for a bigger house, he purchased the paneling and stairway from its hallway and installed them within a new addition to his home in Peterborough.[69]

Following the *Mah-Jongg* craze, George and Grace traveled annually aboard the grand ocean liners of the day. In the summer of 1929, Charles and Abigail joined them. Charles had lost weight and began to feel short of breath. But he shook off his worries and enjoyed his days touring Europe and Egypt.[70] He snapped photos of George and Grace seated atop camels near the Sphinx and Great Pyramid (even in the desert heat, the brothers wore wool suits, the ladies furs). They sailed the Nile where the two brothers rehabilitated one of George's most beloved inventions, his 1887 creation, *Chivalry*. George clung to his belief that the chesslike game of *Chivalry* was the best he had come up with in his nearly fifty years of inventing games.

On this cruise, *Chivalry* was "reincarnated" into an improved game whose major alteration was its name, *Camelot*.[71] Armies of knights and men still took the field with the aim of reaching the opponent's castle space while protecting their own. Multiple jumps over friendly pieces ("cantors") and multiple captures by knights ("charges") were possible in a single turn. Both a two-player and a four-player "tournament" version would be published (and eventually a smaller, fast-playing variant named *Cam*, as well). George hired celebrities, such as comedians Laurel and Hardy, to appear in publicity photos showing them playing *Camelot*.[72] George was determined, this time, to make his reincarnated favorite succeed. Its sales, modest at first like *Rook*'s had been, grew with each passing year. *Camelot* received strong endorsement by game reviewers and was accorded a place in compendiums of standard game rules, such as *Games for Two* in 1930 by Mrs. Prescott Warren, who dedicated her new book to George Parker.

These had been, indeed, good years. But a national crisis now arose and such times proved short lived.

The Depression Begins

George Parker remained a believer in blue chip stocks and AAA bonds, but his enthusiasm for them had waned before he went to Egypt in 1929. He was alarmed to see volatility gripping the market during the heat of summer and it lingered upon his return. September's wild gyrations turned into a rout in late October. George had sold many of his personal holdings before this downfall, but found no solace in his good fortune because, while he may have preserved his family's finances, he knew that his business might not escape the repercussions of a recession. Prior experience indicated that sales of traditional games picked up when recessions hit because there was less work and people had more idle time. But their propensity to play games was offset by retailers' credit deterioration. What good was shipping games if dealers failed to pay for them?

The huge losses suffered by investors suggested that what was coming this time would be more than a nasty recession. President Hoover urged big business to maintain prices and hold onto its employees. Companies did, at first. But demand for big-ticket items, like cars and appliances, soon nose-dived. Inevitably, prices dropped and millions became unemployed. (At the height of the Depression, one-third of all U.S. workers would be without jobs.[73]) Parker Brothers still gained, initially. Demand perked up for card games and *Pastime Puzzles* came back into vogue. It seemed that as unemployment rose, people were occupying their free time by playing games or searching for that elusive puzzle piece, just as they always had during recessionary times. And, for the moment, retailers were still paying their bills.[74]

Pastime Girls were again a mainstay at Parker Brothers. But the increase in puzzle sales led to a dilemma. There was no space available to expand puzzle production, so the firm arranged to lease the vacant livery owned by the HP Hood dairy company, a football field's distance from the factory. Material storage and the sanding function were moved to the ground floor and the jigsaw operation relocated to the second floor of the barn. In winter, the Pastime Girls had to wear coats and boots while cutting puzzles because the barn was unheated.[75]

The cost of *Pastime Puzzles* had risen to two cents per piece. A three-hundred-piece puzzle cost six dollars (over seventy dollars today), so puzzle-renting libraries once again became popular. In New York City, a

Miss Josephine Flood opened the Picture Puzzle Mart on Park Avenue. She was particular and often came to the Salem factory to pick out the puzzles she wanted to offer for rent to the ladies of New York society. She favored large puzzles with highly detailed pictures. These took longer for puzzle fans to assemble and therefore earned her more rental fees. Society women, in general, continued their love affair with *Pastime Puzzles*. It was not uncommon for a chauffeured limousine to pull up to the main entrance of the Parker Brothers plant with a wealthy passenger desiring to buy fifty or more puzzles for the pleasure of her friends in the coming year.[76] By mid-1932, this second *Pastime* craze began to abate. Competitors were now making cheap die-cut cardboard puzzles by the tens of thousands. George Parker was reluctant to compete because of the "cookie-cutter" nature of these low-quality puzzles, as compared to the uniqueness and durability of his three-ply wooden puzzles. But George soon relented and authorized other vendors to make cardboard puzzles for his firm. After business contracted, the Pastime Girls moved back into the factory. (HP Hood tore down its barn and eventually replaced it with a concrete-block, single-story garage, which Parker Brothers later acquired.[77])

A sudden fascination with backgammon gripped the country in 1929–1930, thanks to the introduction of the doubling cube that aroused the gambler's instinct in many a new player. Any firm could make this generic game and Parker Brothers quickly put seven versions into production. *Diabolo* was also brought back, hoping that it might spark the fancy of a new generation. (It didn't.) *Camelot* was temporarily stymied by backgammon's popularity but garnered rave reviews among members of "society," who acclaimed it as the next great "thinking" game in newspaper columns.[78] George believed the life of his revised game would exceed his own, if his business could endure. In 1931, Charles was seventy-one; his health was failing along with his good humor. George reached sixty-five: the age of retirement for most of his workers. As much as he wished to close his rolltop desk and move permanently to his country home in Peterborough, New Hampshire, circumstances conspired to quash his desires. There was still no one to whom he could confidently pass control of his business.

Since the beginning, Parker Brothers Incorporated had been organized along simple lines. The brothers ran the firm while a number of empowered foremen and foreladies ran each department and managed the hiring and administration of workers. It was possible for a gifted worker to rise to the rank of foreman, but no higher. The office had a small array of accountants and bookkeepers and a few managers, like Paul Haskell of purchasing and Ben Hunneman of sales (Grace Parker's brother Earnest also served as a manager). But these men did not have the scope of experience to be replacement candidates for the founder. Edward Parker's son Foster might have been a candidate, but he chose to leave the company to open an auto dealership in Boston. Charles's surviving daughter, Mary, had married businessman Channing Bacall in 1919. They had two children. Channing had attended Harvard and had become an executive at the Champion Lamp Company, but had no interest in switching to Parker Brothers.[79] Feeling alone and overwhelmed, George accepted an eighth principle. He realized that he must seek out help if the business was to endure.

Robert Barton

In 1931, George's last surviving child, Sally, married a tall, thin Baltimorean named Robert B. M. Barton at Brookwood. In September 1932, Sally gave birth to their first child, a son named Randolph Parker Barton. His grandparents began to take train rides to Baltimore to visit their grandson and his parents.[80] Robert Barton impressed George. He had degrees in both history and law from Harvard and worked for his father's legal firm. For eight generations, his family had produced an attorney who could trace his roots to President George Washington's first chief justice, William Marshall. Barton's grandfather had served as an adjutant general for Stonewall Jackson. After the war, he moved from Virginia to Baltimore, hired a tailor to replace the brass buttons on his uniform with black buttons, and opened up a legal office. He slept on its sofa until he could afford the cost of renting an apartment.[81] George observed Robert Barton's stern intelligence and detected in him the right qualities to lead men and women. Thereafter, he began to entice his son-in-law to join Parker Brothers and train to be its leader. Barton came up to Salem to see the operation, but was dismayed by its plant management and dated manufacturing methods. He did not jump at the opportunity.[82]

In early 1932, the banks in Salem failed, just before Franklin Roosevelt took the oath that would make him the nation's thirty-second president. George used his game savvy to steady the sagging morale of his workers. He had "Parker scrip" printed to pay them until he could get cash from the First National Bank of Salem. Merchants in town willingly accepted the scrip. After Roosevelt's election and his bank holiday, the nation's financial institutions reopened and the Parker scrip was redeemed.[83] That same year, George was saddened when brother Charles's health finally forced him to retire. For a while, he seriously contemplated the sale of his firm to a rival. But this option, however unthinkable it would have been in the 1920s, was virtually impossible now. Who among his weakened competitors had the money to buy him out? Milton Bradley had made a costly acquisition by purchasing McLoughlin Brothers. Milton Bradley's investors weren't likely to have the means to now buy Parker Brothers. The firm of Selchow & Righter, makers of *Parcheesi*, was much smaller than Parker Brothers. No other game or toy company in the United States had the muscle to make a fair offer. George pondered how Grace would handle the resultant estate mess if he suddenly died.[84]

Shortly after Charles's retirement, word reached George that Robert Barton and his father were at an impasse over policy. Robert's father felt that all clients are good clients; his son disagreed. Robert Barton had personally thrown out of the office a man who bilked investors out of hundreds of thousands of dollars. Robert, young and idealistic, despised his kind. During college, he had developed empathy for labor after working summers in a machine shop and on a farm. In contrast, his father mainly represented businessmen, both the clean and the corrupt.[85] George Parker took the opportunity to renew his efforts to persuade Robert Barton to join Parker Brothers. The brash thirty-year-old finally agreed, on one condition—after a reasonable period of training, he must be named president, with full authority to run the business. George weighed his options and agreed to Barton's demand.[86]

Barton and Sally moved north to Chestnut Street in Salem, Massachusetts, with young "Ranny" in tow. Their presence brought many joys to the family, but their mutual happiness was dampened by the harsh reality of the declining business. The "common recession" had turned into the Great Depression. Robert Barton felt the need to act quickly.

He absorbed what he saw and heard inside of Parker Brothers and began to advise his father-in-law on how to reduce costs and improve efficiency. He was surprised to find that the firm had no printing equipment. He asked George, "How can this be?" Barton observed that every item assembled and shipped from the warehouse included several printed components.[87] Barton also believed that Parker Brothers had an antiquated management structure. His first priority was finding a trustworthy insider to help him bring about change. He recognized a "bright light" in the manufacturing department, a slide-rule-carrying, notebook-toting foreman named Donald B. Jelly.[88] With Jelly's careful analysis, Barton was able to demonstrate to George that buying printing presses was a smart move. Fortunately, the finances of the firm were still strong. Two large one-color presses were purchased for cash, each capable of printing a box wrap or a game board label big enough for the firm's largest game. A smaller press was purchased to print smaller items like game rules and simple cards.[89]

When Barton became president in 1933, George Parker assumed the position of chairman of the board. From this vantage point, he would serve as Barton's mentor and control new product selection and development. Barton was satisfied with the arrangement. He didn't have an ounce of desire to be a game inventor, although he felt that he was developing a pretty good eye for what would sell. His first year at Parker Brothers had not been easy, however. Employees viewed him suspiciously, like an outsider. And he found working with his father-in-law to be difficult. He often had to take issue with the stubborn Mr. Parker, much as he had with his own father, regarding outdated ways of conducting business. But Barton soon realized that George Parker held the key for his own success. Like his father-in-law, Barton was a believer in managing for lasting success. When the elder explained how experience had led him to a series of gamelike principles that sparked his business success, Barton was quietly impressed. He did not regard these laws as the outdated ideals of an old man. Instead, he felt that he could profit by applying them to his "new way" of running the firm. As an attorney, he knew the importance of playing by the rules while exploiting them to his firm's advantage. He knew he needed a winning move to turn things around, and the guts to exploit it. And while he had great resolve, as would be demonstrated time and again in the coming years,

Barton embraced the importance of patience during adversity—he would not risk capital until a sound opportunity presented itself.[90]

With Barton came the birth of Parker Brothers as a modern, organized business. Under George Parker, it had often been a loosely structured family affair. Shortly after becoming president, Barton assembled a staff of talented leaders, without consideration for family ties. As he was to opine in later years about George Parker, "He was a brilliant man in many ways. Very well read, a beautifully [self]-educated man. . . . But he knew little about business management. [He was a] man who simply could not associate good men with him."[91]

Robert Barton shored up George's weakness and quickly put together his staff. Fellow Harvard graduate Paul Haskell became purchasing agent. Ben Hunneman was promoted to vice president of sales. Don Jelly was elevated to vice president of manufacturing and his predecessor was let go because he stubbornly blocked attempts to modernize the firm. Barton's secretary, Helen Mitchell, recalled that she would periodically bring the brainy Jelly a thirty-inch-square manufacturing report. He would look at the maze of figures and quickly point out all the trouble spots.[92] A twenty-three-year veteran, Charles Phelps, became superintendent of the factory, responsible for keeping it operating smoothly and supporting Jelly's manufacturing efforts. Young Leroy ("Roy") Howard was promoted to editor. Save for George Parker, he was the firm's entire R&D department. (Howard would periodically enlist the aid of other employees to help select and design each year's game line.)

Donald Jelly and Charlie Phelps had good foremen working for them, like Henry Sullivan of shipping, and one especially outstanding forewoman, Agnes McGee, who ran, and would run, the collating (assembly) department until the early 1960s. Her responsibility was to see that the right games were assembled each day with precisely the right count of parts inside each box. Every game was packed entirely by one worker and then inspected by another before a box lid was telescoped over its box bottom. McGee employed only women who abided by her overriding rule—no talking on the job. She believed that talking led to distraction and distraction led to improper collating. Her goal was music to Barton's ears: zero defects. Her voice was also heard when materials for new games were being decided upon. Games had to last; she was as passionate in this belief as George Parker. Consumer response verified the success of her efforts. Very few letters were received from consumers complaining about a missing piece or card, or a box that split, or a game board that warped. And McGee intended to keep things this way.[93]

Shipper Henry Sullivan was to work for Parker Brothers for forty years, almost as long as his cousin Henry Fitzpatrick. His job was to schedule the trucks and train cars that brought raw material to the factory. When finished games came down from Agnes McGee's department, they were stacked in the warehouse in "chimneys"—that is, four-sided stacks, hollow in the center. There were no cardboard storage or shipping cartons, so the stacks had to be built correctly to prevent them from falling and harming the goods. When orders were filled, the order boys would carefully remove games from the top of a chimney, load them onto a cart, and move them to the shipping department where a wooden shook had to be assembled to pack a store's order for shipment. Some big accounts, like Macy's, ordered so many games at a time that its loaded shook would weigh five or six hundred pounds and required three men to move.[94]

Once packed, it became Henry Fitzpatrick's task to get a shook delivered to its customer. George Parker believed Henry Fitzpatrick to be among the most talented shippers in the country.[95] Barton concurred. But employees like Fitzpatrick, McGee, and Sullivan had adopted a "wait and see" attitude about Barton. Sally explained this to her husband. The Yankee tradition required the evaluating of a person over time before coming to judgment. To win their confidence, Barton made a habit of walking through the plant, saying hello, and getting to know his workers personally, as had Charles and Edward before him. He was both amazed and impressed with what he found. Entire families, like the Fitzpatricks and another named Cahill, were working for Parker Brothers! Husbands, wives, aunts, uncles, children—even a grandparent or two. Many had been at Parker Brothers since the time that *Pastime Puzzles* first took off, more than twenty years earlier. And they hadn't remained for the wrong reasons. They were good workers; they had pride in what they did, nicknamed "Parker Pride." They produced quality products. They wanted to work here, despite the fact, as Barton now knew, that Parker Brothers was not a high-paying employer.

Barton's empathy for labor clearly influenced the direction of his moral compass, even though increasingly he was seen as patrician and distant. He was determined to learn and foster the reasons for the devotion of Parker Brothers' work force. He made it known that his door was always open. An employee with a problem or suggestion need only schedule time through Barton's secretary, bypassing his or her foreman. He also focused attention on the industry of which he was now a part. He lacked a real knowledge of who was who in the toy business, which he felt was a barrier to his success as president of Parker Brothers. He went to New York and met with the leaders of the Toy Manufacturers Association (TMA) and asked to join. They first laughed at this young man's naïveté before explaining that you just didn't become a member of the board of the TMA. You worked your way up by serving on committees and then getting elected to higher positions. So Robert Barton agreed to work his way up from the bottom. (Within a few years, he was serving on the board and eventually became its president.) He also set out to build ties to his community, most notably by joining the board of Salem Hospital. He would soon serve as its president, as well.[96]

The firm had only two field salesmen in the United States when Barton became president. One was based in the New York sales office, long-time employee Harry Phillips. The other was rotund Albert Richardson, who had risen steadily from his humble beginnings as a Parker Brothers office boy. Fifty-six years of age in 1933, he managed to cover the bulk of the country for Parker Brothers, despite not knowing how to drive a car.[97] Each year after the toy fair, he would pack great steamer trunks with samples of the firm's product line and hit the rails. Before leaving, he would send ingenious, custom-illustrated postcards to his many accounts, informing them that he was on the road and would visit their city shortly. He personally composed the limericks or clever messages on each year's card. Like most "drummers" of his era, after Richardson reached a city and set up his products in his hotel room, he would contact his major customers there—mainly department stores and big wholesalers—and invite them to a presentation. Before Prohibition ended in 1933, he carried a concealed stock of bootleg liquor below the false bottom of one of his trunks. The spirits were an enticement to ensure good attendance, along with his big supply of cigars.[98]

Sorry Times

Robert Barton got word from the London office of a board game that was selling very well in England. It was entitled *Sorry!* and was made by W. H. Storey *&* Co. outside of London. With George's consent, Robert Barton paid $25,000 to purchase the U.S. rights for *Sorry!* even though George viewed it as just another variation of *Parcheesi.* Barton appreciated its novel features. It used a deck of movement cards instead of dice, had special "slide" spaces on its paths where opposing pieces could more easily be knocked back to "start," and was easy enough for a six-year-old to play. Barton reasoned that if U.K. consumers were purchasing *Sorry!* so would U.S. game players.[99]

Meanwhile, George Parker increasingly lent his efforts to the Essex Institute in Salem, whose goal was to preserve and publicize historical matters. He volunteered to contact and persuade well-known personalities to conduct lectures at the institute. Among them was Hendrik van Loon—an influential U.S. author, history teacher, and journalist, who had immigrated to the United States in 1903. He became an Associated Press correspondent, covered World War I, and, after the war, began to write books. His many popular histories include the best-selling books *The Story of Mankind* (1921), *The Story of the Bible* (1923), and *America* (1927).[100]

George Parker was so impressed with van Loon that he decided to publish a travel game bearing his name and likeness. *Hendrik van Loon's Wide World* game appeared in 1933. Van Loon himself drew the illustration of the world for its board. The game was big and handsome, with metal airplanes and steamships serving as the playing pieces moved to complete a voyage between two distant city spaces. In this era before widespread air travel, *Hendrik van Loon's Wide World* aimed to satisfy the dream, among young and old alike, of exotic foreign travel in real life.[101]

Cardboard "jigsaw" puzzles had rapidly gained ground in the U.S. market because they were affordable, even in hard times. One of the makers of these puzzles was an English company named John Waddington Limited. Victor Watson Sr. headed the firm with help from his son, Norman Watson. Norman had two young boys named Victor and Beric. The family nature of Waddington's mirrored that of Parker Brothers and it seemed fated that the two firms would become close. Waddington's was a leading printer and playing card maker in England. However, in 1933, they were persuaded to publish a game consisting of cards printed with letters and scoring values. Its object was to form and lay down words. The game was called *Lexicon* and, after correcting some early marketing mistakes, Waddington's turned it into a huge seller. Robert Barton agreed to license it for the United States and planned to introduce it in 1935.[102]

Sorry! would be the first game to bear the Parker Brothers "signature" logo, penned by George Parker. Previously, a plain typed "Parker Brothers" name had been printed on each and every package the firm produced. For many years the only real logo to appear on the firm's packages was the image of a sailing ship accompanied by the words "Made in Salem, Mass., USA."

Barton's first year as president of Parker Brothers was a brutal one, in the stark judgment of the firm's books. The firm's sales in 1933 declined for the third year in a row and it suffered a loss in excess of $100,000.[103] Never had such red ink been spilled in the history of the firm. Attrition claimed the jobs of more and more employees. As Robert Barton accepted the inability of the country to shake itself out of the Depression, it became clear to him that being president of Parker Brothers might be a short-term affair. If Americans did not buy games, the firm would not survive, no matter how much he modernized it. Barton, well connected from his Harvard days, knew several people who worked for the Roosevelt administration. They were anxious. This Depression was a monster to deal with. It resisted taming. With each passing month, its choke on the economy meant less free money in consumers' hands.[104]

George Parker had been able to patiently play his back game because his firm continued to earn profits throughout the Depression and had money in the bank. The harsh reality was that Barton had neither to aid his desire to wait for fortune to change.

Drastic times called for drastic measures.

Chapter Four

Rolling Doubles

1934–1952

THE LOSSES HAD TO BE REVERSED. THIS COULD ONLY come about through lowering costs or increasing sales. The prospects for the latter were nil unless, somehow, a "miracle" game, which the company did not yet own or even imagine, dropped from the firmament. And unless enough of Parker Brothers' infrastructure was preserved beforehand, such a miracle would transcend the weakened firm's ability to exploit it.

Robert Barton's patience was ironclad, but he needed time, and a lot of luck, if his patience were to pay off.

Black Monday

On a Friday evening in March 1934, prior to what became known as Black Monday, George Parker sat at his desk and carefully penned two words onto its left side, below the rolltop's track: *Noblesse Oblige.* He later explained that he felt compelled to record, for posterity, his deep sense of obligation for his family of workers at a time when the means to discharge that obligation was expiring.[1]

Fifty-one years had passed since he had published his first game. Hundreds had followed, including many giant successes. The 1934 catalog listed more than 260 items, and yet their combined sales were but a third of the total sales for 1929, when the Depression had just begun. On his office wall hung the childhood photographs of his deceased sons and old photos of his two brothers. Edward would have been seventy-nine. Charles was now seventy-four, retired for two years, clinging precariously to life. None of them could help him now. The one man who could—upon whom he placed all hope—entered and closed the office door.

Robert Barton stood rigid and impassive as always. His small lips tightly pursed, his wire-rimmed glasses reflecting the bulbs in the lights hanging from the ceiling. He tapped the sheets of accounting paper clutched to his chest. "We'll be lucky to ship $400,000 worth of games this year. We're back to where you were before *Pastime Puzzles* entered the line. Should I read you the item-by-item forecast to demonstrate how I came up with this number?"

George took off his glasses. As he cleaned the lenses with his handkerchief, he said, "Yes, yes, fine enough." This expression had been heard hundreds of times by nearly everyone in the company. It was a typical "GSP" response to a business topic that he found unpleasant but could not argue with. As usual, it led him to go "sailing" (change the subject), as his employees called this tactic. He began to speak of his brother and how he had so often "frazzled Charles" by coming up with one more unplanned game that needed financing. Charles would complain about how stretched the firm's finances were. George would laugh and tell him to pull on the money a little harder. "It won't break," he'd say with a twinkle in his eye.

Barton wasn't smiling. "That's possible, when you've got some money to tug on." Parker Brothers had just suffered its first year of major losses; another loomed.

FIGURE 4-1
Make-a-Million

George Parker's attempt to make people feel rich during the Great Depression.

"How can we not be doing better? All those people out there with no jobs, nothing but time on their hands."

Barton was somber as he explained how it was one thing to have a little money to throw around, but another thing entirely to have nothing. Barton detected on his father-in-law's face, beneath the white mustache and Vandyke beard, a look of denial. His own spirits sank. He felt like an executioner come to tell a grieving father that no pardon had come through from the governor, and that not just one, but all of his sons and daughters were doomed. "You want *me* to do it, don't you?"

George sighed. "I can't. You have to."

Barton understood. George S. Parker had been a hero of Salem for so long, he could not bear the thought of becoming its goat. In contrast, Barton was still seen as the cool, distant "black knight" from Baltimore. He had been president for a year, the worst twelve months in the company's history. The idea of anyone other than George Parker running the firm was absolutely foreign to the dozens of employees who had been with the company through its glory years. But then in 1932 came this green attorney, this dour husband of George's smiling daughter Sally, who knew nothing of games or of their hometown, Salem, Massachusetts. He had yet to be Parkerized in the eyes of the employees, who wondered about his sense of commitment, purpose, and belief in earned mutual support.

Parker Brothers had endured as a big, happy family.[2] George was now its grandfather, Barton its adopted father. In two days' time, his "children" would know the lengths to which a father must sometimes go to save a family.

The following Monday morning, Barton fired all the workers of Parker Brothers—every one of the "Parker 100" that, since 1930, had survived the gradual whittling down of the work force. Loyal employees like Henry Sullivan of the traffic department were speechless. Not just because they had lost their jobs, but because they were saddened by the apparent end to the great company they loved to work for. There were no benefits, no farewell checks—another sign of how dire things must be for the firm. Sadly, the workers concluded that even resilient Parker Brothers had been taken down by a monster known as "the Great Depression"—a fiend that had also stolen the jobs of their friends from local employers, including Sylvania, Naumkeag Cotton

Mills, and United Shoe Machinery. It was only as the shaken workers were leaving the building that they were told it might be a good idea to come back that afternoon.

Numbed by the morning's crushing blow and not knowing what else to do, virtually all of the workers acted on the suggestion. As they milled about, rumors began to spread—there would be severance checks, or maybe a stack of games each worker could try to sell to raise some money. Some thought the Parker family would offer vouchers to be honored when the plant was sold, but others scoffed at this idea—who'd want to buy a sixty-year-old building that was only good for making games? The last rumor had a basis in fact. The prior year, George had seriously explored selling out, believing his business had no future without him at the helm. But Barton's arrival had given him pause. Barton's secretary now appeared at the main door and asked everyone to form a line. No one anticipated what would happen next.

Jobs were available. Parker Brothers would not shut its doors.

Everyone was invited to apply for the new openings. The bewildered men and women filed up to a table covered with spreadsheets, behind which sat Barton and Donald Jelly. With typical efficiency, both men decided the fate of them all. Capable employees got their old jobs back. Talented ones were singled out for promotion. Those who were expendable were told, "Sorry, there's nothing for you now." These would go home, despondent, for the second time that day. None of the new openings paid anywhere near the wage of the old positions they replaced. But Parker Brothers wasn't dead after all, and those reemployed were assured the firm could now make ends meet—at least until the end of the year.

When it was over, Barton returned to his office, wiped his glasses, breathed a sigh of relief, and asked for an aspirin. He had performed the first major layoff in the history of the firm. And by so doing, he kept it alive long enough to seize the opportunity of a lifetime.

The Philadelphian

Not long thereafter, a burly unemployed man from Philadelphia submitted a game about buying and developing real estate. George played it, as he did every game that came Parker Brothers' way. This game proved intricate and surprisingly innovative. But all of George's instincts told him that it would not go over with the masses. It was far too complicated, too technical, took too long to play. George turned to Roy Howard and said to his editor, "Unless I change my mind, wait a few days, then have a letter sent that convinces this fellow his game doesn't stand a chance, so he'll leave us alone."[3]

Roy Howard and Barton talked about the game a few days later. Howard had found it to be "a very interesting" moneymaking game. "Mr. Parker is still opposed, isn't he?" Barton asked. Howard said yes. Barton nodded without comment. "Well, do as he says and have the letter go out." The letter Howard wrote mentioned "fifty-two fundamental playing errors"—an exaggeration aimed at convincing the inventor not to bother Parker Brothers again.[4]

By the end of 1934, Barton and his team had managed to limit expenses sufficiently to break even.[5] Given the dim prospects for 1935, Jelly suggested soliciting printing business to help pay off the new presses. Barton, determined to make his investment pay off, suggested that Jelly send purchasing agent Paul Haskell and Charlie Phelps of manufacturing into Boston to solicit contract printing. George regarded this as an act of desperation.

By 1935, 20 percent of U.S. workers were still without a job—this despite the massive social programs of Roosevelt's New Deal. The average family earned $1,500 a year. Bad weather turned Midwest farms into a dust bowl. Over 2 million school children went without education due to spending cutbacks. An average of 900 banks failed each year—and the Dow-Jones average, which had surpassed 380 in 1929, had declined for three years and now hovered at 100. Hand-cut cardboard liners kept old shoes in service. Clothes were mended and mended again before being handed down. Food was scarce on many tables. Soup kitchens were a fixture in cities large and small.

For many, the agony of the Great Depression did not end until 1941, thanks to either a job offer from a military plant or a draft notice. For Parker Brothers, it came via a phone call in early 1935 to Sally Barton. On the line was a friend who lived in Philadelphia. She wanted Sally to know about a game she had played that was quite the local rage. Sally relayed this to her husband, adding, "It's called 'the Monopoly game.'"[6]

Barton stopped what he was doing. The unemployed man's game was called "the Monopoly game." Barton asked his vice president of sales, Ben Hunneman, to look into this. Hunneman reported back that the John Wanamaker department store of Philadelphia had taken a flier on the game last fall. And yes, it had sold through all it could get, which amounted to a few hundred pieces. The toy chain F. A. O. Schwarz had sold out of about a hundred copies. It came packed in big white boxes. Barton's interest was growing. Hunneman went on to say that after Christmas, the buyer at Wanamaker had ordered "a lot more" of a cheaper edition on consignment.[7]

Barton told this to George and got his blessing to reconsider buying the rights. But George still voiced reservations. He was bothered by the disappointing sales of his own cure-all for the Depression—the card game *Make-a-Million*, which was actually no more than a variant of *Rook* with "dollars" replacing points for scoring, and an added "Tiger" card, which greatly affected the dollars earned. The 1934 catalog proclaimed the game a "New Best Seller" and called it "remarkable"—this before one piece had been shipped.

Barton immediately opened negotiations with the unemployed Philadelphian, Charles Brace Darrow. The biggest stumbling block to a deal turned out to be the remaining inventory. Darrow had just taken delivery of 7,500 games and most were lying in storage. George worried that it would be difficult to sell the 5,000 or so pieces his firm would be forced to buy. But the latest sales reports from Philadelphia persuaded Barton that at least that many, if not more, of the *Monopoly* game could be sold. On March 19, he met Darrow in the Parker Brothers showroom at the Flatiron Building in New York City. Darrow, like most Americans, had no idea of the difficulties faced by Parker Brothers. He was awestruck to meet the president of the country's best-known game firm amid the glamour of a New York skyscraper. Barton saw that he was eager to make a deal. In particular, he admitted being overwhelmed by the headache of making, financing, and storing its inventory. Barton sensed that he could gain concessions if he adopted a tough posture. But he respected the risk Darrow had taken to launch the game commercially and offered the Philadelphian more than enough to cover the cost of his inventory. He also offered Darrow a profitable royalty on all subsequent sales. He asked Darrow if he was the sole inventor of the game, as the contract would so state. Darrow said that he was, and the deal was inked.[8]

The Monopoly Game

When the inventory arrived from Philadelphia, George and Grace Parker were away in Europe.[9] Barton urged his troops to get the *Monopoly* game into production as soon as possible. Jelly had orders to use as many of Darrow's components as possible in the first run of the new Parker Brothers edition, the design of which was about to undergo discussion. It was quickly concluded that $2 was the most that people would pay for the game. Parker Brothers' first "standard" edition would consist of a separate board and a small box filled with playing equipment: play money, little green wooden houses and red hotels, an orange deck of Chance cards, and yellow Community Chest cards (named after a public charity that had originated in Cincinnati). There were also colorful title deeds and dice. Parker Brothers' two-color box label was quickly designed using a few graphic images rendered by Darrow's designer for his "white box" set.

FIGURE 4-2

The *Monopoly* Game Craze

1936 Monopoly *flyer.*

The Prevailing Game Craze MONOPOLY is now spreading to all parts of the World. Its popularity in America is the greatest ever attained in games.

MONOPOLY is now made in the following editions, which are obtainable from your Dealer.

$2.00 MONOPOLY SET No. 6. Blue or Black-bound Board. Complete outfit for from three to seven Players, in separate box. Price, $2.00

POPULAR EDITION No. 8. Board bound in Pebbled Green. Separate box contains complete equipment for from three to eight Players. Special-slip Money, Metal Tokens, larger Hotels and large Dice. Price, $2.50

WHITE BOX EDITION No. 9. This set is a great favorite. Entire equipment is contained in a large white box, which now has a removable "Bank," i.e., a compartment section which greatly aids in the handling of money. Grand Hotels are stamped in gold and the set is equipped for from three to ten Players—with a double supply of Special-slip Money. Being a medium priced set, many consider it the "best buy" in MONOPOLY sets, and it certainly gives great satisfaction. Price, $3.50

$5.00 EDITION No. 10. Handsome Box and Board, each bound in Brown Pebbled Leatherette. Special-slip Money and removable Compartment Bank, which facilitates the Banking. With large size Tokens and Grand Hotels. A very practical edition—well worth the price. Price, $5.00

GOLD EDITION No. 12. Houses and Hotels of beautiful Ivoroid. Removable Compartment Bank. New Money with a high gloss finish which makes it a pleasure to handle. Board and Box in Gold Binding. Large size Tokens. A beautiful and practical set with which it is an added delight to play. Equipment for from three to ten Players. Price, $10.00

No. 25, DE LUXE EDITION. This is the finest set made. The board is made of handsome composition in beautiful lacquer colors and highly finished. The Houses and Hotels are made of Ivoroid, removable compartment Bank, new slip finish money, also new metal money and large size Tokens in gold finish. Equipment for from three to ten players. A set that will do credit to the finest living room or to the most exclusive club. Price, $25.00

AT ALL DEALERS OR BY MAIL

PARKER BROTHERS, INC., SALEM, MASS., NEW YORK, LONDON

George was so concerned over the "flaws" in the game's rules that he had requested Howard to develop rules for a short version and a time limit variant of play. George finalized them after his return from Europe. These rule variations would be included with every game to leave the Parker Brothers factory. (Ironically, George seemed not to recall his earlier thinking that people currently had "nothing but time on their hands.") George Parker was still a stickler when it came to the wording of his rules. He prided himself on the fact that a set of rules that he had written in 1895 could not be mistaken as having come from any other pen, and was just as easy to comprehend in 1935 as forty years earlier. With his editorial standards to guide him, he went about the task of rewriting the rules of Darrow's *Monopoly* game, which he found to be incomplete and filled with ambiguities. (Three days alone were spent debating the wording of the rule regarding throwing doubles.[10]) Darrow's game did not come with tokens. Players were instructed to use little objects from around the house, such as thimbles and buttons. Charm bracelets also served as a source of tokens. This inspired the use of small metal playing pieces that resembled everyday objects. Thus were born the Iron, Thimble, Shoe, and other tokens so inimitably associated with the *Monopoly* game. No effort was made to change the design of any of the game's components, including the game board. However, George did not favor the plain design of Darrow's play money. New Parker Brothers money would be phased in after its design was completed. In subsequent production runs, the colors of the properties on the game board were enhanced and a few graphic flourishes (like the treasure chest on the Community Chest spaces) were added. Income Tax originally called for a payment of $300 or 10 percent of holdings. This was soon reduced to $200 or 10 percent. If the game proved successful, illustrations would be added to the Chance and Community Chest cards, but not to begin with. Otherwise the game retained Darrow's imprint.

As the date neared when Agnes McGee's collating department would start assembling Parker Brothers' first *Monopoly* games, George cautioned Barton not to make too many copies until some indication of retail movement occurred.[11] His strong feeling that the game would be too complicated for the majority of players compelled his caution. The *Monopoly* game invited players to become real estate tycoons. They moved endlessly around its continuous track of spaces until all but one ran out of money and went "bankrupt." Title deeds were acquired as players purchased spaces on the track. When a player owned the two or three that comprised a color group, he could begin to purchase houses and eventually hotels, and place them on the group's spaces. A player paid rent when landing on an opponent's space—and the rent climbed with each house erected on it.

Money changed hands constantly between the "bank" and the players. Trading was not only encouraged, it was often vital to get a group and begin development. This could take a while, and bankrupting all the players save one might take hours. For these reasons, George thought the game would cease to be played except via his abbreviated versions. Word of mouth would otherwise grow negative and the game would then fail.

Sales, however, were good from the beginning and George packed up his worries. He soon recommended publishing a deluxe edition of the game. Hope began to spring within the firm that they might have two winners.

George Parker now looked ahead. The *Monopoly* game might well flourish. If the game really took off, his competitors would issue knockoffs to get in on the action. He was still pained by the confusion and lost sales caused by competition during the great *Mah-Jongg* craze of the 1920s (which had given birth to Principle 7). So he suggested to Barton that a patent be applied for to protect the *Monopoly* game.[12] Darrow's copyright had been acquired and the trademark for its name had been registered, without opposition. That was sufficient in Barton's mind. He did not feel patents held much water when it came to protecting board games. But he yielded to his father-in-law's insistence and contracted the firm's Boston-based intellectual property attorneys to prepare an application. A patent must be applied for in the name of its inventor; this patent would bear Darrow's name. Once issued, a patent can be assigned to a business entity. Darrow would assign his patent to Parker Brothers. By doing as his father-in-law wished, Barton was blessed again by Lady Luck. The patent office returned a record of a 1924 patent for a game called the *Landlord's Game* that bore a resemblance to the *Monopoly* game. This patent would stymie the one for the *Monopoly* game unless Parker Brothers owned it as well.

When George heard of the conflicting patent, a light went on. He *knew* the inventor of the *Landlord's Game*! Her name was Elizabeth Magie

Phillips and she had presented her game to him in 1922 or 1923 (and perhaps an earlier version many years before that!). George remembered that she had flattered him, calling him the "King of Games." He had let her down easy, explaining how her invention, which espoused the Single Tax Theory of activist Henry George, was "too educational." George also found it boring, but he didn't voice this. Instead, he recommended to Mrs. Phillips that she protect her idea via a patent. Now, twelve years later that bit of friendly advice would either come back to haunt him or prove to be a stroke of genius.

Auspiciously, it proved to be the latter. Barton urged George to take a train to Washington, D.C., to meet with Mrs. Phillips in Arlington, Virginia, where she lived with her husband. Since George felt responsible for having urged Mrs. Phillips to apply for her patent, he agreed. (But at the moment, he was distracted by the disappearance of his dog, Nero. Ads were placed in local papers. Fortunately, on the morning of his scheduled meeting, Nero was found.) George concluded a deal with Mrs. Phillips to buy her patent late on the evening of November 5. The patent had been of little benefit to Mrs. Phillips and was due to expire in a few years time. Of greater importance to Mrs. Phillips was what she requested and got as part of the deal—Parker Brothers' agreement to publish three of her games in coming years, including an updated version of the *Landlord's Game*. With the Phillips patent in hand, the patent for the *Monopoly* game was issued on the last day of 1935.[13]

Benjamin Hunneman learned that a game was already on the market that bore a resemblance to the *Monopoly* game. He informed Barton that a firm in Indianapolis, Knapp Electric, was selling a game called *Finance*. It sold for only $1 at retail. With sales of the *Monopoly* game picking up, indications were good that it would enjoy reorders for the fall gift-buying season. On principle, Barton and George did not want a competitor sharing their success. Again, Barton held a meeting in his Flatiron showroom, this time with the president of Knapp Electric. Knapp was a maker of electric educational items. His game, *Finance*, was a sideline. Knapp had purchased its rights from its inventor for $750. Barton put enough money on the table for Knapp to agree to sell him *Finance* outright, including its entire inventory.[14]

By Christmas of 1935, a quarter of a million *Monopoly* games had been sold. Parker Brothers' sales rebounded to over $500,000 and Barton's cost controls had yielded a small profit.[15] Everyone inside of Parker Brothers had reason to celebrate. Many former employees had been re-hired; Parker Pride was back. The printing presses had been kept busy and prospects looked good for 1936. But no one, including Barton, could imagine how good. So, as was typical, all the "seasonal" laborers the firm had hired in the fall were waved good-bye in mid-December.

Barton met again with Darrow, this time in Boston. It was clear that Darrow's game had been based on an idea that had been germinating elsewhere, apparently beginning with the *Landlord's Game*. Barton informed him that Parker Brothers had already made a significant investment to protect his game. He wondered if Darrow would support the firm with its legal costs. Darrow, still unemployed, was not ready to do so. Darrow had, indeed, lost his job as a plumbing salesman. Out of work, he had tried several ways to make money before he came to publish the *Monopoly* game. He had played a handmade game with friends of his wife, following a dinner invitation back in 1932. The handmade game had, in turn, been borrowed from friends who lived in Atlantic City—the inspiration for the property names found on the *Monopoly* game board. Darrow had so liked the game that he decided to make copies and sell them to other friends and acquaintances. Darrow agreed to a revised deal that granted Parker Brothers worldwide rights and exonerated him from the burden of legal costs in return for a more reasonable royalty.[16]

Barton accepted George's belief that that there were only a few basic types of games and that all other games were but "nuances and shades of difference" of these. Since it seemed likely that the *Monopoly* game evolved from the *Landlord's Game*, Barton decided to recognize both Darrow and Phillips in the publicity that now began to appear for the game. Barton came to admire Darrow, as he would state often in later years.[17] He liked his courage. Darrow had taken a sizable risk by investing his meager savings to publish the *Monopoly* game. Through his own pen, and that of a hired artist, he had established a unique look for the game and its board spaces. He had managed to interest retailers to purchase it at a time when most stores were reluctant to try anything unproven, especially when offered by a novice.

Across the Atlantic, Victor Watson Sr. of Waddington's received a copy of Parker Brothers' *Monopoly* game, sent by Barton. It arrived on a

Friday in December 1935. He handed it over to his son Norman, who was running the firm's playing card division, and said, "Look this over and tell me what you think of it." Norman's household was consumed by the *Monopoly* game that weekend. "I never found a game so absorbing," he recalled later. "I was so enthusiastic. We had to have it for the Commonwealth." Norman persuaded his father to place Waddington's first-ever transatlantic phone call to the man to whom he had licensed his *Lexicon* game—Barton. It was also the first transatlantic phone call received in Parker Brothers' history. Given the enthusiasm and commitment he heard in Victor Watson's voice, Barton agreed immediately to license *Monopoly*'s rights to Waddington's for continental Europe and the British Commonwealth, except Canada.[18] The decision to license the *Monopoly* game would change Waddington's. No longer would it just be a printing and "playing card" company. *Monopoly*'s impact on Parker Brothers would be even more profound.

The Masterstroke

In accordance with his ninth principle—bet heavily when the odds are long in your favor—George urged Barton to put all the company's resources behind the *Monopoly* game and forget making other games. It was better to apply everything Parker Brothers owned to maximize *Monopoly* shipments given the marketplace's insatiable appetite for the game. He was convinced that every dollar wagered would return a windfall. Unlike his vacillation with *Mah-Jongg*, this time he would not hesitate and give his opponents a chance to compete. He would redeem himself.

The "flood" began after New Year's Day. The post-Christmas trickle of orders for the *Monopoly* game turned into a torrent. It seemed that every *Monopoly* game purchased for Christmas had been played by many people—all of whom wanted their own copy, no matter what their financial plight. So many orders for the *Monopoly* game arrived in the mail and by telegraph that the firm had to store them in wicker laundry baskets in the hallways. All the workers sent home in December were quickly rehired.

Demand this strong, early in the year, pointed to big success—perhaps the biggest in the long history of his firm. Additional manufacturing and storage space was leased in the city of Salem. Production ramped up. Keeping the books for the deluge of orders soon overwhelmed the small Parker Brothers accounting staff; an outside accounting firm had to be contracted. The first one, a prestigious company in Boston in need of work, took one look at the mountain of uninvoiced sales and politely declined—citing the job as being "impossible."[19]

The machines inside of Parker Brothers now began to whirl twenty-four hours a day, seven days a week. Robert Barton persuaded Foster Parker, George's nephew, to leave his auto dealership in Boston and come back to work for Parker Brothers. Barton needed Foster to supervise the nighttime third shift. In appreciation, he was soon elected treasurer. With Foster's help, production reached 20,000 games a week.

Foster hired new workers faster than ever before in Parker Brothers history. One of those hired was a wiry seventeen-year-old trade school graduate who could operate a printing press, a self-proclaimed "punk" —an inexperienced kid—named Louis Vanne (at the time, Vanikiotis). Honed by twelve-hour shifts, Vanne quickly became Parkerized. He had been playing basketball one evening when Charlie Splane, foreman of Parker Brothers' small printing department, sought him out. "You want to go to work?" he asked Vanne. "Sure," Vanne replied, thinking he might be needed for a few hours. He soon found himself working the long night shift. The three Miehle printing presses that Barton had purchased were going around the clock. Each was able to print only one color at a time. Two of them were fourteen-foot-long "horizontal" presses, capable of printing big sheets of paper for game board labels and box wraps. The third was a three-foot-long "vertical" press for smaller jobs, such as game rules. Vanne was assigned to one of the horizontal Miehle machines. His goal was to print 20,000 *Monopoly* game board labels per shift with black ink. His counterpart on the day shift would arrive, clean the press, and then print the same labels with red ink. The next day, the yellow and blue colors were added to complete the job. Box labels were printed in two colors and therefore took two shifts to complete a run. The "scariest" part of the printing came next, when sheets needing varnish were packed up and shipped to Boston. Varnishing sealed the inks, prevented smudging, and offered some protection against spills. It was mainly applied to box labels. When the varnisher didn't set his process correctly, the sheets would stick together, forming a "brick" several feet tall. Vanne was always relieved to see the truck return from Boston with a load of correctly varnished labels. He worked seventy-two hours a week and earned $27. (He was the only member of his family with a job. At home were his unemployed father, mother, and two younger siblings, all of whom now depended on him.) Twenty-seven dollars week was considered a decent wage, even if it did take seventy-two hours to earn it.[20]

Demand climbed to 35,000 games a week. George continued to encourage Barton, Phelps, Jelly, and Haskell to fill the demand, despite a growing sense of desperation. Instead of looking for printing jobs, they were seeking out printers, assemblers, box makers, and token manufacturers. All of Salem was mobilized to help. So great was the need for production that Barton paid a visit to Father Zubcyk of Saint John's Church in Salem and asked for his support in requesting the State of Massachusetts for permission to work on Sundays. (Parker Brothers' workers were mainly Roman Catholic.) Barton offered one concession. "I'll limit the shifts to seven hours, so your people will have time to attend Mass." Father Zubcyk declined, retorting, "I will only say yes if you run three *eight-*hour shifts. My people need all the money they can get, and the church needs their contributions. I'll hold Mass around your shifts." Barton smiled and shook Zubcyk's hand. The request to the Commonwealth of Massachusetts was approved.[21]

If the *Monopoly* game required only printed sheets of paper and cardboard, Barton and company could have satisfied every consumer. Obtaining enough wood houses and hotels was also not a problem. They were made in northern New England and shipped to Salem in potato sacks. To color them, Parker Brothers' woodworking department dumped them into galvanized tubs filled with dye, and dried them under mild heat. The cast metal tokens were made with molds. Parker Brothers' Midwest vendor could acquire as many molds as needed. Box production wasn't an issue as boxes could be made as fast as their labels were printed. There was but one bottleneck in production: the fabrication of game boards.[22]

Made like a book cover, each game board required two pieces of cardboard to be joined with a cloth hinge, then wrapped with an outer "jacket" before a printed game board label was mounted on the other side. After the finished board was closed, a small printed label was applied to its jacket to identify it as a *Monopoly* board (important for merchants looking to match the right game board with each box of game utensils sold). Game board manufacturing required special gluing machines, a moving belt, and workers with the right touch to align the labels properly. Parker Brothers had insufficient amounts of all three, so Barton decided to utilize his Toy Manufacturers Association (TMA) relationship with the sales leader of rival Milton Bradley. George A. Fox had cofounded the TMA and he believed in industry cooperation. Furthermore, his firm was still struggling with the impact of the Great Depression. Parker Brothers' recent success had amplified the gap between their sales. For these reasons, Fox was keen to accept Barton's proposition to make *Monopoly* boards for Parker Brothers. "I know you need this business; I know you'll charge a high price, that's okay," Barton told his friend. But Milton Bradley's board of directors vetoed the idea—competitive practice overruled economic benefit (although Milton Bradley subsequently licensed the *Monopoly* patent from Parker Brothers in order to market a competitive game—which also enjoyed enduring success—entitled *Easy Money*). Undeterred, Barton ended up ordering more board-making machines. There being no room for them in the Parker Brothers factory, he made arrangements with shops in Salem to take them in and learn how to make game boards under the direction of his best workers.[23]

Until this solution could be implemented, Barton decided to suppress demand by raising the price of the standard game from $2.00 to $2.50—an unheard-of increase for its day. This did reduce the inflow of orders until the board-making equipment came on line. A new $2.00 edition was then reintroduced (with smaller money and wooden tokens). Sales took off once more.[24]

During 1936, Parker Brothers marketed six different versions of the *Monopoly* game, ranging in price from $2 to $25 ($325 today!). This most expensive set came with a wood game board and a brass-handled chest lined with trays that held the game's components, including Bakelite houses and hotels and metal coins for added money.[25] When the Parker Brothers accountants closed the books on 1936, 1,810,000 copies of all editions had been sold and the firm had earned an unprecedented $1,000,000 profit.[26] Nineteen thirty-three's nasty loss had been avenged, and then some! Armed with an abundance of cash, Barton struck a deal with a man in Texas named Rudy Copeland for a game called *Inflation*, which resembled the *Monopoly* game. He offered a financial arrangement whenever a similar game surfaced. By mid-1936, Barton had, indeed, acquired a "monopoly" on the *Monopoly* game. George and Barton prevented a flurry of similar games from confusing the market, as had occurred during the *Mah-Jongg* fad, and they had managed to satisfy the desire of nearly 2 million Americans who wanted to own a copy.[27]

The cash infusion from *Monopoly*'s sales paid for another two-story extension to the rear of the plant (a third story would later be added). Within its light blue interior came more manufacturing equipment and several more Miehle printing presses, improved layouts for the manufacturing departments, and more office space for the growing managerial staff. Atop hardwood floors, interrupted by massive blue painted wooden posts, light machinery of many types was installed—including one machine that wrapped a sheet of clear, brittle cellophane around the interior of game utensil boxes. This permitted consumers to open the packages in the store and see what was inside without the pieces becoming lost. Cellophane was the third type of plastic used by Parker Brothers (following Celluloid and Bakelite). It had been invented in Switzerland in 1908 and was licensed to the giant DuPont chemical company in 1923 for U.S. manufacture.[28]

Waddington's enjoyed great sales for its *Monopoly* versions in both the United Kingdom and France. But in Germany, its licensee (Firma Franz Schmidt) suffered—because the most valuable property on its Berlin-based board (Insel Schwanenwerder) happened to be where most of the

WADDINGTON'S PRINTING WORKS
Wakefield Road, Leeds 10, England

WHERE WADDINGTON'S PLAYING CARDS AND GAMES ARE MADE

FIGURE 4-4
John Waddington Company Ltd.

Parker Brothers' U.K. partner.

Nazi leaders had their homes. Minister of Propaganda Josef Goebbels did not want his party associated with capitalistic wealth and quickly denounced the game. Leaders of the Hitler Youth petitioned Schmidt to stop producing the game. Ironically, an Allied bombing raid later destroyed the Schmidt warehouse and the remaining copies.[29]

As 1937 approached, *Mah-Jongg* and *Diabolo* once more clouded George Parker's thinking. Remembering how quickly their fads had ended, he grew anxious that the same fate might befall his current bestseller. He wrote Barton to "absolutely cease making" the game in the event of an abrupt end to its popularity. Barton resisted, fortunately. The game continued to sell well in 1937, albeit at half the pace of the prior year, and George's memorandum was posted in the factory for years as a reminder of how the success of the *Monopoly* game had bewildered even George S. Parker (who, apparently, didn't mind).[30]

To further capitalize on the success of the *Monopoly* game, it was decided to place Darrow's picture on the new *Bulls & Bears* game and make it appear that Darrow was the inventor of this stock market board game.[31] Despite four package changes, sales of the game were disappointing. Once again, an old adage was proved: Consumers don't care who invents or markets a game or how many stores display it. They only care if it appears interesting and proves fun to play. Apparently, *Bulls & Bears* didn't measure up on either count.

Endorsements

Monopoly's sales continued to slowly decline as the 1930s gave way to the 1940s.[32] The firm cut back to two shifts and then to one. Games that could not be produced during the *Monopoly* craze now reentered the line, and George unleashed his pent-up desire to publish new games. The stature accorded him and his company enabled him to establish a dialogue with favored national leaders and to convince several well-known U.S. authorities to lecture at the Essex Institute. George also persuaded four of these notables to endorse games ("manuscripts of game designs"), which Leroy Howard would create and he would edit.[33]

They were Lowell Thomas, Melvin Purvis, S. S. van Dine, and Boake Carter. Thomas was a famous commentator, author, and explorer. Purvis was the United States' most famous FBI agent, the man who cornered notorious bank robber John Dillinger. S. S. van Dine was the pen name of author Willard Huntington Wright, who created a popular detective named Philo Vance. Carter was a highly respected reporter. In March 1932, Carter was behind the microphone at a radio station when the infant son of Charles Lindbergh was kidnapped. He was also famous for his quote, "In time of war, the first casualty is truth." All four of these games were prestigious, if modest, successes. Only Carter's game, *Star Reporter*, would endure (without his name attached after he died in 1944).[34]

Transition

With George's attention divided between Parker Brothers and the outside world, the leadership of his firm began to churn. Foster Parker returned to his auto dealership in Boston after the need for him to supervise added shifts disappeared. Charles Parker succumbed to his illness in December 1936; George lost his closest friend and the man to whom he owed the existence of Parker Brothers as a viable business. Albert Richardson, the heart of the company's sales effort for decades, grew sick and was forced to retire. (He died in March 1940.[35]) Parker Brothers' sales force had always been lean. Now its lone traveling salesman was gone. Barton had a difference of opinion with sales leader Hunneman, and Hunneman soon departed. Replacements were sought out—among them, an impressive sales manger named Stanley James, and Foster's son Edward ("Eddie") Pickering Parker, who had graduated from Harvard with a degree in economics. Eddie joined the firm in 1934 and was assigned to the New York sales office to begin his management training. From the outset, Barton detected special leadership qualities in the charismatic grandson of Edward Parker. (Eddie's younger sister Barbara also joined the company, serving as a bookkeeper for many years.[36])

In New York, the TMA was looking for a single building to house the showrooms of its members. The old Fifth Avenue hotel, built atop the grounds of the old Hippodrome circus at the corner of Twenty-third Street, became available.[37] It was refurbished into fourteen floors of modern showrooms. In 1937, Parker Brothers said good-bye to the Flatiron Building and moved one block across Broadway to its new sixth-floor office and showroom. Three years later, a second showroom was opened in the Merchandise Mart of Chicago, and another sales ace (Eddie Hefferman) was hired to run it.[38]

As the 1930s ended, the U.S. economy was coming back, slowly but surely. The *Monopoly* game had reminded people of how captivating playing a good game can be. And given *Monopoly*'s clout, sales of longtime favorites—such as *Rook, Pit,* and *Flinch*—rebounded. *Sorry!* and *Crossword Lexicon* remained strong sellers. George Parker and Roy Howard continued to issue a flurry of new games, including one based on the popular radio cowboy—the Lone Ranger—and a win-the-presidency game called *Politics.* Another new offering, the *Pinocchio Game,* was based on the first Walt Disney property licensed by Parker Brothers.[39]

Barton's aim was to strengthen the finances of the company in the event of another disruption to the economy. While George expanded the product line, Barton looked for ways to economize. He began to contemplate the wisdom of exporting games to the London office. He suggested to George that they consider licensing Parker Brothers games to Waddington's. George was stubbornly proud of the London office. It had served as an outpost for the sale of Parker Brothers games in Europe, and had acted as the firm's eyes and ears to detect the emergence of new games there that could be licensed for the United States. Establishing it after the turn of the century had been a bold risk; a breathtaking decision for its day. But Barton felt that the London office had outlived its usefulness. Parker Brothers games were expensive in Europe because their components were exported from the United States, not made locally. And he was swayed by the logic of the Watson family, who advocated that each firm license its hit games to one another. Waddington's proposed to close its Canadian office. Thereafter, the only thing going back and forth across the Atlantic would be money from royalties. Its existing arrangements for *Lexicon* and the *Monopoly* game could be the basis for a more comprehensive deal. Waddington's would make and market leading Parker Brothers games throughout the British Empire (except Canada) and Parker Brothers would sell the best Waddington games in the United States and Canada. Barton tried to persuade his father-in-law not to renew the lease of 8 Great Turnstile Street in London. George listened to his son-in-law but could not bring himself to make this decision just yet. Barton was frustrated.[40]

Increasingly, George saw things in a romantic light. Barton felt that his father-in-law placed disproportionate significance on the symbolic value of the London office, or the importance of converting *Chivalry* to *Camelot*, or refining the rules of *Finance*, or championing the *Ping-Pong* trademark via tournaments long after Americans stopped caring if they bought a *Ping-Pong* or a table tennis set. By contrast, Barton's lack of appreciation of his passions made George doubt his son-in-law's loyalty. At first put off by such an allegation, Barton wisely realized that he was engaged in a tug of war with an elderly man who didn't want to let go of the business he had founded. He decided to use restraint. Barton had learned to live by George Parker's principles, and to these he added one of his own: Hold your ground when your position is strong and wait for your opponent to weaken.

The Traveling Mr. Parker

Barton suggested that George spend more time at his Peterborough, New Hampshire home, Brookwood, where his mind could be free to invent new games. George agreed. To reach Brookwood, George had to drive there. After years of walking to work in Salem, he came to rely on a member of the household staff to chauffeur him to work—or he relied on his own questionable driving skills. He owned a Ford convertible and he had a tendency to head right down the middle of the street because it was more comfortable riding on its crown. If he should notice a friend, he often waved with both hands. When he parked in the spot at the front of the factory building, he usually forgot to turn off the motor. (After he had ascended to his second-floor office, a lady in the order department on the first floor would rush out to turn off the motor and retrieve the key.) In New Hampshire, many of the local roads were unpaved and hilly. It was not unusual for a driver to have to ask his passengers to disembark in order to surmount one of the steeper hills. On one such occasion, George could not get the Ford over the top, despite many tries. So he asked Grace to step out while he tried again. He succeeded this time, but deep in thought, he forgot about his wife for the next half a mile. He finally pulled to the side—and waited for her. After she had walked the distance, she gave him a piece of her mind. He replied, "Yes, yes, very well, Mother," and resumed both their journey and his deep thinking.[41]

The Parkers looked forward to their annual summer vacation. Accordingly, they ignored the caution of friends and the headlines, and embarked on trips to Central Europe in both 1938 and 1939. While in Berlin, George saw firsthand the growing presence of the military and the Gestapo under the control of Adolph Hitler in 1938. Two weeks later in France, they were caught in the grip of tension between England and Germany when Prime Minister Neville Chamberlain met Hitler to decide the Czechoslovakia issue. "Peace in our time," said a joyous Chamberlain upon his return to London. (Back home in Salem, the plant was damaged during the onslaught of the Great Hurricane of 1938, which hit the East Coast without warning.) In another trip in August of 1939, they experienced the first days of World War II, arriving in England from France on the day the Nazis invaded Poland. George doggedly kept his ten days of appointments in England, after receiving gas masks for his wife and himself, before returning to the United States by ship just as U-boats started to probe the Atlantic.[42]

George feared that support of Great Britain would be a wasted effort and would ruin the value of the dollar. He had an overwhelming desire to see the United States remain on the sidelines. He wrote to friends in Congress to influence them to keep the United States neutral. But even as he was lobbying Congress, he was preparing for the worst. He may have become a romantic in the eyes of Barton, safe from the rain under the strong roof his son-in-law had built over their heads, but he was wise to reality. George Parker respected the odds. And odds were that, despite his best efforts and those of many others like him, President Roosevelt would help Great Britain against Germany in order to prevent the war from reaching U.S. shores—much like President Wilson had done in World War I. In time, U.S. troops would again be fighting overseas. The *World's Fair* game his firm published in 1939 celebrated world peace, but like the fair itself, it was not the current reality.

Parker and Barton determined to be ready when conflict swept away the peace. Each had a different idea of how to do so.

War Games

After Germany overran France and Norway in 1940, it began to attack England by air. Norman Watson of Waddington's informed Barton that Winston Churchill had asked his firm to maintain card and board game production by any means possible. Churchill felt it vital for morale that diversions be available to the English people. This was a challenge for Waddington's because its playing card material came from Norway, which was now in the enemy's hands. Later, Barton was glad to learn that his partner had devised a way to laminate two sheets of thick paper together to make ersatz cards.[43] The practicality of the Brits served as inspiration for Robert Barton and George Parker.

George's memories of World War I guided his decision making as the new decade began. With President Roosevelt rearming the nation, George knew that rationing of vital materials was inevitable. With his firm's bank account full, George went on a buying spree. He stocked up on essential materials like paper, cardboard, metals, and even truck tires that he felt would be in short supply in the coming years.[44] Several warehouses were leased around Salem to store them all. At one time, twelve carloads of paper and cardboard were waiting to be unloaded on the firm's siding.[45]

The last significant games to enter the Parker Brothers line before the war were the *Game of Oil, Contack,* and *Dig.* Cardboard was their main material. *Oil* challenged players to discover which spaces on the board yielded gushers, upon which were placed pylon-shaped wooden "derricks." *Contack* contained dozens of triangular printed "dominos." They were laid down in three directions rather than two as in the traditional domino game. *Dig* was a frantic word game that contained printed letter tiles and special wooden "picks"—the gummy end of which resembled a gavel. When the gum was moistened, a pick could pick up a cardboard letter tile by tapping on it. The object of *Dig* was to pick up letters that composed a word and then arrange them in order. The word had to fit a category specified on a card. A familiar image appeared on each of these cards—the mustachioed but as yet nameless man from the *Monopoly* game. He was seen with a pick over his shoulder, the art taken from that game's "You are assessed for street repairs" Community Chest card. This was the first time that the friendly little financier would help sell a Parker Brothers product other than the *Monopoly* game.[46]

On Sunday, December 7, 1941, George was in his garden at Brookwood when Grace rushed out of the house to tell him what she was hearing on the radio. War had come, not from across the Atlantic, but from across the Pacific—the Japanese had attacked Pearl Harbor, Hawaii. George called influential friends. He recorded the treachery in big letters in his diary. At work, two days later, he asked for and got a financial assessment of his firm. Inventory and buildings were valued at $180,000. Accounts receivable came to $335,000 and the firm's bank account held $67,000 cash. These amounts represented the sum at his disposal with which to combat the uncertain future.[47]

While George Parker prepared to defend his firm, both Eddie Parker and Robert Barton made up their minds to defend their country. Even before war came that December, twenty-eight-year-old Eddie Parker had volunteered to join the navy. His competency in piloting sailing vessels helped him to rapidly move up the ranks.[48] Barton, at age thirty-eight, was determined to volunteer after he failed to land any meaningful war contracts for his firm (save for some cardboard sorting boxes needed by General Electric in early 1942). He first approached the army. They agreed to make him an officer, but would only assign him to a desk job in the United States. Barton was too proactive to be content with a permanent desk job. He decided that his chances for action were higher if, as with Eddie, his nation could benefit from his boating experience. So he approached the navy. The navy, he knew, would not accept him unless he passed an eye examination. To do so, he needed some help. He managed to "borrow" a standard eye chart, memorize the letters on it, and narrowly pass the test before being accepted into active service. He was assigned to the navy's flight simulator program in Washington, D.C., and later moved on to an assignment in Manhattan, promoted to the rank of lieutenant. He once took his older son, Ranny, to see the giant battleship *Missouri* under construction in the Brooklyn Navy Yard. (Guards chased them off the ship once they caught sight of the twelve-year-old.) The Japanese were destined to sign the surrender documents, ending the war, on the deck of this ship. Barton eventually pulled strings and joined the command of a destroyer escort assigned to a convoy bound for Great Britain. His ship harassed several U-boats before arriving in England shortly after D day.[49]

Eddie Parker distinguished himself in battle; under his command, his destroyer escort—the *USS Wyman*—sank at least two Japanese submarines. The White House commissioned a painting of his vessel. Eddie was heavily decorated and achieved the rank of lieutenant commander before receiving leave in August 1945. He was slated to command a new destroyer in the upcoming invasion of Japan, but the atomic bombs dropped on Hiroshima and Nagasaki alleviated that need. (Eddie later admitted a premonition of dying at the hands of a kamikaze pilot, because his ship would be among the vanguard of ships protecting the invasion fleet.[50])

In addition to these two family members, dozens of key Parker Brothers employees were either drafted or volunteered to serve their country. Not all came home. George ordered the erection of a plaque in the firm's lobby to honor those who served and those who gave their lives.

George was seventy-five when 1942 began. His childhood friends from Medford High School were either dead or retired. He, the most successful of his peers, was unable to call it quits because of the war. After Barton and Eddie entered the navy, George needed help. He persuaded Foster Parker to once more return to Parker Brothers and run the factory. The two Parkers jointly managed the firm for the duration of the war.

Their wartime leadership was impeccable. George made a series of business decisions that were, perhaps, the best since his early years. Relying on his principles, he approached the challenge like a master game player, planning several moves ahead, with an eye on the day when the game would be won and the war would be over.

He minimized layoffs, reducing the average employee's work hours in order to retain as many skilled employees as he could on a part-time basis. Where possible, women filled jobs left vacant by men. He applied his latest principle (number 10) as well: when opportunity narrows, focus on your strengths.[51] George concentrated production and dwindling raw materials on the very best games in his line. Substitute materials were used wherever possible (wood for metal, cardboard liners for cellophane, etc.). Very few new products were published, most notably those designed to bolster patriotic spirit, like the *Army Air Corps* game. Curiously, a game entitled *South American Travel* was introduced in 1942 despite the war—another indication of George's belief in vicariously fulfilling the dream of Americans to visit foreign lands. The "airplane" movers in this game, which were to have been made with die-cast metal, were instead made of cardboard and wood.[52]

George issued only one catalog during the war. The cover of the 1943 catalog was a patriotic red, white, and blue. An American eagle and many military planes appeared in a sky over an ocean filled with a carrier task force and a shoreline occupied by an artillery piece and a tank. A letter written by George Parker appeared on the inside of the cover.

Twenty-five years ago, the United States of America was fighting a war that was the worst the world had ever seen. Today we are fighting an all-out war that dwarfs the last one. Our every effort must go towards winning the struggle that threatens to engulf us.

Parker Brothers' games played their part through 1917 and 1918, keeping up the spirit of the men in the various services, and today our games are being played wherever our troops are stationed.

We are adhering to our ideal that Parker Games must "Look well, play well, and sell well," and while curtailment of essential materials will eventually necessitate minor changes in some games, the playing qualities of the games will not be changed.

At home, people are turning more and more to games to pass away time formerly spent in other pleasures. We will do our part to see that Parker Games are worthy of the trust that over two generations have placed in the games that are "The Standard of Excellence."

The select few games provided to the government for the millions of servicemen, at home and abroad, included *Sorry!*, *Contack*, *Rook*, the *Monopoly* game, and a kit comprising four standard games. Servicemen of all ranks appreciated them. With three hours to go before the Allies invaded North Africa, one of the biggest fans of Parker Brothers games relieved his stress by playing the *Monopoly* game—General Dwight D. Eisenhower. Marines played Parker Brothers games onboard ship, especially the night before an early dawn invasion of a Pacific isle. Airmen played *Sorry!* in their barracks between missions. The army maintained a supply of Parker Brothers board games behind the front lines, in rest and recovery areas. Canteens were stocked with *Rook* and *Touring* for soldiers to play when off duty. Wounded soldiers in hospitals were distracted from their misfortune by playing *Flinch* or *Rook* or *Contack*.[53]

When Parker Brothers veterans, such as Louis Vanne, came home on leave, they were invited to the Parker Brothers factory for a party and all the games they could carry away. Vanne would load up a big box before catching a series of trains back to Norfolk, Virginia, where his ship was based. Along the way, more of his shipmates would join him on the rails and he would begin to parcel out his supply of games. By the time Norfolk was reached, his buddies each had one or two games to bring aboard the ship. They were played endlessly during the long, boring voyage back to their battle zone.[54]

The Monopoly Secret

When allied airmen began to risk their lives flying missions over occupied Europe, Parker Brothers' English partner found a way to use the *Monopoly* game to come to the aid of those who were captured by the Germans. The British War Office worked with a select group of Waddington staffers to modify *Monopoly* boards for insertion in games that the Red Cross would deliver to Allied prisoners of war. These men carved out precise depressions in the unfinished game boards and, before applying their labels, filled them with low-profile compasses, files, and maps that depicted escape routes from the prison camp where each game was to be sent. (The maps were printed on silk because silk did not rustle when opened. Waddington's had perfected this process to such an extent that virtually all British flyers climbed into their warplanes with a Waddington's map secreted in the heel of one of their boots.) Hidden among the games' play money was real currency—German, Italian, or Austrian. It is not known how many airmen escaped thanks to these *Monopoly* games, but 35,000 POWs did break out of prison camps and reach partisans who helped them to safety.[55]

Salem in Wartime

In Salem, unemployment was minimal, largely due to Parker Brothers' success. The business of selling games actually became easier as the war progressed. Concentration of production caused sales of Parker Brothers' best games to rise each year. Sales of the *Monopoly* game, for example, whose annual sales had dwindled to 150,000 units by 1939, rose steadily to 650,000 units by 1945.[56] Competition was of little concern. Parker Brothers had stocked up on paper and cardboard; the competition had not. European games had disappeared from the U.S. market. Parker Brothers' demand quickly exceeded supply. The challenge was to maintain enough stock of raw materials to keep up with demand. Foster Parker and Paul Haskell managed to do so. Henry Fitzpatrick and Henry Sullivan found ways to move their goods—a daunting challenge because the military had commandeered much of the nation's rail and truck capacity.

George now found time to collect and self-publish his poems. Three hundred copies of *Random Verse of Here and There* were printed and bound in 1944. Among its fourteen poems was "Old Salem," which he dedicated to its servicemen and women. Its final verse:

There be those in far off lands,
Bound by the tie of birth,
Who love her as they may not love
Another spot on earth!

War's End

As the war neared its end, George Parker began to contemplate, with sadness, what it held in store for him. He did not fear the impact of the next business setback, or the pain of rising prices, or an attack by competition. Instead, the war's conclusion would bring about the end of an idyllic period when he had successfully run his firm, unchallenged from within or without. Foster had been a loyal lieutenant during these past three years, faithfully carrying out George's decisions. But the return of Robert Barton and Eddie Parker would change this dynamic. At seventy-eight, George was fully aware of his own mortality. He would have to yield his turn and pass the dice to the younger generations. Yet, his pride urged him against returning control to his strong-willed, prosaic son-in-law. As Barton's tour of duty approached its end, George fell victim to his impulses and confronted his daughter's husband. He asked Barton to return to Parker Brothers, but not as its president. Without blinking, Barton informed his father-in-law that if his position was not restored—and strengthened—he would move his family to Seattle. This was the equivalent of a call and raise in a game of poker. Was Barton bluffing? When Sally told her father that her husband was dead serious, and that she backed him, George folded his hand. The thought of his grandchildren on the opposite edge of the country, three days away by train, was unthinkable. (George had vowed never to enter an airplane after his son Richard had died in the plane crash back in 1921.) George reflected on the inevitability of what he must do and, in a moment of acceptance of his advanced years, turned a page and adopted Principle 11—Be a gracious winner or loser. Don't be petty. Share what you learn and what you have.

He then issued a carefully worded memorandum to his son-in-law. Within its two single-spaced pages, he agreed to bring Barton back as president and to add "general manager" to his title. He set forth how he would bow out of involvement in new game development, once Barton had an alternative. George accepted his need to relinquish control in order to make his firm an institution that would prosper far beyond his years. He also provided for the disposition of his stock following his death. His majority ownership would go to his wife Grace but would be voted by daughter Sally, Barton's wife. This meant that Barton would dominate the firm following George's death. George specified that their firstborn son Randolph was to inherit the stock at Sally's discretion. George set forth his desire that the high standards of the business be preserved, his principles adhered to, and that its prestige "increase" for the benefit of future generations. He foresaw an eventual sale of the company, but expressed his desire that it remain within the family for at least "some generations."[57]

In old age, George Parker bowed to the need to be as gracious in defeat as in victory. He put aside petty concerns and decided that, on principle and by virtue of his belief in noblesse oblige, he should share what he had learned and earned with his son-in-law, daughter, and grandchildren. Barton was struck by his father-in-law's sweeping change of heart and agreed to honor his requests.

The war ended in August 1945. Demobilization commenced at break-neck speed. The returning soldiers, airmen, and sailors wanted nothing more than to get married, find a home, and raise a family. And after they did so, they wanted to have fun—often by playing the games they had come to enjoy while in the service. It seemed that an enduring loyalty had blossomed from George Parker's decision to provide games to the military. *Monopoly* and other Parker Brothers games were very popular with returning GIs and their families.

Shortly after VJ Day, a tribute to George Parker was published in the *Saturday Evening Post.* On October 6, 1945, the *Post*—one of the nation's biggest magazine weeklies in this pretelevision era—ran a major picture story on George and the firm he had led for more than sixty years. While Parker Brothers had been the topic of many prior magazine mentions, this was the first time a national periodical featured not just the company, but the man who founded it. It was entitled simply "Game Maker" and was written by Pete Martin. The lengthy article outlined George Parker's career and the business he and his family had built. It featured color photos of George playing *Camelot* with daughter Sally, *Pastime Puzzle* Girls at their jigsaws, and nostalgic shots of several historical games. Charles Parker's daughter Mary was also pictured (supervising a play test session). The publicity helped to establish a positive image for the firm in the minds of war-weary Americans. Their toil and losses had won the war. They were tired of hardship and sacrifice. They had earned the right to have fun once again. The *Saturday Evening Post* pictured the man who had devoted his life to putting smiles on their faces.[58] Given his white hair, rosy cheeks, and stocky build, he was the image of Father Christmas.

George Parker admitted to being humbled by the article, especially its opening. Martin began his story by mentioning that Fulton Lewis Jr., a famous radio commentator, had effortlessly explained the Parker Brothers' game of *Finance* to his eleven-year-old daughter, thanks to the clarity of its rules. Lewis contrasted these rules with the opaque, sixteen-page booklet written by the government for merchants engaged in the buying and selling of coffee beans. A suggestion was made that the man who wrote the *Finance* rules be hired to teach the government how to write simply and clearly.

By late 1945, sailor Louis Vanne and scores of other former Parker Brothers employees returned to work at the factory. With raw materials arriving unabated at the warehouse, the smell of glue and paper and ink hung in the air, reminding these returning veterans that they were back working inside Santa's workshop—not fighting in the devil's crucible. Lieutenant Robert Barton was again in command of operations. Captain Eddie Parker returned in early 1946 and was promoted to the position of executive vice president. Foster Parker stayed on as treasurer. With these three leaders on the job, George Parker was determined to fulfill his desire to live a more leisurely life in New Hampshire. He entered semiretirement.

Before doing so, however, he breathed new life into the wartime-constricted line. George knew exactly what lead game he wanted to publish as soon as the war ended. It was a novel and fun-filled stock market game entitled *Rich Uncle*. For the first time, the little man from *Monopoly* fame was given a name—Rich Uncle Pennybags—and his familiar image appeared on the cover of the game and on every "Daily Bugle" newspaper sheet found inside. A one-piece board pictured all thirty stocks and was inserted upright on the back of the box bottom—which served as the bank and held the game's supply of Daily Bugles and stock certificates. Dice were rolled on each turn to determine which of the stocks paid a dividend. Their price changed throughout the game and players had a blast on their way to accumulating winnings of $50,000. *Rich Uncle* was created and patented by Henry Todd of Dayton, Ohio—one of the hundreds of ordinary people who bombarded George Parker and Roy Howard with new game ideas each year in the hopes that theirs would be among the few chosen for publication.[59]

A prime tester of new Parker Brothers games was grandson Randolph Parker Barton, the apple of George's aging eyes. (Since Randolph was his paternal grandfather's first name, the family came to call the youngster "Ranny.") During the war, while his father was serving in the navy, Ranny's grandparents often invited him and his younger brother and sister to their Brookwood estate. There, they would play games. George never grew tired of playing and experimenting with games. He often wanted to play five or six times in a row to see if he could uncover a flaw or oversight in the game's rules. Young Ranny grew weary of this long before his grandfather did.

As Ranny grew more capable, George stepped up their competition. Playing *Camelot* became his obsession. George didn't seem to mind if his grandson beat him in simple children's games, but his demeanor changed over the *Camelot* board, with its knights, men, and castles. He played to win each three-game series. Ranny's skill improved steadily and soon he gained the upper hand. His grandfather, childishly adverse to losing the third game of a hotly contested set, would manage to slip his rigidly starched cuff onto the corner of the board and wreck the position of the men as he jerked it upward to reach for a piece. "Oh, I'm terribly sorry," he would exclaim as he fumbled to replace the pieces in their alleged former positions.[60]

George doted on his grandchildren, Ranny, Sally, and Richard. He loved to take Ranny on long walks in the woods of his three-hundred-acre estate, often returning late for dinner and to a scolding by Grace. Ranny came to treasure these walks and often asked his grandfather to prolong them and "be late" in their return. He recalled that his grandfather *always* dressed formally and was never seen without his jacket and tie—even when wearing knickers for these wooded walks. Sadly, Ranny was to witness the beginnings of his grandfather's demise due to what was then considered dementia—the losing of one's memories and resultant mental confusion—which today we now know as Alzheimer's disease. Ranny was alone at George's side one evening after dinner in 1947, as the two of them walked out of the home in Peterborough and looked over at the twinkle of lights on Mount Monadnock. George suddenly said to his grandson, "Well Bradstreet, the lights of old Salem Common certainly are bright tonight."[61]

Shortly thereafter, George came to work with less frequency. Robert Barton had a small elevator installed for his father-in-law, who was finding it difficult to mount the stairs to his second-floor office. George still expressed concern that, without the government funding a wartime economy, a recession or even a depression might soon grip the nation. But under President Harry Truman, the country surged ahead, not backwards. And Parker Brothers' sales climbed to levels not seen since 1936, surpassing $2 million. In 1949, George and Grace moved back to Salem where aid was closer at hand to help battle his illness. They bought an historic home on Essex Street. A small staff tended to the household and prepared their meals.[62]

Factory Conflicts

Without George Parker's intrusiveness, Robert Barton had the firm on the move again, but Louis Vanne wanted to bring it to a halt. Emboldened by his training in the navy and his newfound leadership skills, he thought the time was right to unionize the print shop. While there had been union threats in the past, none had ever reached a vote. It was not because the family quashed the attempts; it was simply that after the workers got a better understanding of the pros and cons, the cons outweighed the pros. Vanne thought differently this time. He felt that the firm's printers were underpaid compared to printers at other firms in the Boston area. Union officials began to call on Barton. He kept them off the factory floor and instead arranged for meeting rooms for their presentations. He had a sense of how labor thought and his daily contact with his employees convinced him that they did not want a disruptive work place. He carefully began to remind his printers of all the unofficial benefits they received by being a valued member of the Parker Brothers team. As had been true for decades, employees in financial trouble were still granted loans, many of which were cancelled. Those with long-term health problems got treatment courtesy of the company. Many who got sick were paid in their absence. These acts were not the result of policy and they were not publicized. And it was this goodwill that Barton relied upon to keep the union out of Parker Brothers. When the union vote was taken, Parker Brothers won by one vote. (Barton later learned that the vote was rigged. The real vote would have been overwhelmingly in favor of management, but to avoid embarrassment and potential loss of jobs, enough employees were persuaded to vote for the union to make it appear to be a close election.[63])

Vanne assumed that he was a goner. Sure enough, the next day he was summoned to Barton's office. Standing before the boss, with knees shaking, the stern-faced Barton shocked him by extending a hand and saying, "You gave it a hell of a fight, Louis. Now go back to work. We need men with your drive here." Without fanfare, Vanne was granted much of what he set out to achieve. Wages in the print room were improved. Barton approved the purchase of the first two-color press for the print shop. Vanne's wages went up again when he was promoted to the first of several managerial positions. (He would remain with Parker for many years until his retirement in the 1980s.[64])

Instead of exerting his power and sending a message of fear to his workers, Barton resorted to compassion and thereby blunted further desire to unionize. Shortly thereafter, he instituted the firm's first pension plan. He had to convince George to part with $100,000 (a big chunk of the firm's profit that year) to fund the initial plan. Thereafter, profit sharing would augment each employee's pension and a separate cash bonus was also awarded just before Christmas. The funded pension contribution provided longer-term security. And wages would henceforth be set to rival those of the big employers in town, particularly Sylvania Electric. At employee meetings, Barton often reminded his workers that he didn't set their wages, the local competition did. Doing so took away any advantage a union could hope to provide, and eliminated the need for union dues.[65]

The improved employee compensation may have been sparked by Vanne's failed union attempt, but the means to do so stemmed from the firm's continuing sales success with games like *Pit, Sorry!,* and especially *Monopoly.* It was and would be the company's quintessential game, the one for which the firm would forever be known. Its success verified the culmination of all the lessons and principles learned and laid down by George Parker. The triumph of these enduring games gave Parker Brothers a base it could count on, year after year. *Monopoly's* sales alone enabled its leaders to live comfortably and to share its annuity with their employees. While many employees still thought of Barton as haughty and dogmatic, there was no doubt that he had become Parkerized. He had earned their trust. Barton's only setback in the plant during this time occurred when Donald Jelly, his trusted head of manufacturing, tendered his resignation due to a pending divorce. Charlie Phelps took his place.

Soon after, an incident occurred that employees would later nickname the "Solomon Incident." A former army major was hired in the shipping department. Barton had questioned the man before his hiring, wondering why he wasn't seeking a higher position. The reply was that he had expended his desire to give orders. In the ensuing months, the man grew restless and soon was engaged in a daily argument with a fellow worker in the department. Their differences threatened to boil over and disrupt the entire plant. Barton finally accepted that he must take care of this personally. The easy way out would be to fire the former officer. But mindful of the benefit of having not fired Vanne, he deliberated and settled on a much different tack. He assembled all the workers in the big third-floor collating department. He called forward the two squabbling workers and pointed to a table whereon were piled sheets of blank paper and a box of pencils. "I'm going to let your fellow workers decide your fate. Each will be given a piece of paper and a pencil and will be asked to decide which of you should be fired—or both. I will abide by the majority's outcome." Before doing so, Barton gave the two workers a chance to reconcile. Knowing they both would be fired if a vote were taken, the two huddled privately and made peace. The peace endured.[66]

The Monopoly Man

One of the great, unsolved mysteries in the history of Parker Brothers is the identity of the artist who created the little mustachioed man who, in 1936, began to grace the game's Chance and Community Chest cards and who eventually became the game's icon.

The first *Monopoly* cards made by Parker Brothers replicated the plain text style used by Charles Darrow. But sometime during late 1935 or

FIGURE 4-5
Mr. Monopoly

Two of Albert Richardson's calling cards (left); two sketches of "Little Esky" from covers of Esquire Magazine *(right).*

early 1936, a freelance artist was commissioned to "dress up" the cards. In fact, at least *two* artists were given the task. One came up with a design now known as the "pencil sketch" version. Each of these cards featured different characters, rather than a common icon, coupled with the text of the original cards. Parker Brothers made some of these, but put most into storage. But when the remaining inventory turned up, they found their way into games assembled in the late 1930s.

The second artist came up with the idea of a central character to grace many of the cards within the two decks. This little man was characterized by a big white mustache, a friendly countenance, a bald head (when not covered by a top hat), and the overall appearance of a wealthy financier. He was a family man; his wife appeared on a card, his three nephews on another. He had many acquaintances, including a policeman who hauled him off to jail occasionally. But he did not have a name (as least not yet).

While the name of his creator remains a mystery, the source of his likeness can be narrowed down. The unnamed *Monopoly* man was inspired either by Parker Brothers salesman Albert Richardson and his annual selling cards or by the clay molded character—"Little Esky"—who graced the cover of the popular men's magazine *Esquire* for many years. Richardson's caricature was often pictured with a top hat, bigger than life, riding a locomotive or pulling steamer trunks down a railroad track. Perhaps the artist hired to draw Richardson's calling cards subsequently drew the *Monopoly* man. "Little Esky" had a big white mustache and a top hat. He looked like an elderly financier (albeit a lecherous one), not dissimilar in appearance from the kindly financier drawn for the *Monopoly* game. Perhaps the unknown artist combined an appreciation for both the Richardson caricature and Little Esky.

In 1946, the *Monopoly* man got a name. Parker Brothers published the stock market game *Rich Uncle* and featured his likeness on its box cover and identified him, on the many Daily Bugle newspaper sheets found inside, as "Rich Uncle Pennybags," the man who ran the town.[67]

Other games followed over the years, graced by his likeness. Eventually his family and associates were given names, including wife Marge Pennybags; nephews Randy, Sandy, and Andy; and Jake the Jailbird.

(In 1999, Parker Brothers conducted research and determined that Rich Uncle Pennybags was not a memorable name. So henceforth, his name became Mr. Monopoly.)

Clue

As the 1950s dawned, one of the last cogent things George Parker said to Robert Barton was, "Don't forget what I taught you." Barton liked to think of this advice as George's final principle. As Barton later would opine, "It really was his Principle 12. Namely, ignore principles 1 to 11 at your own peril."[68]

George's mind soon faded into shadows and Barton stepped fully into the light. The fate of Parker Brothers would depend on how he reacted to the glare. Feeling alone, he acted on one of George's principles—he sought help. He went to Leeds, England, to visit Waddington's, then invited its leader, Norman Watson, to extend a trip to New York and come to Salem as his houseguest.[69] He wanted his British counterpart to feel the warmth of small-town America. The two men saw strength in an alliance and concluded their long-delayed pact. Like Parker Brothers, the John Waddington Company Ltd of Leeds, England, was getting back on its peacetime feet. One of the first successful postwar games published by Norman's firm was a clever "whodunit?" entitled *Cluedo*. The game had been invented during the war by a former government actuary named Anthony Pratt, with help from his wife, who designed its game board. Material shortages delayed its introduction until 1948.[70]

Barton licensed it and Roy Howard went to work "Americanizing" the game. A freelance designer created a stylish package and game board, which depicted the first floor of a mansion. Parker Brothers published it under the name *Clue—The Great Detective Game*. It started its rise to success in 1949. The game challenged each player to determine the murderer of the mansion's owner Mr. Boddy (perhaps Miss Scarlett, Colonel Mustard, or Mrs. Peacock?), in what room the murder took place (e.g., the library, conservatory, or billiard room), and what weapon was used to commit the dastardly crime (e.g., the lead pipe, candlestick, or wrench). Three cards, secreted in an envelope, comprised the correct "solution," which players arrived at by making "accusations" and eliminating false clues. *Clue* was easily playable by an eight-year-old and great fun for an adult, whose interest in the game was enhanced by popular detective programs now appearing on a new medium—television. Thanks to *Clue*, Parker Brothers' sales reached $2.6 million in 1949.

The staying power of the postwar expansion worried more business leaders than George Parker. An uneasy suspicion pervaded the Truman years that, without a war, a second crash would occur. This worry was captured in a Parker Brothers game called *Boom or Bust*. The center of the board featured a removable panel of prices that could be flipped over. When a "boom" occurred, prices were high and players made lots of money. When the economy went "bust," the panel was flipped and players endured low prices and suffered poor returns on their holdings.

Competitor Milton Bradley had also recovered during the war by supplying game kits to soldiers. Now, for the first time since their acquisition of McLoughlin Brothers in 1920, the firm began to market games that would rival Parker Brothers' (including *Monopoly*-derived *Easy Money*, educational *Go to the Head of the Class*, and the children's fantasy game, *Candyland*).[71] In Minneapolis, a little company named Schaper Manufacturing Company began marketing a plastic build-a-bug game named *Cootie*. Pressman Toy of New York, original makers of Chinese checkers in the United States, began to expand. Long Island's Selchow & Righter Company, long dependent on the venerable *Parcheesi*, agreed to make boards for a word game entitled *Scrabble*. It would soon acquire the marketing rights for the entire game.[72] But none of these firms worried Parker Brothers at the moment, for the company continued to enjoy its status as the nation's largest maker of games.

Channing Bacall

Management was bolstered when Charles Parker's grandson Channing—daughter Mary Bacall's son—joined the firm in 1949 following his graduation from Harvard. While his degree had been in American colonial history, this modest, bespectacled descendant of Charles Parker quickly picked up the requirements of his new job—running the tabulating department—thanks to a sharp, analytical mind and true enjoyment for his place in the family business. The "tab" machines in the first-floor department were state-of-the-art cumbersome electric calculators. One was as big as a desk. It was used to handle the payroll and to process customer orders. Its operator had to organize a stack of punch cards that comprised the customer's identity, each item ordered, and its quantity. After inserting the cards, the machine would print the customer's order, a "picking" slip for the shipping department, and an invoice to send the customer.[73]

George, Charles, and Edward Parker, circa 1878.

George's first game, Banking, *1883.*

George, high school senior, 1884.

1880s Parker Brothers games.

Parker Brothers
stationery and
original factory
photo, 1892.

George and Charles Parker, circa 1892.

Early games whose box bottoms served as game boards.

George (back), holding son Richard; Charles (front left) and Edward (front right), 1901, at Shirley Hill, Massachusetts.

Grace Parker (front right) with sons Richard (back right) and Bradstreet (front left) sitting next to driver, Mr. Getchell, 1902, at home, Salem, Massachusetts.

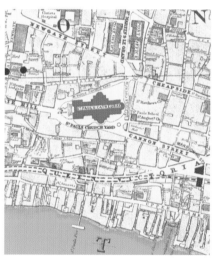

Richard Parker (left), Bradstreet Parker (center), and Edward's son, Foster (right), 1903.

The red dots on this map of Victorian London mark the first locations of the firm's offices.

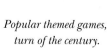

Three of the greatest Parker Brothers card games.

Popular themed games, turn of the century.

An early action game.

George play testing a card game with three ladies from his office, dressed in Gibson girl style.

Pit *postcard, 1905.*

A quiet game of PIT.

Pastime Girl at her jigsaw, 1909.

The Sea-Going Wood Basket puzzle.

A steel Diabolo *with molded rubber ends.*

George with daughter,
Sally, 1910.

Bradstreet, the
"rebel" son, 1918.

Richard Parker,
the dutiful son, 1919.

The plant Edward H.
Parker managed,
as seen from the
railroad behind it.

Edward H. Parker, 1914.

Three games based on the Great War.

Two attempts to diversify.

(From left to right) Henry Fitzpatrick, Albert Richardson, Ben Hunneman, George Parker, and Earnest Mann (George's brother-in-law) at a company summer outing, 1928.

Assembling Mah-Jongg *games in Shanghai, China, 1924.*

Debutante Sally Parker.

Charles Parker, 1925.

*Robert Barton—the man
Sally would marry in 1931—
at Exeter graduation.*

The new Parker Brothers warehouse, 1925.

1921 version.   *Three Lindbergh games.*

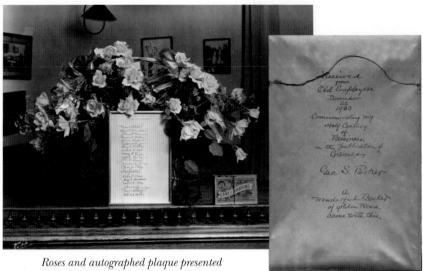

*Roses and autographed plaque presented
to George Parker on the fiftieth anniversary of the
firm in December, 1933.*

Back of plaque.

*Sally, Charles, and George
in Cairo, 1929.*

George and Grace on camels, 1929.

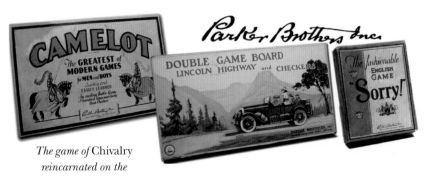

The game of Chivalry
*reincarnated on the
Nile in 1929.*

1927.

1934.

Management in 1935: (from left to right) Roy Howard, Robert Barton, Foster Parker, Paul Haskell, Charles Phelps, Don Jelly, and Chairman George Parker, seated at his rolltop desk.

Edward P. Parker, Foster's son, Harvard University graduation, 1934.

Louis Vanne printing on a Miehle press, 1937.

Monopoly's success paid for a major line expansion in the late 1930s.

Lt. Commander Eddie Parker sank two Japanese submarines while skippering the destroyer escort USS Wyman.

Forty-one-year-old Lt. Robert Barton (left) and shipmates aboard the destroyer escort, USS Jeffrey.

USS Wyman.

George Parker's Brookwood *estate.*

English Monopoly *board, modified for Allied POWs, showing the location of hidden files, a compass, and a silk map.*

George Parker's book of poetry.

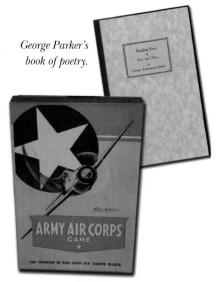

A Parker Brothers WWII game.

Grace Parker donated two stained-glass windows to the First Unitarian Church of Salem, dedicated to her husband, George, and their sons, enhanced with a reference to Camelot.

Charles Parker's grandson, Channing Bacall, serving in France, 1952.

"Chimneys" of Monopoly *games.*

Fred French cutting Monopoly *money (left); two ladies banding the bills, 1954.*

Bing's not-so-lucky game, 1954.

Keyword *did not blunt* Scrabble's *sales in 1953.*

Scoop, *licensed from Waddington, 1956.*

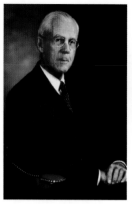

Three Parker Brothers presidents—Ranny (left) and Robert Barton (center) and Eddie Parker (right)— play testing a game, circa 1958.

Robert Barton.

Channing Bacall.   *Ranny Barton and* Risk *in New York City showroom, 1968.*

Magazine ad, Christmas 1960.

Craig Nalen of General Mills (left) hands Robert Barton a check to buy Parker Brothers, February 24, 1968.

New president, Eddie Parker.

Bill Dohrmann, head of R&D.

Michael Habourdin (left), Ranny Barton (center), and Victor Watson (right).

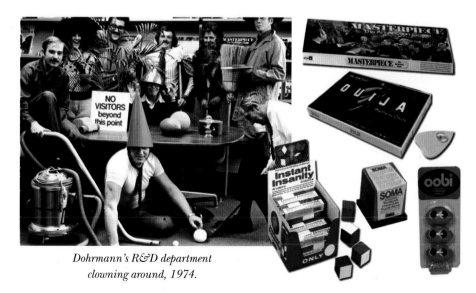

Dohrmann's R&D department clowning around, 1974.

Notable products, 1967–1973.

Beverly office building, 1982.

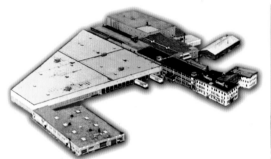

Salem plant at its greatest extent, 1984.

Rich Stearns, president from 1984 to 1985.

John Moore, president from 1985 to 1991.

Monopoly *championship, Washington, D.C., 1982. Bruce Jones is the banker; the author is seated to Jones's right, serving as chief judge. Jim Fifield is at the top of the frame.*

Monopoly
commemorative edition.

Video game hits, 1982–1985.

Kenner Parker Toys management. Bob Kinney (chairman), Ron Jackson (CEO) front row, under the clock. John Moore, Parker Brothers president, is behind Jackson.

Kenner Parker Toys became a public company after its spin-off from General Mills.

First day of trading, November 1, 1985.

Popular games from the Kenner Parker era.

Last photo of the Salem factory prior to its demolition in the fall of 1994.

*Ranny Barton (far left) and former staff
at an alumni reunion, 2002.*

*Dave Wilson, president of
Hasbro Games and former
vice president of sales for
Parker Brothers.*

*Parker Brothers classics under
license to Winning Moves Games.*

A few of Parker Brothers' many current hits.

At about this time, news articles began to appear about devices known as "computers," which the military had purchased. They were as big as a house, had thousands of vacuum tubes, and required a lowly recruit to walk around all day replacing tubes that went bad. Bacall also witnessed the sight of many other "lowly recruits" who were hired to jack up the building, acquired in 1901, to align its floors with the original building on Bridge Street. Gangs of workers pulled levers in sync to slowly inch the old building higher. To Bacall, it seemed like a scene from a Roman war galley where countless rowers pulled in unison to the beat of a drum.[74]

When the Korean War started, Bacall was among those Parker Brothers' employees who were drafted to serve their country. He joined the signal corps and was stationed in France. Fred French of the printing department was another. He had worked in the printing department for only two years when Uncle Sam came calling. He had known George Parker from an earlier experience. He recalled his days as a teenager, when he had clerked a soda stand in a drugstore at the Hawthorne Hotel. George had maintained a room there when he lived in Peterborough, New Hampshire. George would come in daily for a Coca-Cola—but insisted that teenaged French first wash a glass in his presence before pulling the soda tap to fill it.[75]

Goodbye, Mr. Parker

When the Korean-era workers left for the service, George Parker waved good-bye to them and also to his second-floor office facing Bridge Street. Helen Mitchell, his longtime secretary, agreed to resign to become a private assistant for George and Grace. Mitchell was with "GSP" through his final days.

George S. Parker died on September 26, 1952, at age eighty-six. His ashes were laid to rest in the family's gravesite at Harmony Grove Cemetery alongside those of his brothers and sons. Despite a terminal prognosis, doctors had kept him alive for weeks through the urging of Grace Parker, who could not bear to see her husband depart this earth.[76] Condolences poured in from far and wide. His obituary notice appeared in many newspapers. They noted his fifteen Atlantic crossings, memberships in fraternal and social organizations (such as the Essex Institute in

Salem and Union Club of Boston) and his directorship in banking and industrial circles (such as the Naumkeag Cotton Mills and the Naumkeag Trust).[77] Suppliers and loyal accounts wired their condolences. The associations he had been a member of passed memorial resolutions. Grace Parker was inundated with flowers. Gifts to charities, such as the Children's Home in Cincinnati, were made in his name (in this instance by the U.S. Playing Card Company, which had supplied the decks for many of Parker Brothers' most successful card games).

The officers at Parker Brothers paid their respects and looked ahead to a future without the guiding hand of the man who, for sixty-nine years, had provided a moral, ethical, and strategic vision for their firm. A comment George made to Pete Martin of the *Saturday Evening Post* could well have served as his epitaph, and inspiration to those he had entrusted to carry on after he was gone:

> After all is said and done, games help the world along. Making games is something you can look back upon with pride and not a particle of regret.

Following her husband's death, Grace Parker, with help from Helen Mitchell, commissioned a stained glass window for the First Unitarian Church of Salem. At its base appeared a dedication to George and their two sons, along with imagery and a reference to his most treasured game, *Camelot*. (Grace Mann Parker would survive her husband by twelve years, passing away in 1964 at age ninety.[78])

Robert Barton now held the fate of the company solely in his hands.

Chapter Five

Running Up the Score

1953–1968

Spread Holiday Cheer
All Through the Year
Give FAMOUS PARKER GAMES

WITH HIS FATHER-IN-LAW GONE, THE MOMENT Robert Barton had awaited for many years was at hand. He was undisputedly in charge of the firm. Barton took command a few weeks before former General Dwight Eisenhower won his next command, as president of the United States. Both men faced uncertainty, change, and problems caused by growth.

New Game Plan

Eisenhower would struggle with war in Korea, Russian atomic spies, the threat of global communism, and the need to bolster allies in Europe. At home, the dollar was worth half as much as in 1935, but inflation could not hold consumer spending in check, so insatiable was the country's demand for new housing, cars, clothing, and entertainment.[1]

The nation's problems affected Parker Brothers as well, but in a more positive way. Barton's main challenge was figuring out how to make all the games the country demanded, due to growth in leisure spending and the desire of consumers to escape the worries of the postwar world (which seemed to multiply on a daily basis). His main obstacles included the rising cost of raw material, a shortage of manufacturing space, and the loss of young female employees who retired to have children. Barton relied solidly on his staff to solve these challenges. Eddie Parker was now his executive vice president. Eddie's father, Foster, was his treasurer. ("The treasurer runs the mill," he often told Foster, who was saddled with the responsibility of overseeing both manufacturing and the firm's finances.) Channing Bacall was in the army but would return to added responsibility. Ranny Barton, in college in Virginia, also looked forward to his turn in the family business.

The children of the World War II generation—the "baby boomers"—were becoming the largest segment of the nation's population. For the most part, they had not known poverty, depression, or war—and their parents wanted only the best for them. They would be responsible for driving the amazing growth and maturation of the once-small U.S. toy and game industry into a multibillion-dollar powerhouse.

It was fortunate that demand for existing games seemed limitless, because the firm had lost its creative force and its editorial guidance with the demise of George Parker. Until Barton could bolster R&D, the sales department would be the key to sustaining growth. Foster Parker was also responsible for the five-man sales force, whose talents and capabilities were constantly stretched. Stanley James, the firm's best salesman, continued to run the New York office, as did Eddie Hefferman at the Chicago office. These two served their regions on a year-round basis. Not so for the rest of the country. The remaining three salesmen lived either in Boston or New York and periodically covered their territories via railroad excursions, as Albert Richardson had done for decades. One was color-blind, another couldn't drive a car and relied on taxis, the third was young and untried. Despite these limitations, the trade placed orders early, and by October production was often booked for the remainder of the year.

To shore up product development, the Salem-based salesmen then shifted their efforts and helped editor Roy Howard fine-tune the next year's product line. A meeting room was provided for them on the third floor of the Salem factory where they played the new games and perfected their sales pitch for the next New York Toy Fair, in February. Paul Haskell was a keen writer in addition to being a skilled purchasing agent. He often helped Howard with new game testing and editing. When feasible, other employees were given Friday afternoon off to join in these game-playing sessions.[2]

Output of the Parker Brothers factory approached a ceiling. To accommodate the next round of growth, management considered a break with Salem by building a facility elsewhere in the country. Iowa was suggested. It was in the middle of the country, close to the vital Chicago market, and could save the firm a lot of freight costs. Salem, Massachusetts, located at one extreme of the three-thousand-mile-long nation, was a poor location to headquarter a firm whose products were mainly boxes filled with air. It put Barton and company at a competitive cost disadvantage. But Salem did have one irreplaceable ingredient—a skilled and devoted work force that turned out millions of high-quality games each year.

On February 17, 1953, a major announcement was headlined in the *Salem News*—Parker Brothers would connect its factory to its warehouse via a $500,000 addition. This would eliminate the need for the material-carrying trolley that shuttled goods between the two. In a letter to the president of the city council of Salem, Barton explained how he and his firm had decided to stay in Salem. A statement within the article tempered the cheer from the local populace. Parker Brothers had, for the first time, seriously considered building elsewhere.

Barton wrote:

> It may interest the Council to know that before deciding on the $500,000 expansion program which the company has at present underway, we investigated the possibility of establishing a branch plant elsewhere in New England or even in the Middle West. . . . But in no instance did any government or its departments extend to us the cooperation that we have received from the Salem city government. It is largely for this reason that we determined upon a policy of expansion in this city, and I am certain that this decision will be for the benefit of both the company and the city of Salem.

The die was cast. Parker Brothers would make a sizable investment that would strengthen, not diminish, its tie to Salem and its thirty thousand citizens for the foreseeable future. Following Foster Parker's financial arrangements, the 56,000-square-foot, three-story structure was built. It came on line in late 1953 when annual sales surpassed $5 million. (There was no bust and, accordingly, *Boom or Bust* did not endure in the Parker Brothers line.) Sales of the *Monopoly* game exceeded a million units for the first time since 1936 and the game showed no sign of losing its status as a "must-have" cultural icon.[3]

In the prior eighteen years, competition in the games industry had done little to arouse the attention of Parker Brothers. But this changed in 1953 when Selchow & Righter claimed ownership of the country's hottest-selling game—a four-player crossword tile game named *Scrabble*. Reacting to this, Parker Brothers quickly published a similar game named *Keyword*, complete with crossword-style game board, letter tiles, and racks. *Keyword*'s significant difference was the inclusion of a deck of "Keyword" cards that provided more scoring opportunity. The public was not dissuaded from *Scrabble*, however, and for the first time in recent memory a game of significance did not bear the Parker Brothers logo on its package. Milton Bradley's sales began to rise rapidly as well. Concentration of effort on its bestsellers was working. Its game operation now supplanted its educational business as the engine of growth for the firm.

In response, Barton began to address new products in a more proactive way. To complement editor Howard's effort, Barton fostered his relationship with John Waddington Company Ltd in the hopes that he could benefit from the import of new hit English games. But none appeared after *Clue*. Turning attention back to his own company, he decided to build an internal R&D group. The first man to join Howard in the development effort was an energetic Parker Brothers employee named Lew Green who, for a decade, had worked the game counter at Macy's in New York City, demonstrating Parker Brothers games. He was passionate about Parker Brothers games and knew them all, inside out. But it would take years before the understaffed group would be self-sufficient.

R&D was not the only undersized department inside of Parker Brothers. There was no marketing to speak of during the 1950s. Store displays and advertising represented the extent of the firm's "marketing" efforts. The print ads at Parker Brothers had previously been written solely by George Parker and placed by two women at a small local agency. They were now in their seventies. Finally, Eddie Parker recommended a change and Barton agreed. An agency in Boston named Badger, Browning and Parcher was hired, with Frank Browning Sr., appointed to lead the effort to modernize Parker Brothers' advertising and "spread the word" about each new featured game. Ironically, Browning's firm had no creative team. It relied on a bright and outgoing freelancer named Jack Wilcher to create the jingles and copy lines that soon would be heard on the radio and seen in Parker Brothers print ads.[4]

Barton did not have much savvy when it came to advertising, but he tried to understand its importance. Browning and Wilcher once came to his office to try and "educate" him. Wilcher, to everyone's surprise, started banging out a rhythm on Barton's round meeting table, while singing a new jingle he had written ("Monopoly, Monopoly, I always land in bankruptcy . . ."). To those in the room, Barton seemed more stunned by the banging on his table than the cleverness of the jingle.[5]

Old-timers were starting to retire, and replacements had to be found. Plant superintendent Charlie Phelps, a forty-five-year veteran, suffered a heart attack and had to leave the firm. He died shortly thereafter. Foster Parker, seventy-five in 1954, grew sick. This heavy smoker was diagnosed with lung cancer and confined to bed. Channing Bacall, now twenty-four, took his place as treasurer with responsibility for the manufacturing, bookkeeping, and tabulating departments. To provide sales leadership, twenty-year veteran Stanley James was promoted to vice president and moved to Salem from the New York office.

After a glorious half century, the last *Pastime Puzzle* was cut, finished, and packaged in Salem. Rising costs had steadily narrowed the market for these exquisite wooden puzzles. Furthermore, the jigsaws used in the 1950s were still the originals from 1908. They often broke down and management was unprepared to replace them. A grand chapter in Parker Brothers' product history now closed.

The search for a new hit game continued. Popular entertainer Bing Crosby lent his name to *Call Me Lucky*. The object of this light strategy game was to capture lucky point cards placed on the spaces of the board. This game became an example of management's determination, with Frank Browning's advertising support, to capitalize anew on popular themes, personalities, and programs. *Call Me Lucky* was only a modest success, but this didn't seem to matter. Sales of existing well-known Parker Brothers games continued to exceed projections and advertising was one important reason. Television had become the dominant medium and Parker Brothers began to use it to its advantage. Dave Garroway was a television pioneer. On January 14, 1952, this tall, knowledgeable gentleman with a bow tie greeted television viewers from Maine to California as the first host of NBC's *Today* show. His laid-back style caught on and led to a nationwide following.[6] He liked Parker Brothers' games and readily agreed to promote them on air, often holding one above his head and another across his chest. The impact was dramatic. Sales of Parker Brothers' staple games continued to rise throughout the 1950s.

Randolph Barton

Randolph Parker Barton had remained outside the glare that shone on his older cousins and father. Despite the devotion and instruction accorded him by his grandfather, Randolph Barton had not inherited George Parker's sense of self-importance. Whereas George had insisted on being called "Mr. Parker," his grandson wanted to be called "Ranny" and preferred to address those he met by their first names as well. He had grown into adulthood bearing a strong resemblance to a youthful, but shorter, Joe DiMaggio. While intent on joining the family business, he was struggling first to get through college. In frustration, he dropped out of the University of Virginia during his junior year and joined the army. Eighteen months in the quartermaster corps, loading and unloading freight cars in Alaska, helped mature him. With new resolve, he returned to school, married his childhood sweetheart—Maud Palmer, a Wellesley graduate—and at twenty-five, joined Parker Brothers following his graduation in the summer of 1957. After six weeks of training, during which he worked in several different parts of the plant, he settled into the product development department and helped Lew Green to update games like *Star Reporter*, *Politics*, and *Pollyanna*.[7] The "build-a-newspaper game" *Scoop* had arrived from Waddington's in 1956. As clever as it was—with a randomizing cardboard telephone that determined if the editor accepted each story card you submitted or not—it became another disappointment. Building a newspaper did not grip the imagination of boomers in this age of television.

Careers

Finally, Robert Barton and staff found a post–George Parker hit. Its success was due to the Space Race, which had begun the prior fall with the Soviets' launch of Sputnik. This event jolted the complacency of U.S. leaders, who suddenly recognized the need for more engineers, scientists, and professionals in all disciplines. *Careers* became the perfect game for the time. Dr. James C. Brown, as associate professor at the University of Florida, had invented and published it. He felt that his game would provide an opportunity, in game form, for youngsters and adults alike to learn the importance of balancing the factors of success in the choice of one's career. Where once Charles Parker had advised his brother George of the importance of satisfaction in a career, Brown's game asked each player to secretly record a balance of fame, happiness, and money in their *Careers'* "success formula," which determined who won. This feature was especially appealing to girls, who typically emphasized happiness while boys usually overweighed money or fame. With secret formula recorded, each player embarked on a journey through many careers— such as business, farming, Hollywood, and space travel—earning hearts (happiness), stars (fame), or dollars signs (money) in different proportion, coinciding with the nature of each career. *Monopoly*-like features were also present—a continuous track of spaces around the board, including a space like Go where one's annual salary was paid and increased, and a Park Bench, similar to Free Parking. Also included were orange Experience and yellow Opportunity cards. And, of course, lots of play money. Learning of Brown's success with his game, Parker Brothers licensed *Careers* in 1956 and published it the next year.[8]

To promote *Careers*, Frank Browning Sr. arranged for Macy's to set up a human-sized game board in its flagship Herald Square store in New York City and fill the store's windows with *Careers* games. New Yorkers responded enthusiastically, and soon the nation was *Careers*-happy. Browning requested and received a bigger fall media budget. He placed Parker Brothers ads in thirty magazines and commercials on sixty television stations. Twenty-five radio towers beamed audio commercials.[9] The media blitz combined to boost sales of most staple games to new heights. Sales reached $6 million in 1957, a 1,500 percent increase from the depths of 1934.[10]

Careers helped finance another strategic addition to the factory. A 14,000-square-foot shipping room was built along its east side, and plans were laid to add two floors atop this single-story addition once it became prudent to do so. The office staff also benefited. The sound of trucks being loaded beneath their windows would no longer be an annoyance; the old shipping department became offices for Channing Bacall's growing financial department. Robert Barton trusted and relied on his young, intelligent treasurer. He looked to him to adjust the "valve" that regulated the flow of money to pay for the firm's growth and its operating expenses. He instructed Bacall, simply, to "keep me out of trouble and don't let me overspend."

Risk

In the summer of 1957, at the invitation of Robert Barton, Mr. Boisseau of Parker Brothers' French partner, Miro Company, came to Salem. While the purpose of his visit was to discuss the possibility of the joint venture and see the operation of his potential partner, he also had with him a copy of a new game entitled "La Conquete Du Monde." The board for this "conquer-the-world" game was quite large. It divided the continents into colored territories, each of which was always occupied by one or more brightly colored wooden pieces, which represented armies. There were hundreds of these in the game—a plastic box full for each of six players, plus many dice and a deck of territory cards. The game was immediately seen as both unique and promising. Barton acquired its North American rights on the spot. But its overt war theme bothered his staff. They also felt that luck played an excessive role in the initial distribution of "territories" and that the game took far too long to play.

It would take the better part of a year to fix these shortcomings. Its title, in particular, was troublesome because educators were questioning the merits of war toys and their sales were on the decline. Many names implying conquest had already been registered with the trademark office; many others were inappropriate for a game intended to be played by families. One day, Parker Brothers salesman Elwood Reeves walked

FIGURE 5-1

Take a *Risk*

Risk *ad, 1959.*

into Robert Barton's office with a piece of paper in hand. "I think I've got it," he said. The word RISK was written on the paper. Barton called others to his office. They agreed this was a terrific name for the new game. Reeves then explained that he came upon the name simply by combining the initials of his four grandchildren![11]

A French movie producer named Albert Lamorisse had invented the game that Parker Brothers now christened *Risk*. He was a minor celebrity in the United States as well, thanks to his movie *The Red Balloon*. To resolve the flaws that Parker Brothers felt marred play, people both inside and outside of the firm were enlisted to play the game. Like the firm's resident salesmen, management had always participated in the testing of new games. Their involvement was one reason why the firm had gotten by for decades with only Roy Howard in the R&D department. They helped him refine the rules of new games by playing them over and over to discover flaws or predictable strategies, which would adversely affect word of mouth.

The biggest need in *Risk* was to speed up play. The winner was the player whose armies eventually occupied every one of the forty-two territories on the board. To capture an adjacent territory owned by an opponent, a player had to wipe out all the wooden armies defending that territory and then move some of his armies into it. To do so, a series of attacks took place. This involved rolling dice and comparing the numbers rolled by each player. One day, while playing against Channing Bacall, Eddie Parker experimented with a rule that permitted a strong attacker to roll three dice in an attack versus two dice rolled by a sturdy defender. This solved the problem. Excitement now rose steadily and a typical game ended with a bang. With Ranny Barton's help, the lesser concerns were soon ironed out and *Risk* was ready to market. It was launched in 1959 with a smart advertising campaign and a hold-your-breath retail price of $7.50. The large board and the cost of the polished tiny wooden armies had inflated the price. A vendor that Miro had found behind the Iron Curtain, in Czechoslovakia, supplied these. Channing Bacall attempted to have them made in the United States, but no U.S. vendor could replicate the quality of the secret Czech process. Despite the lofty price, the aura of the game and its wealth of components made many boys and men place *Risk* at the top of their Christmas lists. *Risk* added a million dollars to revenue in 1959 and quickly repaid the firm's careful attention to its perfection.[12]

The toy industry itself was becoming a media topic, thanks to hot products like the Frisbee, Hula Hoop, and the breakthrough Barbie doll.[13] The next year, Parker Brothers was the beneficiary of another well-publicized cultural happening. Seven years after the death of George Parker, his favorite invention shared its name with a musical on Broadway, Lerner and Loew's *Camelot*. Parker Brothers immediately placed an ad campaign behind the game and watched its sales rise once more.

Expansion

Those who came to know Robert Barton realized that he was an austere man, not given to impulse or frivolity. But Barton knew the importance of daring in order to remain competitive. The epic of the *Monopoly* game was proof positive. Since the 1930s, Barton had plugged himself into the leadership of the Toy Industry Association. From his vantage point, he knew what his competitors were saying, thinking, and—most important—doing. And what they were doing was innovating new products at a frantic pace to satisfy the expanding interests and demands of the boomers. One firm, in particular, held his attention. Mattel, of Hawthorne, California, had begun in a garage in Denver after World War II, and—with its knack of developing innovative toys and memorable television advertising—had become one of the nation's largest toy companies in only a decade. Barton realized that if an upstart, run by a husband-and-wife team, could shake up the toy industry, another might come along that would threaten his games business.

Barton decided to expand his firm's horizon. While he lacked a firm idea of what he was looking for, he knew future hits might lay beyond the confines of a game with a board or a deck of cards. The only limit he would place on his next product acquisition was money. He was unwilling to incur debt, and in this decision he had the full agreement of his staff. Perhaps the memory of Rogers' and Winslow's constraints on George Parker and his brothers had been passed down through their genes. The family would rather defer dividends and plow back profit than ask a bank for a long-term loan.[14]

Barton decided to move beyond board and card games by entering a category of playthings that could be made using his firm's manufacturing prowess. He encouraged suggestions. A woman in the manufacturing department proposed kits to make stuffed animals. Children's quilting kits were suggested as well. Soon, water-coloring kits, puppets, paper dolls, and embroidery cards were added to a diverse line of what now became known as *Pastime Products*. A "King of Fun" logo, consisting of a small *p* and *b* topped by a crown, represented the line. Sales, unfortunately, did not measure up. After a few years, the line was discontinued. The sheets of printed "fur" from the unsold stuffed animal kits were soon seen in driveways all over Salem, each serving as a chamois for polishing the owner's automobile.[15]

Expansion remained a primary goal, but cost control was also a high priority. The most difficult expense continued to be freight. Not only was Salem far from the nation's geographic center, but it was also miles from major intercity highways. This cost disadvantage threatened to make Parker Brothers games more costly than those of rival Milton Bradley. No one on Barton's staff had the stomach to propose moving Parker Brothers out of Salem. Not only was the firm intimately connected with the small city, with each benefiting in the symbiotic relationship, but its supply of labor was also more deeply experienced in game making than in any other part of the country save Springfield, Massachusetts, where Milton Bradley had its factory. To move the firm successfully would require moving key employees. Native New Englanders, especially on Boston's North Shore, were unlikely to relish moving to the nation's heartland, far from the sea, in Barton's opinion.[16]

After careful site investigation and financial analysis by Channing Bacall, the firm reduced its freight burden by building a distribution center in Des Moines, Iowa. Freight car loads of game parts could now be shipped from Salem to Des Moines, assembled, and then trucked to accounts in the Midwest, especially to the lucrative Chicago market.[17] Bacall's proposal proved to be a cost-saver. This new base in Iowa was therefore prime for expansion in coming years.

Next, Barton acquired 40 percent of France's Miro Company. (John Waddington Company Ltd purchased 20 percent and the managing Habourdin family retained the remainder.) The triumvirate began to realize synergy immediately; Miro presented Parker Brothers with another major product opportunity, but not without a complication. A French inventor named Edmond Dujardin had modified *Touring* and recast it as *Mille Bornes* ("a thousand kilometer markers") and it took the French game market by storm. *Mille Bornes* played exactly like *Touring*, its object

FIGURE 5-2
Parker Brothers' Plants

Parker Brothers' Salem, Massachusetts plant through the years (1889–1968), and the Parker Brothers' plant in Des Moines, Iowa, 1962.

being to lay down cards whose kilometer marking totaled 1,000. In addition, *Mille Bornes* contained a broader array of road hazards (e.g., accident card), and remedies (e.g., a repair card), and special cards like "Driving Ace," which accelerated one's progress. Since Parker Brothers already had *Touring*, it seemed unlikely that the firm would want *Mille Bornes*. But Barton and Eddie Parker did not wish to see a competitor selling this card game powerhouse ("Never hesitate and give your opponents a second chance," George Parker would have advised), so they made a most unusual deal. They agreed to take on *Mille Bornes* and discontinue *Touring*. It was decided to retain the French name in order to preserve the continental "glamour" of the new game. The highly promoted 1963 launch of *Mille Bornes*, at $3 retail, began in Chicago and was so successful, it was rolled out nationally. The new card game outsold the *Monopoly* game, unit for unit, that year. *Mille Bornes* was here to stay.[18]

That same year, Barton won approval to purchase the Philips Game Company, of southern Massachusetts, primarily to acquire its best game,

Spill & Spell. Along with the firm's modest line of games came an executive named Hank Simmons, whose research and development experience was badly needed. Longtime editor Roy Howard had retired and his successors had not measured up. Simmons had game savvy and challenged any signs of complacency in new product selection.[19] While Barton came to respect Simmons's expansiveness, the two did not always see eye-to-eye, much as George Parker had contested Barton's views on products during the 1930s and 1940s.

Vice president of sales, Stanley James, wanted a stronger national selling effort. His department got a boost with the addition of permanent offices in Atlanta and San Francisco. The company finally had a sales manager in each region of the country. Gone were the days when Parker Brothers salesmen from Boston or New York made grand selling tours across the country a few times per year.

Barton was keenly aware that rival toy companies were capitalizing mightily on the second material revolution to hit the industry—plastics. Three-dimensional plastic action games were growing the market share of his closest competitors, especially Ideal Toy Corporation. Ideal had sparked this craze with the introduction of a game called *Mousetrap.* While Ideal was a latecomer to the games business, it rapidly became the nation's third-largest maker of games, behind Parker Brothers and Milton Bradley. Barton paid careful attention, worried about the possibility of new rivals entering the games business by mirroring Mattel's innovation in toys. To counter, he began to look for action games that Parker Brothers could make. His firm, however, still relied on wood and cardboard. The first successful action game for Parker Brothers, the "explosive" *Booby Trap*, was made in the factory entirely out of wood (wood frame and cylindrical pieces), aside from one purchased metal spring.

To compete in plastics, Barton would have to invest in plastic molding machines. He did this by acquiring control of Boyden Plastics, a plastic molding firm located in Taunton, Massachusetts (near the Rhode Island border). *Monopoly* houses and hotels would henceforth be made out of colored polystyrene plastic. (Wood was reserved exclusively for the pieces found in deluxe editions.) Games like *Booby Trap* would now be molded out of plastic. While plastic parts would be much cheaper to make than wood parts, the savings was partially offset by the need to make expensive steel molds. Fortunately, a skilled mold-making

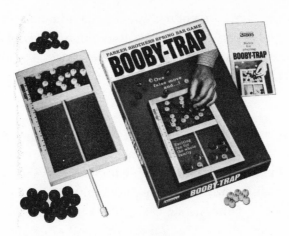

FIGURE 5-3
Booby Trap Game

industry existed in Massachusetts and Boyden Plastics knew how to design and acquire the molds.

More international expansion occurred. Barton and team agreed to establish Parker Brothers Canada and headquarter its new subsidiary in Toronto. By so doing, Parker Brothers instantly enhanced sales of its staple games by 10 percent or more. Licensing deals for Parker Brothers products were soon signed in many more countries, especially for the *Monopoly* game, which added substantial income directly to the bottom line—and started the buildup of global awareness for the Parker Brothers brand.

At home, the American Civil War Centennial kicked off in 1961. That year, Parker Brothers agreed to market a game entitled *1863* to capitalize on the well-publicized event, much as George Parker had exploited military conflicts during his career. The game was invented by three staffers of *Life* magazine, which first published the game at the conclusion of a magnificent five-part series on the war in their May 1961 issue.[20] Their game could be played on a two-page game board spread, but its army and navy pieces had to be pasted on cardboard and cut out with scissors. Mention was made in the magazine of Parker Brothers' forthcoming version. Barton and team believed that *Life*'s millions of readers would play the magazine's makeshift version, then rush out to buy a permanent copy. Unfortunately, either the majority of the readers of *Life* didn't play it, or they were not motivated to spend money on what they had just received as part of their paid subscription. *1863* did not remain in the Parker Brothers line long enough to see 1962.

Edward Parker

In 1963, Robert Barton, at age sixty, designated Edward Pickering Parker as his successor. It was time to plan a transition, even though he committed himself to remain on the job for at least five more years.

Barton felt satisfied with his accomplishments. While never an inventive person like his father-in-law, George Parker, he had licensed many best-selling games—*Sorry!*, *Clue*, *Careers*, *Risk*, and especially the *Monopoly* game—which made Parker Brothers stable, very profitable, and the envy of its competitors. He valued the relationships built with his foreign partners. He had applied sound fiscal planning to the firm and, with the help of Channing Bacall and Eddie Parker, had kept his firm debt free. But prior to designating Eddie as his successor, he debated the same issues as George Parker had many years earlier. Must he continue with the firm until his death? Could he plan a transition and remove the firm's dependency on him? Would he be able to live comfortably on the dividends of the stock his wife owned?[21]

Eddie Parker was no mere second fiddle. He had learned the operation of the firm inside and out and gained Barton's confidence as a vital contributor to products, especially given his role in the development of *Risk* and the acquisition of *Mille Bornes*. If the work force inside of Parker Brothers could have voted on their leader, Eddie would have won by a landslide over Barton. Whereas George Parker had displayed a haughty attitude toward his laborers ("He was like a king leaving his throne whenever he walked through the plant," Louis Vanne once bemoaned), and Robert Barton was seen as severe, although ultimately fair, the workers regarded Eddie Parker as a prince among men. Although he was not tall like Barton, Eddie's physical presence commanded respect, not awe. He was approachable. Most saw him as a "regular guy" who happened to wear a suit instead of worker's garb. His nose pointed straight ahead, not in the air. He wore a smile easily and maintained a compassionate attitude. He had a sense of humility, talked to the workers on their level, understood their problems, and kept both ears open when people spoke. He walked down to the cafeteria at ten o'clock each morning to have a smoke and a cup of coffee—but mainly to sit with anyone who was on break and discuss what they wanted to talk about. In this way, he learned about brewing problems and corrected them before they became serious issues.[22]

Eddie and his wife Natalie had three daughters. Middle daughter Anne, on her first visit through the Parker Brothers factory, was struck by her father's ability to greet each worker by name (there were more than three hundred in Salem now) and the easy rapport he had with them all.[23] Fred French recalls walking down Washington Street in Salem one busy Saturday with his wife, Fabia. Across the street, Eddie Parker spotted them and quickly crossed over. "Hi Fred," he said, shaking his hand, "Aren't you going to introduce me to your wife?" When Fred introduced Eddie to Fabia, she was awestruck that the executive vice president of Parker Brothers had taken time to greet them. Fred was equally impressed—he had met Eddie only twice on the plant floor. (As a contrast, many years later when Eddie returned from a meeting in Fred's office, Robert Barton asked him where he had been. Eddie told him, "I was with Fred French." Barton struggled to recall who Fred French was and what he did.[24])

When Eddie's daughter Anne was nine, she and her friends paid a visit to her father at work. With Eddie distracted, she found herself on the first floor watching the cartons of *Monopoly* games slowly coming down the conveyor from the third-floor collating department. With friendly prodding from the workers nearby, Anne and her friends went up to the third floor and asked to be "loaded" into open cartons and placed on the conveyor. Laughing and shrieking, they were soon on the way back down to the first floor. Once there, with the thrill over, the thought of embarrassing her father made Anne question the escapade and it didn't reoccur. Eddie's relationship with the work force had a similar effect. No one wanted to disappoint him.[25]

Barton had considered Channing Bacall when deciding on his successor, but believed the firm's treasurer was in the right job at the right time and would become Eddie's "number two." Channing and wife Joan had two children. He was very happy in his roles as treasurer, father, and husband. He had kept Barton solidly informed of the firm's financial health, and the family patriarch expected that he would do the same for Eddie when his time came to lead the firm. Channing was regarded as the egghead of the family. He spoke clearly and his words were filled with intelligence. He had developed respect and loyalty toward the firm's workers and, like Eddie, began each day with a walk through the plant to greet them.[26]

Shortly after his hire in 1957, Ranny Barton completed his training in several departments. After Ranny came to know how the plant worked, he joined management as a vice president reporting to Eddie Parker. Robert Barton felt that his son would learn the business much faster, with less intimidation, if Eddie were his boss, rather than himself.

Ranny came to enjoy working for Eddie and they became close friends. Slowly, but surely, he learned "the nuts and bolts of the business" from Eddie, and also from Channing Bacall. His father saw him becoming a key ally for Eddie once he retired. What the elder Barton did not know was that as his son was learning how Parker Brothers worked, he was quietly making mental notes about how to modernize the company. He realized that Parker Brothers' proven but tired manufacturing methods and lack of professional marketing were holding it back.[27]

Leadership Growth

As President Lyndon Johnson stepped out of the shadow of former President John Kennedy, the grandchildren of Edward, Charles, and George Parker began to emerge from the long, thin shadow cast by Robert Barton. In addition, Hank Simmons was becoming a force, thanks to his good eye for products—most of those he endorsed made money—but he was not a member of the family and often pushed in a way a nonowner tends to push, without an eye on the bottom line.[28] However, Simmons did advocate that the firm refresh its corporate symbol, believing the George Parker signature logo to be tired. A new "pinwheel" logo—a blue and white swirl—was soon adopted to appeal to the nation's 190 million people, now recipients of the TV advertising blitz.

While Lyndon Johnson enacted his Great Society and wrestled with the growing war in Vietnam, Robert Barton pondered what it would take to keep his company great and wrestled with its need for growth capital. In 1944, George Parker had requested that Barton keep the company in the family hands for at least a few generations. Barton wondered if that could be done without financial help. If outside investors should gain a significant foothold, might someone other than a Parker or a Barton or a Bacall take over leadership of the firm? Would the discipline forged by George Parker's principles be challenged?[29]

The steady growth in sales—from $6 million in 1957 to $13.3 million in 1965—accelerated in 1966. Sales climbed another 20 percent to $16 million.[30] Channing Bacall had calculated that costs could be reduced further if game boards were also made in Des Moines. A 48,000-square-foot addition was approved to further the facility's success, and it entered service during 1967. Only the print shop in Salem was uneconomical to replicate, so freight car loads of printed box wraps and game board labels continued to arrive regularly from Salem.[31]

Ouija

For the company's next uncanny acquisition, conservative, upstanding Robert Barton put instinct aside. Instead, he put his trust in advice his sales force was giving him. Based on input from retailers, they told him this acquisition would be "a once in a lifetime, can't-miss deal." Barton concurred. With $975,000 in cash and Channing Bacall's blessing, he made the most expensive product acquisition in the firm's history. He purchased the rights for the venerable *Ouija* board from the sons of William Fuld, who had popularized this "Mystic Oracle" four decades earlier.[32]

Backed by a clever print and radio advertising campaign orchestrated by Frank Browning Jr. (who had taken his father's place in the advertising business), *Ouija* would outsell *Monopoly* in 1967—2.3 million copies to 2 million.[33] Once again, the mood in the country drove sales of a Parker Brothers' blockbuster. The Vietnam War was not going as well as President Johnson's administration claimed. The "credibility gap" grew and it seemed that citizens were losing faith in leaders of all types. In uncertain times, reliance on the supernatural always increases. Staid, traditional Parker Brothers began to advertise a classic occult "toy" at a moment of great national uncertainty, reminding a receptive populace that the "mystical oracle" could provide "answers." *Monopoly* and *Ouija* accounted for fully one half of the company's $18 million in sales during 1967, helping the company to earn more than a million dollars in net profits.[34]

William Fuld is thought by many to have invented *Ouija*. Wrong man. In 1891, Elijah Bond received a U.S. patent on the forerunner of the

Ouija board. But the following year, 1892, Fuld purchased Bond's rights in the patent and applied for an improvement. (Evidence of the origins of *Ouija* devices can be found in ancient Greece and China. The Romans were also known to have *Ouija*-like devices.) Notwithstanding where it may have originated, Fuld was bent on exploiting his new acquisition. He founded a firm known as the Southern Novelty Company in Baltimore, Maryland. Years later, he changed its name to the Baltimore Talking Board Company and began to make "Oriole" Talking Boards and *planchettes*—the triangular-shaped moving devices that pointed to letters, numbers, and words printed on the board in order to provide answers to questions. Sales were brisk and Fuld made a great deal of money. A Presbyterian, he had no personal attraction to the mystic nature of the board, save the one time he had asked it if he should build the factory to make the Oriole board, and the board replied "yes." He claimed that he ignored its "mystic" powers thereafter. With its name changed to *Ouija* (the combination of *yes* in both French and German, respectively), Fuld cleaned up during World War I when thousands of U.S. citizens relied on his board to try to learn the fate of loved ones on the front in France. *Ouija*'s enduring popularity inspired artist Norman Rockwell to feature it in his painting for the May 1, 1920, cover of the *Saturday Evening Post*.[35]

When Fuld died tragically in a 1927 accident, his children inherited his business. The *Ouija* board soared in popularity during the Great Depression, and again during World War II. With sales on the rise once more in 1967, Robert Barton made the Fuld brothers an offer they couldn't refuse.

General Mills

As dazzling as were Parker Brothers' sales and profit expansion, the consumption of cash to build inventory, hire workers, and add to facilities seemed unrelenting. There had always been three options to raise cash: bring in private investors, issue stock to the public, or sell the firm outright. Discussion on these options dated back to 1957, but by 1966 it was no longer idle conversation at the regularly scheduled Monday morning management meetings. By 1967, it was a regular topic. Simultaneously, Parker Brothers began to be solicited by other firms and individuals interested in buying it. Barton did not like the distraction and hired Lehman Brothers of New York City to screen these inquiries.[36]

FIGURE 5-4
Bestsellers, 1967

One of those who survived the screening was General Mills, the venerable Minneapolis-based maker of Wheaties and Cheerios cereal. General Mills had decided, strategically, to augment its growth through the acquisition of other consumer product companies. Craig Nalen of General Mills' new ventures team, a Stanford Business School graduate, was on the hunt to find a board game company to buy. He maneuvered his way into a meeting with Milton Bradley, where his Jack Kennedy grin, athletic build, and vibrant personality were met by polite rejection. He then went on to visit Parker Brothers. The Salem factory presented a sharp contrast to the modern Minneapolis office building where he worked. The original 1875 clapboard building fronting Bridge Street continued to house its main offices. The reception area was cramped and lined with the same dark mahogany wood that George Parker had favored. The stairs creaked and seemed canted. The narrow L-shaped hallway at the top of stairs looked like a museum, lined with old display cases containing products, some new, some old. But everything was sparkling clean and one could hear the energized hum of the factory just beyond the small executive area where Robert Barton awaited to escort Nalen into his plainly furnished office. The thirty-four-year-old Nalen studied the thin, rigid man after he sat down behind his desk, but Barton's stern expression, accented by austere wire-rimmed glasses, betrayed nothing of the thoughts at work within his mind. Nalen was not intimidated by the cool reception. He explained how

General Mills could, by acquiring Parker Brothers, provide the working capital needed to modernize the business and foster more expansion. Robert asked his son, Ranny, and nephew, Eddie Parker, to join the meeting. Nalen repeated his pitch. The elder Barton remained impassive and concluded by saying, "Well, I'm not interested." Then he added, "But it will be the younger generation's decision, you know." Despite the added comment, Nalen was certain that Robert Barton called the shots and he would have to be persuaded. Perhaps first swaying Ranny and Eddie could do this.[37]

Nalen had already helped General Mills to buy Rainbow Crafts, the maker of *Play-Doh* modeling compound. This was a good fit because *Play-Doh*'s main ingredient was flour, and General Mills was the nation's largest maker of flour. He was looking at other firms, including Kenner Toys of Cincinnati, Craft Master of Detroit, MPC (a model kit maker), and several European toy companies. None of these appealed to him as much as did Parker Brothers because of its staple product line, conservative nature, and impeccable reputation.

When Nalen finally heard back from Parker Brothers, it was Ranny Barton who relayed the message: "The time's not right, Craig." Nalen reined in his enthusiasm. Throughout 1967, he would contact Ranny or Eddie periodically, invite one or the other to a memorable dinner in New York, and begin to build rapport whenever opportunity presented itself, hoping "the younger generation" might push the elder Barton into negotiations.[38]

Throughout the year, responses to Nalen's overtures were discouraging. Channing Bacall voiced doubts over the wisdom of selling. Eddie Parker wasn't sure it was for the best, for either the family or the workers. Would General Mills want to move Parker Brothers out of Salem and plop it down in the Midwest? But Eddie and Channing could not make the decision on their own. Robert Barton's wife Sally had inherited the majority of the firm's common stock from her father, with the provision that it ultimately go to Ranny. She had vested its voting rights with her husband and oldest son, trusting their judgment implicitly. This fact assured that Robert and Ranny held the cards when it came down to a vote. In late 1967, with the elder Barton approaching sixty-five years of age, he began to think more and more about the benefit of diversifying his financial holdings. He worried about onerous estate taxes that would surely compel the sale of the firm if he and his wife should suddenly die.[39]

Their son Ranny, typically quiet and seemingly aloof, began to make his presence felt. Long concerned about the firm's need to modernize, his eyes had been opened on exactly how to do so. He had seized an opportunity to attend a management program at Harvard and entered the fifth class of the Business School's Program for Management Development. There, he learned the potential of applying modern marketing techniques and the value of modernizing its manufacturing department. He imagined the future, and it was not a continuation of the past. He began to challenge his father's thinking. His father's objectives did not include the likes of M.B.A. marketing people and the investment of millions in new equipment. Robert Barton's goals hadn't changed: protect the good image of Parker Brothers, maintain strong financials, take advantage of golden opportunities, but otherwise build profits and avoid undue risk.[40]

Two factors, however, caused Robert Barton to listen to his son. First, he sincerely wanted to retire and enjoy the company of notable friends, like naval historian Samuel Eliot Morison (a relative) and newscaster Walter Cronkite. Second, the price-earnings ratio of leading toy companies listed on the New York Stock Exchange, such as Mattel, was twenty and higher—an unprecedented markup. Robert Barton's experience had taught him that timing is more important than any other factor when making a business decision—more important than product or resources or reputation. If he waited another year or two and the stock market declined, toy stocks would surely decline as well and the intrinsic value of Parker Brothers to General Mills, or anyone else, would be considerably less.[41]

Robert Barton was also uncomfortable with the alternatives. He didn't favor bringing in investor partners. Their presence would not help him to disengage; the contrary would more likely be true. Selling 20 percent of the family's stock on Wall Street in a public offering would lead to investor scrutiny and adherence to regulations that might hinder the firm's agility or conservative philosophy. He didn't desire that either. So Robert Barton made up his mind. He would make a clean break. He summoned Ranny, Channing, and Eddie to his office one morning toward the end of the year, and pointed to the stock tables in the *Wall Street Journal.* He used the lofty P-E ratios as his justification to sell the firm outright. Now.[42]

The next question he asked was, Is General Mills the kind of company we want to sell to? Unnoticed, Robert Barton had been doing some research. He liked the qualities of the General Mills executives and the cut of their suits. Once he had declared himself in favor of a marriage with General Mills, Ranny, Eddie, and Channing fell in line. Ranny was chosen to be the one to telephone Nalen. "When can you come to Salem?" Ranny asked. Nalen was there, with his boss, the next morning. Robert Barton had already calculated his price, based on "current market value." It was $47.5 million, which was initially rejected as too high. Barton responded calmly that high or not, that was his price. The brass in Minneapolis was consulted. Within an hour, Robert Barton's hand was shook and he got what he asked for. A vote of the board of General Mills made it official. The firm whose icon was known as Betty Crocker would soon own a game company.[43]

Betty Crocker

One of the first questions discussed was whether or not to put Betty Crocker's picture on each Parker Brothers' game. There never was a real Betty Crocker (at least as portrayed by General Mills). She was created in 1921 by one of the firm's predecessor milling companies, the Washburn Crosby Company of Minneapolis. Every year, thousands of letters arrived asking questions about baking, which Crosby dutifully answered. Soon, managers decided that it would be a nice touch to sign the answers personally. They took the last name of a retired Crosby executive, William Crocker, and added "Betty" as a first name because it sounded warm and friendly. A secretary who won a contest among female employees penned her signature. Artist Neysa McMein drew her first image in 1936. He did this by "blending" the features of all the women in the General Mills Home Service Department. As a result, many people believed Betty to be real. A poll had ranked Betty as the second most famous woman in the United States (after the then-president's wife, Eleanor Roosevelt). As time went by, her face was periodically changed to give Betty a more youthful, more professional, and more multicultural appearance. Despite Betty's devoted following and high appeal, thoughtful minds inside General Mills and Parker Brothers decided that good cooking and good game play didn't "mix." So her image was removed from consideration and in its place Parker Brothers was compelled to print the General Mills corporate symbol on its packaging.[44]

The Secret Is Revealed

During the due diligence period that followed, one hundred fifty disputes occurred. Ranny, energized by the potential of the deal, found ways to remove every one of the obstacles that appeared in its path. Ranny believed, wholeheartedly, that his company and General Mills were meant to be on the same team. Nalen soon handed a check for the purchase of Parker Brothers to Robert Barton, and General Mills had its game company.[45]

The family's negotiations to sell to General Mills had remained a well-guarded secret. George Fox, a Parker Brothers manager with nearly twenty years of service in the plant, had his ear pressed to the rail—as, it seemed, did everyone else who worked inside of Parker Brothers. The most credible rumor they detected was that their firm was going public. For a year now, many employees, including Fox, had been salting away whatever cash they could in anticipation of a chance to buy company stock on the ground floor.[46]

On Valentine's Day 1968, Robert Barton asked the employees to assemble in the biggest room in the factory—the collating department on the third floor. Fox watched as, under the lights of the *Salem Evening News* photographers, the elder Barton climbed onto a table, stood rigidly at attention, and faced the expectant gazes on his employees' faces. When the murmurs subsided, he made his announcement—Parker Brothers had been sold to General Mills. Fox's jaw dropped. For an uncomfortably long period, the room fell into complete silence. "You could have heard a pin drop," Fox recalled. The reaction took Barton by surprise, so he added a few important facts. Nothing would change, management would stay on except that he would become chairman and Eddie Parker would become president. This was greeted with strong applause. General Mills would fund expansion of the crowded plant and the purchase of new equipment. There would be opportunities for advancement, maybe even into General Mills for some, and the pension plan would be improved. The last item brought the most approval from the crowd.[47]

Parker Brothers now became another division of the sprawling General Mills "Leisure Group." Kenner Toys had already been purchased; so had Craft Master and MPC. Soon Lionel Trains would be added to the array. European toy companies were falling into line. In fact, Parker Brothers' share of Miro in France, which General Mills now owned, put pressure on Waddington and the Habourdin family to sell their shares in Miro. Nalen and General Mills built the largest toy and game company on the planet.

Privately, Barton continued to disagree with his son over the "M.B.A." culture of General Mills and what its effect might be on Parker Brothers. When Ranny mentioned the importance of building a modern marketing department with product managers, his father responded, "Product managers? We sell *products* here. This is the kind of business where people must grow up in it. What does a fancy diploma have to do with picking good games from among the bad?"[48] When Robert Barton was named chairman of Parker Brothers, Eddie Parker, son of Foster Parker and grandson of Edward H. Parker, became only the third president in the firm's eighty-five-year history. Channing Bacall continued as treasurer. Ranny Barton became executive vice president. His first job was to stop the tide of visitors from General Mills who seemed to show up daily to "kick the tires" and check out their new acquisition.

When the fascination finally subsided, the reality of what had just occurred began to sink in.

A cereal company in the Midwest, which did not share its tradition, its base of operations, its industry, or its hard-earned principles, now owned the game publishing firm of Parker Brothers. How the two would fare together became a topic of great concern in the plant and the challenge of Eddie Parker's presidency.

Chapter Six

New Rules

1968–1984

EDDIE PARKER DID NOT SHARE ROBERT BARTON'S enthusiasm for the sale of Parker Brothers, but he accepted Barton's reasons for cashing out and retiring. It was done. Now he set about making the new marriage work.

The General Mills Era Begins

Eddie instinctively relied on the first four of George Parker's principles to get the most out of General Mills. Under the cloud of an ever-present cigarette, he formulated his plan. First, he set as his goal to secure everything General Mills could offer that would enhance Parker Brothers. Second, he would foster strong relationships with the leaders of General Mills and make sure they understood the culture of Parker Brothers. Third, while he would comply with new rules and systems imposed from Minneapolis, he would shield his people from misguided interference. And fourth, he would dazzle the "Mills" executives with outstanding results. If he achieved the first three, he had no doubt he could accomplish the fourth. Parker Brothers had a much higher ratio of profit to sales than did General Mills, or any of its other acquisitions for that matter. (In 1967, Parker Brothers' pretax profit was over 20 percent of sales.[1]) Surely they too knew the merit of building on success and not tampering with it.

Eddie held the initiative from the start. His personal charm and naval commander's aura captured the respect of Craig Nalen and the rest of General Mills' management team. He capitalized by proposing and then winning endorsement to modernize the organization of Parker Brothers.

He created six functional departments, each headed by a vice president: finance, operations, human resources, marketing, sales, and research/ development. Parker Brothers received its first IBM computer, doing away with the punch-card-hungry, antiquated tabulating machines, much to Channing Bacall's pleasure.

Eddie then received approval to build a huge distribution center, planned before the deal with General Mills. Erected on the west side of the factory, it added 92,000 square feet of storage space for finished games and raw materials. (The old warehouse built in 1925 was henceforth used to store "WIP"—work in progress inventory—such as game boards.) Several loading docks, fronting Bridge Street, improved the receipt and shipment by tractor tailors (railroad deliveries were on the wane). The property it stood upon was purchased from the HP Hood dairy company, whose old office and storage building had to be razed. But the concrete block garage, which had replaced the old barn where the Pastime Girls had once cut puzzles, was not only preserved, it was connected to the new distribution center and converted into a spacious printing plant.

A huge four-color offset press was purchased, capable of producing in two hours what Louis Vanne and his press mates needed forty-eight hours to accomplish back in 1935. With space freed up inside the existing factory, manufacturing efficiency was markedly improved, thanks to studies performed by General Mills' efficiency experts. One of their recommendations, however, did not pan out. They advocated using an automated cutting machine to slice sheets of *Monopoly* money. But Fred French, honed by years of experience, manually cut the bills faster than the proposed machine. *Monopoly* money was, and would continue to be, cut by eye and hand until the present day.[2]

The Departure of Robert Barton

While Eddie was working the General Mills relationship, Robert Barton receded into the background and served as Eddie's adviser. Officially, he was chairman of Parker Brothers, a title once held by George Parker when the two shared power. Just as George had maintained his control over new products, Barton kept his hands in the new product process so that Eddie could focus on the business. But unlike Eddie, who was careful to work within the rules set forth by General Mills, Barton broke them—and with significant consequence.

Not long after the sale a dispute developed between Robert Barton and vice president of R&D, Hank Simmons. Simmons concluded that his contribution to Parker Brothers had gone underappreciated. He wanted a piece of the check Barton had received from the sale of the company and he also insisted on a substantial pay increase. Like Eddie Parker, Simmons had built an early rapport with the General Mills executives, especially Nalen. Feeling secure, he delivered his demands to Barton one morning. Barton was incredulous. Never fully comfortable with Simmons, he remained stone-faced and told him "where to get off." Simmons then played his ace in the hole: He would resign if his demands weren't met. Barton didn't flinch; he accepted his resignation. Simmons had maneuvered himself out of a job. When Nalen learned of this, he was furious. Barton, it seemed, had violated a sacred new ground rule: The hiring and firing of key executives was to occur only after discussion with General Mills. Being called on the carpet by Nalen, whom he dismissed as an unseasoned "thirty-something-year-old," clawed at Barton's dignity. He retaliated by offering his resignation. Nalen accepted it.

The Parker Brothers workers were stunned and confused. But Eddie, Channing, and Ranny knew what had really happened. Robert Barton had used the clash with Nalen as an excuse to walk away "on principle." He had seriously debated retiring when the deal was consummated. But he did not want to be regarded as a mercenary, waving good-bye the moment the check from General Mills touched his fingers. And he wanted to assure the work force that Eddie would have his help in adjusting to life with General Mills. However, Eddie had developed a rapport and gained beneficial results for Parker Brothers far sooner than Barton anticipated. Feeling nonessential, he decided that Eddie "ought to have the show all to himself."

After his brief, incendiary stint as chairman of Parker Brothers and thirty-six years of leading the firm, Robert Barton was gone without fanfare.[3] Back in 1932, he had left his father's law firm in Baltimore in a similar fashion and moved his family north to Salem to help save the company his father-in-law had founded. After an ominous beginning, Barton had succeeded beyond any measure of expectation, growing Parker Brothers' annual sales by 3,600 percent. Parker Brothers had survived and flourished as a result of many of his decisive actions. Especially notable was his support for acquiring the rights to *Monopoly* in 1935. (Nalen later commented that the price to buy Parker Brothers still would have been tolerable if all General Mills got was this one game.)

In retirement, Robert and Sally Barton continued to live in their oceanfront home in Marblehead, a few miles from the Parker Brothers factory. They provided counsel for their adult children and doted on their grandchildren. Barton remained on the board of trustees for Salem Hospital and aided other charities. He would skipper his sailboat until virtually his dying day, many years later.

Eddie Parker was now in complete control. His influence soon extended far beyond Salem. He joined the Toy Manufacturers Association and in time became its president. He held sway on business strategy for the European toy subsidiaries. He cultivated his growing rapport with General Mills to steadily bolster Parker Brothers. A human resources department was created to administer General Mills' acclaimed personnel-evaluation and compensation systems. Eddie agreed to strengthen Parker Brothers' staff by accepting the transfer of two General Mills executives—one to run marketing, the other to serve as controller. With their help, Eddie Parker and Channing Bacall learned how to smoothly navigate the General Mills approval process. Now that both Simmons and Barton were gone, the publisher's philosophy of Parker Brothers was diminished. Eddie recognized that consumers were unlikely to buy outdated board and card games simply because Parker Brothers had copies of them in its warehouse. Consumers were inclined toward new TV-promoted novelties and action games. Thus, it was decided to phase out the backlist. Eddie and staff began to streamline the product line by disposing of slow sellers in the inventory. For example, good-byes were said to postwar favorites *Rich Uncle* and *Dig*.[4]

Instant Insanity and Soma

The timing of the acquisition had another immediate effect on Parker Brothers. It provided the cash needed to ratchet up advertising and counter threats from the competition. Milton Bradley and Ideal Toy were hammering away on TV with commercials for games with "toy" appeal—notably plastic action games. Both firms were publicly owned and could afford these campaigns. By contrast, however, Parker Brothers' mainstay products were tougher to advertise effectively. Only *Ouija* seemed to have TV appeal.

Parker Brothers' nascent marketing staff and new owner urged Eddie to aggressively seek out products that could be effectively promoted on TV. The aim was to leverage prime ad space during the fall gift-buying season to generate hundreds of thousands (or even millions) of units in sales.

In 1968, a new Parker Brothers' product, coupled with this ad strategy, struck gold and cemented the General Mills–Parker Brothers marriage. The new hit was a four-block puzzle called *Instant Insanity*. Its object was simple—arrange the four one-and-a-quarter-inch colorful cubes in a line, with four different colors showing on each side of the line. The tactile appeal of the cubes and their objective were easily demonstrated on TV. A harried-looking Pat Paulsen from the highly popular program *Laugh-In* fumbled with them in the commercial, sweat beading on his forehead as the challenge overwhelmed him. He helped Parker Brothers sell 9 million of the $1 puzzle.[5]

The following year, a three-inch tall, nine-block puzzle named *Soma* was introduced. The blocks were of different shapes. Initially, they came stacked together in a cube. But they could be reassembled into countless other forms, like a dog, house, or cross. *Soma*'s clever commercial featured droll pundit Henry Gibson, also from *Laugh-In* ("Soma do, and Soma don't."). Several millions were sold and the puzzle attracted so many fans that Parker Brothers launched a *Soma* newsletter.[6]

Nerf

In 1970, a completely different kind of product appeared in the Parker Brothers' showroom at Toy Fair. It was not a game, but a colorful four-inch ball of foam, weighing in at a couple of ounces, and packed inside a box with openings that enabled consumers to squeeze it at retail. It came with no rules and no other playing equipment. Players were encouraged to make up their own uses for it.

It didn't start out that way.

Nerf began life as an indoor volleyball game. Its inventors proposed that it be played while sitting cross-legged on the floor. It was one of the

FIGURE 6-1
Nerf Ball, 1970

first new games seen by urbane Bill Dohrmann, a Princeton graduate and recent Parker Brothers recruit who had taken Hank Simmons's place as head of R&D. One day, as members of his department were playing the game on the floor, a group of executives, including Eddie Parker and Ranny Barton, happened upon them. Dohrmann playfully threw the ball at Eddie; it bounced harmlessly off his head. Eddie tossed it back at Dohrmann and the group soon forgot about the game and began to throw it wildly at each other. "That's a ball!" Eddie exclaimed. "A ball that won't wreck the house." It was so decided, then, to sell the ball by itself, without its indoor volleyball net. Three-quarters of a century after successfully launching *Pillow-Dex,* Parker Brothers reentered the indoor sports business.[7]

This episode, as much as any, highlighted the spontaneity and instinct so essential in picking new products in the toy and game field. No General Mills research could duplicate these results. Both Dohrmann and the current head of marketing, products themselves of the General Mills system, quickly learned to loosen their ties, toss aside protocol, and shed disciplined thinking because these didn't work inside the aging wooden walls of the United States' best-known game factory.

The name *Nerf* was proposed and endorsed by two of Dohrmann's designers.[8] It sounded as soft and friendly as the ball itself. In the fall of 1969, *Nerf* was presented to the trade as part of Parker Brothers' new 1970 line. The trade was less than impressed. The idea of charging $2 for a toy consisting of two ounces of foam distressed most of them. The Woolworth's game buyer went so far as to say that he wouldn't insult the intelligence of his shoppers by putting one *Nerf* ball in any of his stores. Dohrmann and company were undeterred, their confidence bolstered by favorable play tests with kids. But, just in case, it was decided to push the launch date forward into January, a month before Toy Fair, with the hope that retail success would lead to big orders at the show.

Aided only by a small TV budget, *Nerf* began to fly off the shelves the moment it was stocked. Some stores sold hundreds per week. Excitement over this first modern Parker Brothers "toy" spread rapidly through the trade by word of mouth, like the great Parker Brothers board games of old. The Woolworth's buyer, humbled, called and asked how quickly he could get twelve thousand.[9]

Parker Brothers had not only a new product but also a new business on its hands. Four million *Nerf* balls were made in 1970, boosting total revenue to $36 million, double what it had been when General Mills acquired the firm three years earlier. Minneapolis was beaming. *Nerf* was destined to become a brand name for an entire line of safe, soft balls—from an indoor basketball with a door-mounted hoop to molded foam outdoor footballs that were easier to catch and throw than their pigskin counterparts. Nalen won national acclaim as a business "wizard." But just as his star reached its zenith at General Mills, he chose to leave for a new opportunity. With Nalen gone, General Mills executive Don Swanson took over as head of all nonfood subsidiaries of the cereal giant. To make day-to-day management more feasible, he organized them into groups. Parker, Kenner, and the lesser toy companies became part of the "Fun Group."

Monopoly Tournaments

In 1972, Bobby Fischer and Boris Spassky of the U.S.S.R. squared off in a highly publicized world chess championship in Reykjavík, Iceland, with underdog Fisher winning. The publicity from this event prompted Victor Watson of Waddington's to suggest a similarly promoted world *Monopoly* championship, to take place in Reykjavík as soon as possible. (Watson had become the leader of John Waddington Company Ltd after his father, Norman, had stepped aside.) Ranny Barton liked the sound of this and so Watson's staff quickly organized the tournament. Ranny was impressed by the media coverage and saw the potential of holding periodic *Monopoly* championships. By 1977, the first true world *Monopoly* tournament was held in Monte Carlo, with champions from more than two dozen countries vying for the crown (actually, a silver plate).[10] Thereafter, a new world championship would be held every few years. Rules and regulations were developed to enable the game to rank with chess, bridge, and *Scrabble* as a legitimate forum of championship competition. Entrants first competed in a series of timed preliminary rounds. Then the five players with the most winnings competed in a final round, without time limit. The last one standing was crowned the new champion.

Building R&D

It became routine for executives from General Mills to be transferred to Parker Brothers, and then brought back for reassignment inside the parent company. Often, employees preferred to remain at Parker Brothers.

One executive determined not to return to General Mills was Bill Dohrmann. Despite having come from a trendy advertising agency in Chicago with an office in a glass skyscraper, the tall, trim, dapper Dohrmann had fallen in love with the charms of Salem and the worn office he occupied. The transformation was completed one morning, shortly after his first Toy Fair. Dohrmann opened a window to clear the stuffiness and found himself inhaling clean salt air, accompanied by the sight and sound of seagulls floating over the water. This compensation was unknown in Chicago or Minneapolis. Like many other transplants, Dohrmann was hooked.[11]

For a while, Dohrmann ran both marketing and R&D. When the task became daunting, he chose to remain as head of R&D and went about building a competent new product team. For the first time in the company's history, artwork and industrial design would be supervised and executed by in-house designers.[12] Not only would they design packages, game boards, and plastic components, but Dohrmann encouraged them to become game designers, and to think like editors as well. There was a need for this versatility. The sales force was constantly in the field, not around to lend a hand as they once had.[13]

Dohrmann's record wasn't flawless, however. Among the most unusual products he sponsored was a novelty called *Oobi*. *Oobi* wasn't a game and it wasn't a puzzle. It wasn't "sliced goods" or a craft or a toy or a fortune-telling device. *Oobi* was a message carrier. It was reddish orange in color, egg-shaped and hollow, and fit in the palm of your hand. Its only decoration was two big eyes looking up at whoever was holding it. Three *Oobi* message carriers were packed on a card that hung on a rack at retail. The back of the card explained *Oobi*'s purpose and how to use it: *"I contain a message to another human being. Please further my journey an inch, a foot, or a mile. Add a note if you wish. Then help me to the next nice person, like yourself."*

Dohrmann believed that *Oobi* could be a word-of-mouth blockbuster, with sales exceeding *Ouija*'s. During its development in 1970, *Oobi* was referred to as "Project O" in the unlikely event a competitor got wind of it and rushed a similar product to market. In 1971, *Oobi* was test-marketed on the West Coast with a television commercial that stated "*Oobi* means love." However, the West Coast public did not take a liking to *Oobi*. Another test market was conducted in the Southeast. Same result.[14] Parker Brothers "got the message" and *Oobi* joined the junk heap of toy history.[15]

While *Ouija, Soma,* and *Nerf* had greatly expanded Parker Brothers' horizons, its core business was stagnant. There had not been a hit board game since *Risk* in 1959. Many pundits thought the era of board games was over because they were, well, "boring" compared to the physical games, puzzles, and toys that now dominated the market. Dohrmann and Eddie Parker disagreed. *Masterpiece* was invented at the nation's biggest and most successful toy inventing firm—Marvin Glass and Associates of Chicago. Glass was a diminutive, homey man, with a passion and ambition twice his size. After World War II, he set up shop and became the biggest purveyor of hit toys and games to the entire industry. His success in spawning action games like *Mousetrap* and *Toss Across* for Ideal Toy Corporation enabled him to build an organization with several partners and dozens of highly talented people. The sleek two-story headquarters built by Glass had Chagalls hanging in the well-lit hallways, but no windows in the design area—to prevent peering eyes from seeing what was going on inside.

Masterpiece placed its players inside an auction gallery. They moved their tokens around a circular track surrounding a portrait of Rembrandt. Miniature paintings came up for bid frequently and evoked rousing auctions. The catch was that the worth (if any) of each painting was unknown (a random value card was secured to the back of each painting before play began). At game's end, the value of all paintings purchased was revealed and the player with the highest net worth won.

Dohrmann flew to Chicago and negotiated with the Art Institute for rights to reproduce the paintings it had replicated on postcards for sale in its gift shop. A tortured genius at Frank Browning's agency came up with the idea for its commercial. It featured sophisticated but flustered buyers competing in an art auction, grappling with fakes and stunned by surprise values. A scene from the commercial was printed on the cover of the package—the first time this had been done in the games business. Another first was the printing of the box bottom with a photo and description of the game. Rising consumer pilferage compelled Parker Brothers to begin shrink-wrapping its games. No longer would consumers be able to open the lid and inspect the components through fragile cellophane. The effort behind *Masterpiece* paid off. Sales totaled 3.5 million units within five years.[16]

Its success, however, was soon compromised. A man named Christian Thee claimed that Parker Brothers had illegally funneled the game's idea to Marvin Glass and Associates and that he—Thee—had submitted this idea to Parker Brothers years earlier. Indeed, Thee had submitted an art auction game with a circular track board to Parker Brothers and several other game makers. He explained in court how he labored for a very long time to create his game. In contrast, Jeffrey Breslow, managing partner of Marvin Glass and Associates, told the court that the idea for *Masterpiece* had come quickly to him, with the details taking less than two hours to iron out. Nevertheless, a Brooklyn Federal Court jury found for the plaintiff and Thee was awarded more than $400,000 in royalties.[17]

Parker Brothers *won* a legal battle of a different sort in 1973. Atlantic City decided to simplify matters for its citizens and visitors by doing away with the streets named Mediterranean and Baltic Avenue. Each of these streets had other names along part of their lengths, much like neighborhood-dependent thoroughfares of London. At first, college students from Princeton attempted to save the streets for the sake of the game they so admired. Then, in January 1973, under the glare of the media's attention, Parker Brothers joined the battle. Ranny Barton went to Atlantic City to argue, with passion, that the two street names be preserved. When the vote was taken, even the city commissioner who had advocated the change voted to keep Mediterranean and Baltic alive. Barton was hailed a hero and when the reporters asked him if this was a victory for the company, he replied that it was a victory for the country.[18]

Changing of the Guard

In the midst of these controversies, the ground was shifting again at Parker Brothers. Eddie Parker, the beloved chain-smoking president of the company, had been diagnosed with lung cancer (as had his father Foster before him and most probably his grandfather Edward before him). Doctors held out no hope, and predicted he would die within six months. When this became generally known, the firm braced for the changing of the guard. That August, while Ranny was on a three-week vacation cruise off the New England coast, several Parker Brothers vice presidents flew to Minneapolis to press their case with Don Swanson to fill Eddie's shoes after he died.

Ranny Barton, the father of three children and a fixture in his community, was comfortable with his life. Thus, he thought long and hard about disrupting it by seeking the high-pressure job. As executive vice president, he was next in line—and he had the heritage, being Robert Barton's son and George Parker's grandson. Nevertheless, he didn't want the job offered to him solely on that basis. But he had done little to make a real name for himself. He so far lacked the conviction and the courage to push Eddie to embrace the changes he felt were necessary at Parker Brothers. In many ways, Ranny was a work in progress.

Although he was not a gifted talker like his cousin Eddie, Ranny had learned to counter his halting pattern of extemporaneous discourse with a smooth presence on stage. He shined during public presentations, such as in Atlantic City. He was congenial and his early grooming by George Parker gave him an aura befitting that of the presidency. As he wrestled with the opportunity, the need to stand up and fight shook him out of his lethargy. He grabbed a sheet of paper and wrote down what he would do if he were president. The words flowed from his pen, clearly and succinctly. Finally, after years of knowing that something must be done to bring Parker Brothers to the forefront of the industry, he had found the words that defined his ideas. Then he placed a call to Swanson and arranged a meeting.

Ranny went to Minneapolis armed with his single sheet of yellow ruled paper. It contained his vision of how Parker Brothers would grow under his leadership. It called for the kind of change favored by General Mills. Swanson called in the CEO of General Mills, Bob Kinney—himself a former New Englander—and together they decided that Ranny had earned the right to succeed Eddie Parker. Ranny became the fourth president in the firm's ninety-year history. Eddie was elevated to the advisory position of chairman. His failing health forced him to spend more and more time away from his office. By October, he was confined to his home in Beverly Farms. Ranny assumed day-to-day control but honored the request of Kinney that no changes be made until after his cousin's death. ("And then make them all at once," Kinney had advised Parker Brothers' new president.[19])

Eddie Parker passed away on January 1, 1974. After the funeral and period of mourning, Ranny did exactly the opposite expected by the many Parker Brothers' veterans who thought they knew the affable but largely passive former executive vice president. He did not sit back and merely administer Eddie's policies. He did not ask his vice presidents for advice. He did not grope for direction. He acted. And he did precisely what he had advocated to Swanson and Kinney, and all at once, as Kinney had instructed.

A reorganization ensued, and opponents and managers that Ranny felt were ineffective were axed. Among them was Channing Bacall, who had done a masterful job as treasurer for many years. However, Bacall was also responsible for manufacturing, which Ranny felt was out of date and poorly run by Bacall's head of operations. When Bacall refused to fire this veteran, Ranny asked Bacall to resign. Then he demoted the head of operations. Next, he asked the sales leader, who had opposed him for president, to step down.

In one fell swoop, Ranny Barton had changed Parker Brothers from a family-run, conservative organization to one now seeking high-flying M.B.A.'s and marketing wizards in a quest to again double sales. Ranny let it be known that even though he was not an expert in any area of the firm, and had no particular desire to become one, he would oversee a group of executives who were experts, and who would deliver results (or else they too would be shown the door).[20]

Beverly

Ranny received General Mills' approval to upgrade its production equipment, to add more state-of-the-art printing presses, and to hire skilled manufacturing leadership. He also won consent to house his new M.B.A.'s, and most other Parker Brothers executives, in a gleaming new office building to be built on a lake in the woods in nearby Beverly.[21] The citizens of Salem complained bitterly, feeling betrayed by the move.[22] But Ranny believed it was vital to change the image of his company from that of a manufacturing-oriented firm to a marketing-directed firm. The times demanded it; its competitors compelled it. In recent years, archrival Milton Bradley had grown stronger and stronger, thanks in part to aggressive TV promotion and a 1962 project that resulted in a sleek, state-of-the art manufacturing plant—raw materials in one end, finished games out the other—located in East Longmeadow, Massachusetts, with a modern office suite atop it.[23]

When the new Beverly facility was ready for occupancy in late 1977, the veterans of Salem's cramped offices were dumbfounded by the size of their new quarters. Each was assigned a spacious cubicle or office; gone were the crowded rooms where many had rubbed elbows. The new building had central air conditioning. And it was beautiful. "It was like entering fairy land," exclaimed longtime sales analyst Barbara McDonough. A winding wooded road and tree-lined parking lots led to a horseshoe driveway before the gleaming glass-covered building. After passing through its front doors, visitors entered a large reception area, graced by portraits of George and Eddie Parker. Broad stairways and landings surrounded an indoor tree located under an atrium that bathed the tree and the stairs in natural light, in stark contrast with the sunless dark paneling flanking Salem's narrow stairway. Behind the first floor stairs, the outer wall of the human resources department was covered by a floor-to-ceiling enlargement of a 1920s company picnic photo at Centennial Grove in nearby Essex. If one studied the life-size faces, Parker Brothers legends like Albert Richardson and Don Jelly could be spotted. It was as if these Parker Brothers immortals were part of a welcoming committee affirming, from the outset, that the Beverly building was, indeed, Parkerized and blessed for occupancy. As one climbed the stairs, raised panels on the walls came into view, each finished with a print of a vintage Parker Brothers game. On a wall adjoining the landing on the third floor hung the massive, framed two-thousand-piece *Pastime Puzzle* depicting a coronation, which a Pastime Puzzle Girl (Mary Cahill) had skillfully cut decades earlier. One could not help but soak in the spirit of Parker Brothers of old, while projecting optimism about its capabilities for the future. The only aspect of the design that jarred the eyes was the trendy orange fabric used on half the panels of the modular office system.

The Beverly office building inspired new, unfettered visions of growth. And Dohrmann's touch for finding great products to secure that growth was immaculate during Ranny's first years in office. A board game named *Payday*, invented by a local designer (Paul Gruen), became a hit in those days of "stagflation" and high unemployment. It seemed that people liked balancing the budget as they moved across the calendar-like game board earning their salary, paying bills that were dealt to their mailbox space, while trying to keep their heads above water. Meanwhile, President Jimmy Carter played a real-life game of national bill juggling as he struggled with stagflation, deficits, and the bankruptcy of many cities, including New York. But as had often been the case, Parker Brothers grew throughout the current downturn in the country's fortunes.

Another powerful seller was the letter cube game *Boggle*. A failure when first introduced as part of a low-priced line of games in 1972, it returned in 1976 backed by a clever subway and billboard ad campaign in New York City. It soon was ringing up sales in cash registers everywhere.

Boggle included a plastic gridded base. Under a clear lid, sixteen letter cubes were shaken until they each fell into alignment in the four-by-four grid. Racing a three-minute sand timer, players wrote down unique words, formed by connecting adjacent letters, as spotted on the grid. *Boggle* was a million-seller by 1977.

Dohrmann and his licensing assistant also made hay with games based on two popular TV shows, *Happy Days* and *The Six Million Dollar Man,* and one based on a humor magazine—*The Mad Magazine Game.*[24]

FIGURE 6-2
Going Mad?

Mad Magazine Game, *a million-seller from 1979 to 1982.*

This game turned game playing on its ear. Its object was to lose all of one's money by moving backward around a board (sometimes while clucking like a chicken). Licensing had provided a controversial source of endorsement since the era of "pep" and the awakening of American culture. In theory, a popular personality or movie or program already had a core audience willing to buy products endorsed by their favorites. But the game-buying public is fickle. Not every program or celebrity engenders the kind of competition that makes for a compelling game. That these three games all sold many hundreds of thousands of copies was a distinctive achievement. Collectively, they added $2 million of profit to Parker Brothers' bottom line.

Delighted with the vibrancy of his firm's new products and their sales, Ranny Barton arranged for both Bill Dohrmann and Dave Wilson, his sales leader, to enroll in the program he had completed at the Harvard Business School.[25]

The Rise of Sales

E. David Wilson was a born leader with unshakable confidence and a magnetic personality. He was also a master strategist who thought beyond the tactics of an opportunistic sales call or the coddling of a buyer. The country's retail environment was always changing. Major chains seemed to have short periods of dominance. Sears, Roebuck and F. W. Woolworth declined in importance, while Toys "R" Us and Child World appeared and rose to new heights. Former household names had disappeared (like the W. T. Grant Company and discounter E. J. Korvette).

Recognizing the constant churn in retailer dominance, he did not allow his team to become dependent on any one of them. Wherever America wanted to buy games, his games would be there. Wilson understood that the key to enduring sales success was to build upon success (echoing George Parker). To do so meant getting more shelf space for his games per storefront, and constantly expanding the number of stores where Parker Brothers games could be purchased. The means to do so were persuasive sales programs and Dohrmann's products (plus great commercials from marketing). His results were the envy of the industry. Unit volume for Parker Brothers games, especially lesser items, was unprecedented. And *Monopoly*'s sales were never higher, often surpassing three million units per year, than during his leadership.[26]

The Anti-Monopoly Trial

While Parker Brothers was regarded as the best of General Mills' many acquisitions, an oversight led to a setback for Ranny Parker and Bill Dohrmann. It began when an economics professor at the University of California at Berkeley changed the name of a slow-selling business game he had invented from *Bust the Trust* to *Anti-Monopoly*. When Parker Brothers heard of this, the firm sued for trademark infringement and demanded in court that Professor Ralph Anspach remove his game from the market. Anspach resisted, having discovered the existence of *Monopoly*-like games prior to Charles Darrow's version, which Robert Barton had acquired in 1935.[27] Barton, now in his late seventies, was asked to perform one more service for his old company. He was called as the key witness for Parker Brothers. When the highly publicized case went to court, Anspach's attorney tried to undermine Parker Brothers' ownership of the *Monopoly* trademark by accusing Barton of having fraudulently acquired the patent for the *Monopoly* game. The attack on his honor was traumatic to the man whose distant ancestor had helped George Washington establish the Supreme Court. Since this was not a jury trial, the judge asked Barton how he felt about the accusation. The elder Barton replied that he was outraged. The judge said that he would feel the same way were he in Barton's shoes.[28]

Initially, the courts ruled in Parker Brothers' favor. The district court held that "monopoly" was not a generic name when Darrow originally began to use it and that the mark had not thereafter become generic. Anspach appealed. The Court of Appeals for the Ninth Circuit agreed that the mark was not generic when Parker Brothers registered it, but in an opinion that shocked trademark lawyers and sent a shiver through trademark owners, held that the mark had *become* generic. The court of appeals adopted a "purchase motivation" test by which the trademark was valid only if consumers, when they asked for a *Monopoly* game, meant that they wanted Parker Brothers' version of the real estate trading game. According to this test, the mark was not valid if consumers did not know or care who made the game. The court of appeals decision implied that if consumers didn't know that General Mills made Wheaties, or that Kimberly-Clark marketed Kleenex, or that Frigidaire was a brand owned by General Motors, their trademarks would no longer be valid.

In response to that decision, Parker Brothers did two things that ensured the protection of the *Monopoly* trademark. First, it settled with Anspach in a manner that preserved the *Monopoly* trademark, obtaining an assignment of his *Anti-Monopoly* mark and then licensing it back to him. Second, Parker Brothers joined with numerous other trademark owners to seek relief from Congress, which soon amended the federal trademark statute to explicitly reject the Ninth Circuit's "purchaser motivation" test for trademark validity.[29]

The Golden Era

As the 1970s neared conclusion, Parker Brothers' staff and burgeoning marketing department bustled with activity inside their modern headquarters by the lake in the woods in Beverly, eight miles from the thriving Salem plant. More than 1,100 employees worked in the firm's three manufacturing locations (Salem, Taunton, and Des Moines). Their combined efforts had fueled the steady rise in sales in every year since General Mills had acquired the New England game company. Building on the foundation laid by Eddie Parker, Ranny Barton had successfully guided his firm by straddling two worlds—the principled tradition he and his veteran workers had absorbed, and the modern practices of the country's highly acclaimed marketing company, General Mills. While the introspective Barton did not stand on a soapbox and preach his dual philosophy, his actions spoke volumes. From the vantage point of a future perspective, the 1970s were Parker Brothers' "Golden Era."

For Parker Brothers' growing corps of upper- and mid-level managers, Ranny and wife Maud established a pleasant tradition. Every year in June, they hosted an outdoor cocktail party at their home overlooking the harbor in Manchester, Massachusetts, where their yacht *Enchanted* lay at anchor (General Mills followed the grain cycle and ended their year on May 31; Parker Brothers had to follow suit). The party presaged the awarding of management incentives and the celebration of yet another record-breaking fiscal year. "Christmas in May," as many called it.

During this era, Ranny had opened the door to greater influence by General Mills because he genuinely believed in the methods and talent available to Parker Brothers from its parent. General Mills listened to him and let him run the show. And why not? He and his company continued to produce outstanding results, no matter what the state of the economy or the mood in the country. It did not seem to matter if the president was named Johnson, Nixon, Carter, or Reagan, or what influence their policies had on the nation's economic well-being.

Beyond financial success, capable people, organization structure, and planning processes were rapidly strengthening Barton's firm. All of these could not have arrived a moment too soon because of a threat, and an opportunity, summed up by one word.

Electronics.

Blips and Bleeps

In early 1975, a husband-and-wife team of astrophysicists from Harvard came to Parker Brothers to pitch Dohrmann on the idea of putting something called a *microprocessor* inside of a game. Just twenty-eight years earlier, a pair of scientists at Bell Laboratories had found a way to replace tomato-sized vacuum tubes with fingertip-sized transistors to make logic circuits. Thanks to the demands of the Space Race in the 1960s, thousands of transistors could now be etched onto a piece of silicon the size of a fingernail.

Robert and Holly Doyle realized that, with the exception of a few simple electrical circuit games made in prior decades, no game existed that replaced the need for a human opponent. These two ex-Harvard professors argued that a game that could react to a player's decisions instantly and intelligently could captivate a large market. They asked, "What's the annual sales volume of *Monopoly*?" Dohrmann replied, "Around $20 million." They smiled and retorted that each of their ideas could easily generate $20 million in annual sales, maybe more—maybe as much as $100 million.[30]

The esoteric games the Doyles showed that day did not spark Dohrmann's enthusiasm, or that of anyone else who saw them. Dohrmann reminded them that Parker Brothers was a family games business. He needed products for three or more people to play simultaneously, to meet the needs of a family gathered around a table. Meanwhile, Parker Brothers' R&D team remained focused on traditional games and on a new building toy called *Riviton* that featured a plastic tool that forced rubber "rivets" into openings on plastic panels, enabling kids to build all manner of objects (not dissimilar in capability to the classic metal *Erector* sets).

Electronic games remained purely a discussion topic. No one yet at Parker Brothers understood how to design, develop, or source electronics. This field was even more foreign to General Mills, so the typically intrusive grain-grinders could provide no help. The Doyles offered to teach, but Dohrmann felt their offer to be premature. Parker Brothers first had to decide if there was even a market for electronic games. He asked about pricing. The answer: probably $30 or more. The *Monopoly* game sold for less than $10. Who would pay $30 for a game just because it had blinking lights and emitted bleeping sounds (if at all) and could be played by only one player at a time?[31]

The Doyles persevered. They had to educate the Parker Brothers executives before they could hope to do business. They came back time and again and gradually began to swing the imaginations of the "prove it to me" leaders and designers sitting across the table from them. The declining cost of entry-level microprocessors greatly aided their cause.

Parker Brothers may have seemed reluctant to add electronic games to its line, but the firm's management was not myopic. The marriage between traditional games and electronics was seen as inevitable. And if Parker Brothers saw this, then so must its rivals. At the New York Toy Fair of 1976, three electronic games did appear and they became the talk of the trade (an auto racing game, a football game, and a nuclear annihilation game). Bob Doyle wrote a letter to Parker Brothers and offered a scolding and a warning: "It should have been *your firm* who launched this category; now you're behind."[32]

Dohrmann pushed harder for a corporate decision to develop an electronic game. Ranny Barton gave his blessing. The question now became: Which one? Some of the Doyles' new ideas, like an electronic pinball game, were just too expensive to consider for now. With some reluctance, a game tentatively entitled Sink the Sub was selected. It straddled the line between the old and the new. It had a game board whereupon several players (destroyer captains) sought to locate an invisible enemy sub (deftly controlled by the electronic brain). It had a few red lights, but made no sounds. Development of its game play was not instinctive to the firm's traditional R&D department, and finding a worthy name was even more painful. Finally, *Code Name: Sector* was adopted, with much gnashing of teeth.[33]

So unsure were the Parker Brothers staffers of the game that they seriously considered keeping it off the market in 1977—until they heard that archrival Milton Bradley was definitely going forward with an electronic game called *Comp IV*. So *Code Name: Sector* made its debut at the 1977 Toy Fair. Its sales were disappointing, perhaps due to the fact that the game was too smart (human players seldom won) and it was *very* expensive—$50 in some stores. Meanwhile Mattel's $20, electronic button-tapping *Football* game was a great seller, proving that electronics priced right, with the right degree of action and challenge, could ring cash registers.

Parker Brothers finally got serious, and by so doing, redirected the future of the company.

The Doyles were funded to develop a better handheld game. Gone was the idea of attaching a horse buggy to a gasoline engine—the analogy of coupling a game board to an electronic circuit box, like *Sector* had. The Doyles came back with something they called "3-T." At first, no one found anything to like about it. Dohrmann was unmoved because all it seemed capable of doing was playing tic-tac-toe (whence the name 3-T, coined by the Doyles). Dohrmann wanted something that couldn't be played with an ordinary pencil and a piece of paper.[34]

The fall of 1977 was approaching and Wilson and his sales team pushed Barton to crack the whip and endorse a new electronic game for the 1978 Toy Fair that would make the buyers forget the disappointment of *Code Name: Sector*. As was often the case, an imminent deadline brought out ingenuity in dedicated, smart people. From the crude beginnings of 3-T came a sleek handheld named *Merlin*. It would be powered by a microprocessor made by Texas Instruments (TI). Pressing the limits of their little "brain," TI engineers found ways to squeeze not one, but six games into the device, which ended up bearing a resemblance to the stylish Princess telephone handset marketed by AT&T.[35] Richard Stearns, a young marketing product manager, came up with the game's name after a winding search through the thesaurus. A former industrial designer turned electronic game designer (Arthur Venditti) helped create most of the six games, including one where a player could input the notes to a popular tune and *Merlin* would play them back upon the press of the repeat function. Early market research damned the game, but sentiment at Parker Brothers was running high and, as in the glory days of George Parker when instinct meant more than analytical facts, the Parker Brothers executives stuck their necks out and went forward, braving the great Blizzard of 1978 to get from Boston to Toy Fair to try to woo the trade.[36]

Once there, they found that the trade needed little persuasion to buy electronic games. They were hot for the category. Parker Brothers' biggest challenge became to convince them to buy and support *Merlin* over Milton Bradley's new *Simon* game. Whereas *Merlin* played six different games, *Simon* was more toylike and could play but one game—but it was very compelling. (*Simon* played a series of musical notes, adding one more to the sequence after each turn. The object was to repeat the sequence exactly to avoid elimination.) As the year progressed and production began, this challenge effervesced into the heat of the market. Wilson's team sold 700,000 *Merlin* games—all that could be made before Christmas.[37]

Meanwhile, after two children choked to death by swallowing rubber rivets from *Riviton*, management cut short its Thanksgiving vacation to plan a voluntary recall. It was a massive effort and cost the company $8 million, but Barton and staff believed this was the right thing to do. While suffering a financial setback, Parker Brothers won the admiration of both the media and General Mills, which properly overlooked the financial implications. Another setback occurred when an operations management miscue enabled the machinists' union to organize the maintenance workers in the Salem plant. But when the maintenance workers could only achieve parity in their wages, further talk of unionizing faded away, and no other organizing would take place inside Parker Brothers.[38]

In 1979, with increased production of *Merlin*, the firm reached a great milestone: It achieved over $100 million in sales.[39] A gala party was held at Crane's Castle in nearby Ipswich, Massachusetts. In attendance that night was Bernard Loomis, whom Don Swanson had promoted from president of Kenner to manage the Toy Group (the new name chosen for the Fun Group). Loomis, a bear of a man topped by a head of thick white hair, was a former street-smart salesman who had risen to prominence at Mattel prior to becoming president of Kenner. At Kenner, he and his team spotted the opportunity—overlooked by most other toy companies—for a merchandising deal around a new movie entitled *Star Wars*. Kenner's *Star Wars* toys became the biggest grossing toy line in history. Loomis had a knack for picking such hit toys and a desire to do the same with games (he adored word games). But it quickly became obvious that Barton and his new boss (and former peer) mixed as smoothly as oil and water. On this special evening in 1979, Loomis abruptly left the party because of a perceived insult. The incident was symptomatic of what had become a very difficult relationship, from which dramatic consequences would soon follow.[40]

Short Circuit

As the 1980s began, Parker Brothers found itself inexorably a part of the third materials revolution to hit the games industry (printed matter and plastics being the first two). The future for electronic games looked very bright and Parker Brothers was determined to follow *Merlin*'s success by introducing many more electronic games. The R&D budget began to swell as the search was widened to find the next blockbuster. The hunt proved more difficult than anyone imagined. Parker Brothers marketed better games than *Merlin*, but time and again they came up short.[41] In 1981, sales hit a major bump in the road. Sell-through of handheld electronic games from all manufacturers began a steady and alarming decline.[42] The culprit was another product of new technology: *video games*.

Two years before this short circuit, Parker Brothers had begun its biggest-ever expansion of R&D and marketing. Marketing leadership, in the person of influential Ron Jackson (formerly of General Mills and Parker Brothers' recent head of finance), was solidly behind electronics. His strong but quiet presence was shifting influence away from R&D and the sales department. He was the new power in the firm behind Barton. With Jackson's urging, Dohrmann was encouraged to build an in-house electronics engineering group and to hire an experienced R&D manager to bolster new product design. For the former he hired pleasant, talented Don Miffitt from Gillette's new ventures group, and for the latter he selected me. I had been running Ideal Toy's game division.

I had been in the industry since my college days ten years earlier when, in between classes, I ran my own game company (Gamescience Corporation) before selling it to a New York firm prior to my graduation. Miffitt, a gifted leader with strong electronic knowledge, quickly found and hired the talent necessary to build the electronic development group. I had the task of molding a cohesive group from veteran Parker Brothers designers and writers.

Dohrmann's third group, product development, soon came under pressure. It needed systems and engineering talent to keep pace with the complex electronic and plastic projects in the pipeline. Tension mounted between it and the operations (manufacturing) department, now under the leadership of a sinewy, results-oriented executive named Joe Marquez, who, like Loomis, had worked at toy giants Kenner and Mattel. Marquez asked Dohrmann to set up a new product tracking system and ensure that new games were turned over to manufacturing earlier in the year.[43] This was an important priority. Both marketing and sales needed to get a "read" at retail before vouchsafing the fall forecast. Unlike previous times, the Salem plant could not respond quickly if demand fluctuated in the fall, because electronics required long lead times to secure parts from the Far East. After further debate, Marquez and Jackson recommended to Barton that a separate department be established, run by a vice president devoted to product development (even though this approach had failed once before). Barton concurred. It was not easy for Barton to take product development away from Dohrmann, given Dohrmann's strong contribution to the growth of the firm in the prior twelve years. But Barton believed that he was effective only if his staff was effective and worked in harmony.[44]

I was asked to manage the new product development group until a seasoned "pro" could be found. My experience at Ideal Toy was invaluable. Ideal was a high-pressure, chaotic company, not unlike Mattel or Kenner. But its R&D department was staffed by dozens of highly competent technical people, who had taught me what makes a good product development department tick. I applied this knowledge, set up the new department, and we hit the ground running. After a dead-end search, Barton, with consent from General Mills, gave me the job on a permanent basis. I would work hand in hand with Dohrmann, who would concentrate on new product research and inventor relations. My task would be to complete the design and engineering of each new product, on time, so that the operations department could make it on the assembly line, on time. Miffitt and his electronic group came to report to me, and I started to hire the designers and mechanical engineers we needed (several from Ideal Toy were happy to join me at Parker Brothers).[45]

Marquez appointed an aspiring manager from his group to work with me on the task force charged with implementing a companywide new product tracking system. High school graduate Tom Dusenberry had started on the loading dock in Des Moines and had soon become manager of safety for the facility. Now, seven years later, he was in Salem and on the rise. He was coolly logical when approaching his assignments and was hungry for advancement. One day, as we were standing outside my Beverly office, I asked him what his ambition was. He pointed across the secretarial pool, beneath the benevolent light of the skylight, and directed my attention to Barton's presidential office. "I want to sit in his chair someday." (He would.)

After Toy Fair of 1981, three more shocks hit Parker Brothers. First, Wilson resigned to become general manger of rival Milton Bradley. Then Jackson accepted a position on Don Swanson's staff at General Mills. Third, the sales of handhelds tanked.

Sales and marketing leadership was abruptly weakened at a time when the company faced its first sales decline since the early 1930s. Workmanlike Dick Dalessio, Jackson's right-hand man, succeeded him. A sales executive from preschool toy maker Fisher-Price replaced Wilson. He saw the decline in sales of electronic games as just the end of another fad. Trends come and go quickly in the toy business. But electronics had become Parker Brothers' claim to fame and their decline was a jolt to the firm's reputation and confidence.

Dalessio lacked the physical and charismatic presence of Jackson. He was a solid, bread-and-butter marketer whose subordinates felt he might be better suited in banking or as a general manager of a less volatile business. He clung to the belief that the problem with handheld games was trade related, not consumer driven. He thought that clever ads directed to parents would persuade them to stay the course and support the company's expensive, snazzy new microprocessor-based games. He and Barton paid a visit to the head buyer of Toys "R" Us to press their case. The Toys "R" Us executive stood toe-to-toe with Dalessio and said, "Would you buy yesterday's newspaper?" Barton knew, right then, that handhelds would not come back in time to reverse the tide.

The Birth of Video Games

As the sales decline accelerated, the first layoff in modern memory occurred. The cuts were especially deep in R&D, where the need for electronic development suddenly seemed as unnecessary as batteries for a *Monopoly* board game.

The Des Moines facility was abruptly shut down to save its overhead, and its manager (Bob Dabrio) was recalled to Salem. Demands on Barton by Loomis began to intensify. Ranny, seemingly out of options, started to wonder if there was any way he could right his ship and regain the sales growth Loomis and General Mills wanted.[46] Where once the "big stick" of outstanding results had enabled him, or Eddie Parker, to speak softly and have the General Mills execs listen in rapture, the recent decline in profits tipped the balance. Influence from above began to pressure him to abandon the conservative principles established by his grandfather and seek growth by taking larger and larger risks.

An expensive addition to the Beverly office building had just been completed to house the expected "forever" growth in electronics-related personnel. One day, Barton walked into the empty addition and said to me dejectedly, "What are we going to do with all this space? We'll never fill it." At the time, I was just starting to earn his confidence. Having returned from the summer Consumer Electronics Show in Las Vegas, I chose this moment to inform Barton that the head of Atari's home computer division had introduced himself during a break, and asked me if he could license Parker Brothers' great board games to make video game cartridge versions. Atari was, by far, the most successful and most talked-about company in consumer enter-tainment. Barton stopped looking at the bare walls and stared at me. So I added, "It seems to me that if they want to license our titles, there may be a market for us out there."

"I don't think General Mills would want us signing a deal with a com-petitor," Barton replied as he thought about the implications.

"I'm thinking that we can do this ourselves," I replied.

I explained that Miffitt and the survivors of the recent bloodletting believed they could learn the programming techniques of the Atari video game system. By doing so, it would be possible for Parker Brothers to create cartridges, compatible with Atari. "But, yes, it would mean that we'd ride their coattails in the marketplace." The latter didn't bother Barton. He recalled how Wilson had urged him to look into "home en-tertainment electronics" before leaving to join rival Milton Bradley. So Barton decided to discuss the topic with Dalessio. Dalessio was opposed. While believing that video games was indeed a promising field, he felt that Parker Brothers should enter it by creating a system that would play board games, perhaps an upward-pointing TV console built into a coffee table's surface. The cost of developing such an idea, at a time of belt-tightening, overwhelmed Barton. He came back to me and asked how much it would cost to decode the Atari system. Miffitt had already given me the answer: $50,000, mainly to fund a highly qualified outside firm who would do it surgically without any connection to Atari's research.

A few days later, Barton took me aside, beyond the earshot of market-ing, and told me to go ahead, to keep him informed of progress, but to otherwise keep this video games project under my hat.

An engineer named Ralph Baer had invented video game hardware in 1966 while working as an electronic engineering wizard at defense contractor Sanders Associates in New Hampshire. An immigrant, his family left Cologne, Germany, in 1938 just before Kristallnacht. At Sanders, his team continually innovated new electronic technology, but Baer's most notable accomplishment occurred when he figured out how to make objects move on a TV screen under the influence of a player with a controller in hand. Dozens of patents soon followed, assigned to Sanders by Baer. The Magnavox television company licensed Baer's technology and produced a system known as Odyssey in 1972. That same year, an engineer named Nolan Bushnell was present at the Magnavox

Profit Caravan demonstration of the Odyssey. Later, with the help of an associate, he built the first coin-operated game—*Pong*. It became enormously popular and Bushnell was soon (incorrectly) identified as the originator of video games. His success led him to found Atari, and by 1979 his firm's Video Computer System became the rage of the country. Sanders defended its patents in court and Bushnell and Atari signed up for a license of the Baer patents. Many others followed. (Parker Brothers would not run afoul of these patents, as it intended to make software only for hardware systems like Atari, made by companies which had licensed the Baer patents.[47])

A few weeks after my informal meeting with Barton, I invited my boss upstairs to the electronics department. There, in the lab where so many recent handheld games had been brought to life, sat a TV screen, an Atari video game system, and a young engineer seated next to a smiling Miffitt. The engineer flipped a switch and a picture of the train icon from the *Monopoly* game appeared on the screen. He then picked up a joystick and maneuvered a cursor over a column of colored bars. Whenever he clicked on a bar, the train changed to that color.[48] That was it, pure and simple. Now it was Barton's turn to smile. He asked me to invite Dalessio to see a repeat demonstration.

Although Dalessio had reservations, Barton suggested that he put some people to work to come up with a plan for marketing a video game cartridge or two. Dalessio assigned this task to Stearns, the young product manager who had championed *Merlin*. Stearns, who had the time and the enthusiasm, was aided by a "man without a home" named Bill Bracy. Bracy was ten years Stearns's senior and had served mostly in financial capacities during his General Mills career. But at Parker Brothers, he was given a chance to develop marketing plans. As there was no room for him in the third-floor marketing department, he was "exiled" to an office in the personnel department on the first floor, behind the photo of the 1920s picnic. He and Stearns became a matching pair. Each was deeply religious, a proud father of a brood of kids, and innately intelligent. Their pairing led to better and better arguments for Parker Brothers to enter the video game race.

The pace of development picked up a bit with the team in place. Then, one day in June, the alarm was sounded. Jim Fifield, the latest General Mills executive appointed to lead the Toy Group, called for a meeting in New York. The topic was to be video games—and which division within the Toy Group would enter this vital category.[49]

Bracy poured himself into writing a masterful, surefire marketing plan. Miffitt and I developed a convincing "show and tell" that laymen could quickly grasp. Stearns became the nervous, excited champion who coordinated all of our efforts. Dalessio decided not to make the New York presentation. He seemed reluctant to be associated with a strategy about which he had grave doubts. And he felt that Stearns's fluid understanding and enthusiasm would be more effective. Whatever the reason, his decision would cut short his own career at Parker Brothers and catapult that of Stearns.

Stearns and I reviewed our presentation to Barton on the Eastern Airlines shuttle to New York. The date was July 28, 1981. I had the flu and worried about my coherence. Nonetheless, Barton liked what he saw and heard—but he cautioned us both to not appear smug once the meeting convened.

At 200 Fifth Avenue, the studious-looking, dark-haired Fifield chaired the meeting in a conference room in Loomis's new marketing and design office ("MAD" for short). Loomis and his top assistant were already there along with the president of Kenner (Joe Mendelson). Each group had a plan. MAD presented "Operation Leapfrog"—the creation of an elaborate video game system that would outdo Atari. Kenner proposed licensing the groups' great properties to Atari, and not taking a risk internally. Parker Brothers set forth its strategy of programming video game cartridges—first for the Atari system and later for Mattel's Intellivision and then home computers. The Stearns/Bracy marketing plan suggested that $15 million worth of two cartridges could be sold next year, with lucrative profit margins. I demonstrated our ability to program them. The meeting ended on a high note. Loomis and Mendelson endorsed the decision by Fifield to appoint Parker Brothers as keeper of the video game flame for the group. They acknowledged that we had the best chance to deliver product next year. Fifield, for his part, did not reveal his emotions and the eyes behind his black glasses appeared remarkably vacant. But his Clint Eastwood–like posture and cold voice conveyed directness not previously heard from any General Mills executive. He admonished Barton not to think small. Fifteen million dollars was nothing in a business that was already over a billion dollars at retail. He instructed all three of us to let nothing stand in the way of a major video game introduction at Toy Fair, 1982.

Star Wars and Frogger

In the months that followed, we programmed two games. The first was based on the most recent *Star Wars* movie. Created from whole cloth by the software group, it would be ready by the next Toy Fair.[50] The second game, which came later, was based on a moderately popular arcade game named *Frogger*. As a result of the momentous meeting in New York, Stearns and Bracy began to spend a part of each workday in video arcades. By watching what games kids played and experiencing them personally (with gusto), they came to recommend which titles could be hits if made into video game cartridges. That was step one. Step two was convincing a property's owner to consider doing business with Parker Brothers, which as yet had no presence in video games. A Parker Brothers license was still a pig in a poke, compared to Atari or Mattel. But Stearns did have one argument the two hardware giants could not match: Parker Brothers would program cartridges for *all* hardware systems. This was a pure boast in 1981, because as yet the video game engineers could only program for the Atari system. But they had a swagger and were confident the next system to give up its secret would be Mattel's Intellivision (and eventually Colecovision and every other home computer system of merit).

Stearns and the marketing department at Parker Brothers were thinking several moves ahead. One day in December, after a blinding snowstorm, Denny Miller (Channing Bacall's successor as head of finance), the company's attorney, and I flew to Los Angeles to finalize and sign a contract that broke all the rules. Sega, owners of *Frogger*, had entertained a bidding war for the rights to its game. With Fifield's support, the absolutely unheard-of figure of a half-million-dollar advance and a healthy royalty won the deal for Parker Brothers. In Parker Brothers' ninety-eight-year history, no game had even been licensed with a royalty advance a fraction of this amount. A sense of do-or-die prevailed. Toy Fair was two months away and the first line of software code would not be written until this deal was signed. The contract took forty-eight hours to negotiate and write, thanks to the wondrous new device in the possession of Sega's attorney—a word processor. In less than ninety days, one of our bright young programmers delivered a spectacularly faithful equivalent of *Frogger*.[51] It so happened that the frog-hopping, horizontal log-and-lily-pad scrolling of the arcade contest was perfect for the amazingly crude and limited computer chips inside the Atari hardware.

Several Parker Brothers executives, most especially Barton, began to court the makers of arcade games. They were mainly in Japan. After I made a side trip to Hong Kong, where the Toy Group had a large engineering and buying office (more and more of Parker Brothers' games were being sourced in labor-cheap China; almost all of Kenner's toys were made there), I flew directly to New York City. Toy Fair had begun. After reuniting with my wife, Anna, in our hotel room, she told me, "Ranny Barton called. He wants to see you right away." It was nine o'clock in the morning and I was hoping to sleep until noon, to shake off the effects of the twelve-hour time change.

By ten o'clock I was in Barton's office at Parker Brothers' showroom on the sixth floor of the 200 Fifth Avenue Building, fully expecting to see my boss brimming with excitement over the trade's reaction to *Star Wars* and *Frogger*. ("Phil, your guys did it! We're going to do fifty million in video games, this year!") This was not what I heard—even though Barton already knew that the video game sales forecast was jumping by the hour and might exceed *$100* million before Toy Fair ended the next week. I was startled by the stressed look on my boss's face. "Phil," he began somberly, "it's not enough to do two. We've got to get six out this year, or more. Money is no object. Whatever you'll need, you'll get. But you got to turn the heat up and do more."

I soon learned that, prior to my arrival, Fifield had been galvanized by the video game fervor whipped up by the trade's press. They were reporting that video games were the biggest thing to hit the toy industry in history. Mindful that his outposting as head of the General Mills Toy Group was a proving ground for his ability to lead the parent company, Fifield was beginning to play what we soon came to understand was an aggressive chess match. Parker Brothers was his key piece. His powerful ambition made him see Parker Brothers' video game business (and to a lesser extent, Kenner's brilliance in toys) as the means to escort him across the board to checkmate his rivals within General Mills. If these twin efforts doubled or tripled the sales of his group, and ratcheted up profits accordingly, he would have little trouble persuading his mentor, Bruce Atwater, chairman of the company, to award the crown to his protégé.

Late February was traditionally a sanguine time for the employees of Parker Brothers. With Toy Fair over and the pressure off momentarily, there were smiles and jokes and the traditional dinner hosted by the sales department to say "thank you" to the marketing and R&D staffs. On the surface, there was more reason than ever to celebrate after Toy Fair 1982. It was conceivable that the company's sales would double in the space of the next twelve months.

The toy and game business is, to be sure, a "fashion" enterprise. Trends come and go. Veterans learn to savor the highs, not knowing when the next peak might come. George Parker's principles, seemingly imbued in everyone inside of Parker Brothers, made people patient when times were lean, determined to exploit success when times were good, and always careful to protect the firm's long-term image by offering products with both quality and durability. But the stress lines I had seen on Barton's face bore witness to a worry we all soon felt. The firm's legendary reserve, which had always served it well, came crashing to earth. George Parker had agonized over the right card game to succeed *Pit* before he purchased *Flinch*. We didn't yet know if the appeal of *Star Wars* and *Frogger* would connect with kids before the next round of similar games would be in production.

Parker Brothers' recovery from the handheld blues only increased demands on Barton from above to push harder on the growth pedal. Throughout the firm's history, money had been very carefully budgeted and expended. Few companies, private or public, could match the finesse by which Parker Brothers nurtured and protected its cash, while simultaneously investing in the future. This pillar of conservative management was being replaced by an edict from Fifield to spend as if the printing presses in Salem were capable of producing legal tender and not just *Monopoly* money. (In a touch of irony, the prize awarded to that year's winner of the world *Monopoly* tournament, held in Washington, D.C., was a *Monopoly* game stuffed with real money.)

The vacant office space that Barton had fretted about in 1981 quickly filled with squads of electronic engineers, technicians, marketing product managers, graphic artists, mechanical engineers, and the swell of staffers in other departments needed to cope with the growth brought on by video games. More and more of the brightest talents in the company were assigned to support video games, at the expense of the company's core of traditional games. In retrospect, it was as if Toy Fair had been a giant reeducation seminar where the teachings and experience of a century were discarded. The old king was dead. All hail the video game king. Naturally, this attitude adversely affected the morale and self-worth of employees not assigned to the big, sleek, expensive video game line. Barton and others made real efforts to correct this tilt, but to little avail.

Dick Dalessio, who had tried to resist the Fifield tide, fell into disfavor with the head of the Toy Group and was soon unemployed. The pressure on us deflected our ability to contemplate its significance—Fifield, more and more, was telling Barton what to do. Barton next acceded to Fifield's request that Parker Brothers create a separate electronics division. That meant forming two parallel sales, marketing, and R&D organizations, each headed by an executive vice president. Stearns was made executive vice president of the electronics group, with Bracy elevated as his vice president of marketing. Bruce Jones, former market researcher and family game director, became vice president of traditional marketing and reported to a green M.B.A. from General Mills. Even more M.B.A.'s arrived to fill out the expanded marketing staffs. Dohrmann, unhappy with the changes he had experienced, took another job and bid farewell to the Parker Brothers R&D department that he had once regarded as his reason for jumping out of bed in the morning, eager to get to work.

Word began to reach Dave Wilson at Milton Bradley of Parker Brothers' shift in emphasis. Parker Brothers' former sales leader had not enjoyed success with video game products at his new employer, but he now saw an opportunity to exploit Parker Brothers' shifting attention. Over the next few years, concentration on traditional games and the 1984 purchase of his company by toy maker Hasbro provided the means and the money to make Milton Bradley number one, by a sizable margin, in nonelectronic game sales.[52]

The Death of Principle

Despite decoupling from tradition, by the end of the fiscal year in 1983 Parker Brothers' sales exceeded everyone's expectations, including Fifield's. The surplus profit was quickly invested in massive off-season TV advertising, in typical General Mills fashion, to create more brand awareness. This gusher of money caused another ratcheting up of expectations from Fifield. His "six" jumped to "twenty" and soon marketing was under the gun to offer these in as many as 150 variations to satisfy all the different hardware systems competing for kids' attention. In my development group, the number of video game programmers jumped from two to twenty to forty—with at least that many external programmers under contract. Back in 1981, when Barton asked me to trim my department's budget, we had to make do with $2 million to accomplish the development of the entire new product line. Now, it was typical to require and get this much for a new computer or a suite of development workstations or whatever new technology was needed to satisfy the appetite of the video game–hungry public. Royalty advances for hot game licenses were in the seven figures. Sales leader Bill Brett responded to the scale of money invested in sizzling presentations by competitors Atari and Mattel—and newcomers Activision and Imagic—by investing a million dollars on one massive trade show. It would preview our 1983 video game line to every important customer in the country. When the two-day event ended, orders for well over $100 million had been written. Swanson was amazed, both at the expenditure and the orders taken. He told Brett that General Mills had never experienced anything like this. Video games were the biggest new product category in the long history of their business. Parker Brothers, since 1968 a significant contributor to its parent firm's profits, was now caught in the glare of General Mills' spotlight—like a suddenly popular Hollywood starlet at a premiere. And Fifield seemed well on his way to accepting his Academy Award in Minneapolis.

If only the curtain could have dropped then. There would have been thunderous applause in the theater and everyone on stage would have gone home a hero or heroine. But after the conclusion of the dazzling video games sales show, the magic gave way to sobered reality.

As great arcade titles like *Popeye* and *Q*Bert* neared production and "can't-miss" licenses like *James Bond, Spider-Man, GI Joe,* and *The Lord of the Rings* were undergoing final testing, clouds appeared on the horizon. Video game hardware reached a saturation point, and its technology was not advancing quick enough to satisfy the desire for visual realism of the nation's youthful players. Despite a slew of new titles, sales began to slow at retail. Atari announced a huge loss. This megacompany, owned by Time Warner, went from fair-haired prince to ugly goat when its red ink caused a sizable decline in the price of Time Warner's stock.[53]

As George Parker had once cautioned against expecting the *Monopoly* boom to continue, Barton, Stearns, and Bracy concluded that similar restraint had to be enacted to contend with the nascent video downturn. The head of human resources (Al Zink) was told to stop hiring people and get ready, instead, for layoffs. That summer, the Toy Group's global conference was held at the beautiful La Montreaux Palace hotel in Montreaux, Switzerland. Upon arrival, Barton was invited to see Fifield in his penthouse suite. Fifield led Barton onto the balcony, with its magnificent view of Lake Geneva. He was cordial as he asked about the sales forecast. Barton, in businesslike fashion, told his boss the truth, as was his duty: The fiscal 1984 sales program was a dream; it was unattainable and Atwater would have to be informed because Parker Brothers' shortfall would affect General Mills' earnings. Fifield grew testy, then adamant. In a chilling voice, he told Barton to make the program happen, and to avoid any contact with Atwater because he, Fifield, was the sole communicator from the Toy Group to General Mills. He came close to calling Barton a coward. Deeply upset, Barton walked out of Fifield's suite knowing that the Montreaux conference was effectively over before it began, and that he had lost all ability to make the right decisions for his firm. When Atwater arrived two days later, Barton had to button his lips and present the sales program as if it were secure.[54]

Perhaps, if Fifield—bright, well trained, and gifted—were a lifelong toy leader like Loomis, he would have taken the advice of his field general. However, his goal was to influence Atwater and leap back into a position of prominence at General Mills. Through his irrational response, he had exposed this clashing goal to Barton—who now had no illusions about the consequences that lay ahead. Verification came quickly, and rudely. Many of the video game orders taken at the megashow evaporated as the market decline accelerated.

For Barton, the satisfaction he had always felt growing up in the games business was replaced by frustrated agony as Fifield tried to will the sales program to happen. Despite the hoopla and massive new product and marketing efforts, Parker Brothers barely surpassed the previous year's sales total, when only two video games, with remarkably little investment, had generated well over $100 million. As the sales program dwindled month by month, most employees of Parker Brothers felt their pride dissipate as well. By the end of 1983, video game manufacturers collectively lost $1 billion. To maintain Atwater's confidence, Fifield manipulated a "breakeven" for the current fiscal year (which ended in May 1984). The reserves on Parker Brothers' books were drained. Brett's sales department had to cash in every favor with the trade in order to write millions of dollars of spring sales, mainly for nonvideo merchandise. The overburdened Salem work force was physically unable to ship all of the orders before the end of May. So officers, managers, and staffers from the Beverly office building lent a hand, working evenings to help get the orders picked, packed, and loaded onto trucks in time. Fifield presented this to Atwater as a heroic achievement, another Parker Brothers miracle.

Decision for Ranny Barton

Of course, the orders stole business from the next fiscal year and the arm-twisting of the trade damaged Parker Brothers' standing with its key customers. But the future be damned. Only the present counted.

With each passing day, Barton's alarm etched itself further on his face. His skin sagged, dried, and became blotched with red. He gained weight. He held fewer staff meetings and spent more time alone in his office. But in the fall, he seemed to recover. His appearance began to improve and the added weight began to disappear. His staff noticed a new-found resilience. He seemed less affected by the doom that hung so thick it seemed one could touch it like a heavy fog. Layoff after layoff now took place, which Barton weathered with aplomb.

What none of us knew was that Barton's new composure was due to a dramatic, and secret, decision. He had confronted Fifield, in the only way he knew how, in order to send a message beyond him to the office of the chairman of General Mills. Barton told Fifield he was resigning as president of Parker Brothers. Fifield, rattled, tried to talk Barton out of his decision. Barton held firm. Fifield, no fool, knew Atwater would probe and want to know why one of his most successful managers, a man who was only fifty-two, would want to cut short his career. Could this be the same determined man who had arrived in Minneapolis only ten years earlier carrying a piece of yellow-ruled paper that outlined his long-term vision for the firm his grandfather had established?

Barton made one concession to Fifield. He would remain until the following spring to help pick his successor and achieve a smooth transition. Like his father and his grandfather, he would then serve as chairman, for a brief period. Barton knew of only one person with the talent, experience, and favor at General Mills who could fix Parker Brothers: his former head of marketing, Ron Jackson. At this moment, Jackson was president of Talbot's, a women's clothing subsidiary of General Mills. Fifield was dead set against this choice. He regarded Jackson as a strong adversary and realized that Jackson would have Atwater's ear before he agreed to set one foot back inside of Parker Brothers. (Barton foresaw the damage done by Fifield to his firm as being irreparable unless someone also replaced him as head of the Toy Group.)

In April 1984, Barton revealed his decision to his staff, then went downstairs to the cafeteria and told the assembled crowd of employees, who gasped and shed tears. He tried to put a good face on his announcement, offering as motives a desire to do less traveling, spend more time with family, and engage in added community affairs. When asked if he were being forced out, Barton squelched such speculation, but did not reveal his true impetus. He was proud, he added, of having helped take the firm from sales of $35 million in 1974 to well over $200 million in 1983.

Ranny Barton was easily the most unassuming, most hands-off of the four family members who had run Parker Brothers. But he had achieved its most spectacular growth. To do so, he had relied on his grandfather's principles, his father's expansiveness, his cousin Eddie's skill at handling General Mills, and his own practice in hiring the best talent he could find.

Privately, Barton, the gifted sailor, admitted sorrow for leaving the helm of his ship while it was in such troubled waters. But in fact, he had surrendered the wheel months before.

After a hundred years, the Parker family no longer claimed control of the firm George S. Parker has started with only fifty dollars and an entrepreneur's unlimited dream.

Chapter Seven

Back to Go

1984–1991

JAMES FIFIELD WOULD STRENGTHEN HIS CONTROL OF
Parker Brothers through his choice of Ranny Barton's successor.
And he would do so, arguably, without regard for long-standing
principles, a credo of permanence, and a sense of obligation to the
workers. The words uttered by the Toys R Us buyer who once confronted Dick Dalessio expressed well the new reality. Parker Brothers
tradition was "yesterday's newspaper."

Richard Stearns

Richard E. Stearns, twenty years Ranny Barton's junior with only three
years of officer's credentials under his belt, was appointed president.
Those of us who rooted for him shook his hand and pledged our support. Inwardly, we were relieved that we had not suffered the same fate.
This tall, fast-thinking Wharton Business School graduate had many ad-
mirable qualities. He had lifted himself out of a difficult childhood
through hard work and intelligence. He absorbed volumes of information instantly and had boundless energy. He was devoted to his wife and
family. He was agile and trim, although his bushy hair had prematurely
grayed. Stearns had a gift for public speaking and was blessed with a
quick wit. He could vanquish the somber mood in a meeting by mim-
icking the voice of his favorite character, Popeye ("Olive, that plan dis-
custipates me"), or with a sudden quip. When asked how he viewed the
monthly business review in Fifield's New York office, he replied, "I'd
rather be in a dentist's office having a root canal."

Ranny had coached and encouraged Stearns during the video games
roller-coaster ride. He liked him and had promoted his career. But he

had also advised Fifield that it was just too premature to thrust Stearns into the president's chair. Ranny saw Stearns's marketing talents as not sufficiently developed for general management. For example, Stearns's enthusiasm for new projects made him a hands-on guy who was reluctant to delegate. He had been trained to win big by taking large risks, and needed to learn the art of prudence. He had the onus of explaining, on a monthly basis, the backslide in video games sales, which tarnished his winner's reputation. As with Robert Barton, years earlier, the work force had not yet accepted Stearns as "Parkerized." And his single-department experience had not prepared him for the myriad issues raining down on the corner office desk.

By contrast, Barton's choice, Ron Jackson, had experience in human resource management, had been a vice president of both finance and marketing, was well known by the work force, and currently held a president's title.

But in Fifield's all-or-nothing game, Stearns was the only choice. Bill Bracy observed, "Fifield did not want someone who could contest his will." Most Parker Brothers vice presidents concurred.[1]

With Ranny gone, Fifield and his staffers dictated the operating decisions they wanted Stearns to enact inside of Parker Brothers. When a closed-door meeting was convened at Parker Brothers to identity "bodies" for the next layoff, Fifield attended. When asked why he was present, Fifield's reply was, "The head of the Toy Group is going to know everything, right down to the cost of the glass stones in your *Pente* games." Among the truly disastrous decisions was the consolidation of all manufacturing of the various Toy Group companies into "TGOD," which stood for Toy Group Operations Division. Tough-as-nails Vic Rado became the master of all production for every company in the Toy Group. Although he was a highly experienced leader in toy manufacturing, he seemed to exhibit little regard for the human consequences of his decisions.

TGOD and New Ventures

Joe Marquez, who had guided Parker Brothers' operations group so successfully, was transferred to the Toy Group's Mexican marketing subsidiary. The Salem factory and the Taunton injection molding facility now reported to Rado, not Stearns. This significantly impeded Parker Brothers' ability to respond agilely to shifting marketplace demand.

Compounding the error, most of the molding machines in Taunton were shipped to a new molding and manufacturing facility in the Border Zone of Mexico, where the mortar was still drying and the untrained work force was light-years away from the competence of the Parker Brothers' manufacturing people whose jobs had been eliminated. Years earlier, when Channing Bacall had advocated a comparable decision—the establishment of a facility in Des Moines—a year of painstaking preparation and planning had been invested before the first shovel of dirt was excavated. Rado told everyone he would go from plan to production at full capacity in six months.

Several Parker Brothers and Kenner manufacturing executives were compelled to relocate to San Diego and were given the impossible task of achieving Rado's six-month deadline. There was no contingency. It was all or nothing. While the buildings did go up in time, chaos reigned inside. The desolate landscape of northern Mexico had insufficient infrastructure to support the buildings. Managers couldn't drink the tap water. The office walls were bare because the paint was "stolen" every day and then repurchased from the "yonke" yards in the neighborhood, only to be stolen again. Several of the transplanted executives suffered physical and mental breakdowns.[2] At the same time, the director of manufacturing in Salem (responsible to Rado for traditional game output) suffered a heart attack after being told to impose a pre-Christmas layoff on his beleaguered workers.[3]

In addition, Toy Group management was forcing "global branding," which meant that each new license taken by Kenner or Parker Brothers was to be exploited by every other toy group company, in every country, whether it made sense or not. For example, Kenner's cute *Care Bears* toys had to be made into numerous Parker Brothers board and card games and video game cartridges, and sold throughout Europe, where customer affinity was not as strong as in the United States. Equally damaging was the edict that Parker Brothers diversify into other categories in order to offset the decline in video games. Soon, the old-line game firm was selling children's books and records as well as a new line of construction sets (this time with no small parts that kids could choke on). Each of these ventures required relationship building to reach new buyers who had little or no experience with Parker Brothers. These new businesses also required the firm to take more inventory risk. And the seminal decisions required by these businesses further diluted management's time, especially after Bracy was transferred to Kenner. (Since Stearns regarded the older, more experienced Bracy as his confidant and sounding board, this move was deleterious to the youthful president.[4])

None of the new ventures succeeded for more than a few months. So many unsold children's books clogged the company's warehouse, with no sales prospects, that hundreds of thousands were given to a Native American charity in Arizona. Toys "R" Us soon reported a massive return of Parker Brothers books to their local stores. (Toys "R" Us had a "no receipt required" return policy at the time.) Returns also came back from the children's record line, often through strong-arm tactics the likes of which Parker Brothers had never experienced in the generally reputable toy trade.[5] Delays in getting to market with the *Construction Company* line allowed competitors to scoop most of the business not taken by industry leader Lego. There were no sustained hits, either, on the traditional side of the game business—save one. A young graphics department designer (Jim Englebrecht) suggested offering a fiftieth-anniversary commemorative edition of the *Monopoly* game in a tin package. A novel idea for its time, it entered the line in 1985 with a sales forecast of 50,000 units. It sold *350,000* units, verifying the enduring appeal of this classic game.

Heading for the Exit

For the first time in Parker Brothers' long history, there was a noticeable exodus of talent, especially in the electronic engineering group. Among them was Don Miffitt, who left to start his own development firm. Despite layoffs (Parker Brothers' employees dropped from thirteen hundred to eight hundred between 1983 and 1985), the company still had layers of underutilized management and redundant positions. The lean, fit athlete that once was Parker Brothers gave way to a bloated, depressed beast with seemingly nowhere to turn. Financial leader Denny Miller told Stearns that he knew how to make a lean Parker Brothers profitable at under $100 million of sales, but could not foresee how to do so if a higher number was sought by continuing to compete in the high-stakes, low-margin world of new ventures and electronics. In effect, he was saying that all the sweat and effort expended to grow the firm over the past ten years had been for naught.

In May, the General Mills Toy Group had reported a $21 million write-down due to TGOD and $10 million of losses at Parker Brothers due to video games. Shareholders and the financial press blamed the cereal giant's inability to manage its nonfood business as the culprit, especially the Toy Group. In reaction, Bruce Atwater and the General Mills board of directors studied alternatives. In a dramatic move the following January, the Minneapolis firm announced its desire to retrench, concentrate on its food businesses, and sell its toy and fashion operations. There were no takers, so General Mills reluctantly decided to give these companies to its shareholders by spinning them off into freestanding operations.

Fifield, at first, was sanguine. He was slated to be the chief executive of a publicly traded corporation, answerable only to a board of directors, without an intervening parent company. But General Mills would be accountable for the health of these companies at the time they were "spun." Atwater dug deeper, and asked for advice and opinions about the leadership of the Toy Group. Among those he consulted was Ranny Barton, who was now free to offer the truth about what had happened at, and after, the 1983 Montreaux conference. In May 1985, in Minneapolis, Atwater asked for Fifield's resignation. This occurred prior to what many inside of Parker Brothers feared Fifield was set to do—liquidate the game company and fold its brands into Kenner Toys in Cincinnati. (Fifield, however misguided in his handling of the Toy Group, later applied his skills with better results in a successful career in the music industry.)

To Ranny's relief, Atwater persuaded former Parker Brothers executive Ron Jackson, currently president of Stride Rite shoes, to return and become president and CEO of Kenner Parker Toys. E. Robert Kinney, former chairman of General Mills, agreed to serve as chairman of the board for the new firm.

By selecting these two principled leaders, Atwater gave Parker Brothers a chance at redemption.

Ronald Jackson

It now fell to conservative Ronald J. Jackson to restore the ethics and values that had served Parker Brothers so well during the first ninety-eight years of its history. His 1985 return to Kenner Parker Toys was welcomed by nearly every employee. They suddenly felt a reason for hope. Jackson was tall, slender, and graceful. Coupled with his light brown hair, delicate glasses, and placid expression, he bore an uncanny resemblance to Robert Barton. But whereas Barton was austere, Jackson was friendly and engaging. Underneath it all beat the heart of man who cared deeply for Parker Brothers and was determined to restore its pride and its values—even if he had to clean house of old friends to do so.

In appearance, the Salem factory had hardly changed since the days Jackson's office was located there in the mid-1970s. The Beverly office building was also physically untouched. Only the Taunton molding operation had disappeared, but a few of its machines had been relocated to the old Salem armory, which was connected by a hallway to the Salem plant. There was a significant continuity in personnel. Many of the people at Parker Brothers were old friends and acquaintances; veterans peppered each department. On the surface, it looked like Jackson's goal of rehabilitating Parker Brothers would be effortless, methodical.

It wasn't.

People had been changed by the video game experience and the realignment of the values they had held dear for so many years. Mutual trust and pride had broken down. Parker Brothers could not be revitalized merely by declaring that all was well and by changing the name on the company's masthead.

The new firm would be known as Kenner Parker Toys, Inc. (KPT). For the first time in its history, Parker Brothers would be a cog in a publicly traded company, not merely a small subsidiary of a giant corporation. The necessary due diligence, paperwork, and financing would be finalized by the fall. Before this process was complete, Jackson, alarmed at the sagging fortunes of the former Toy Group, fought determinedly for a better capitalization than General Mills proposed. General Mills had a fiduciary responsibility to assure survival of KPT for a reasonable period of time, but not indefinitely. This meant that Jackson and his new team would have to stem the losses and regain profitability quickly. This was important for another reason: The quicker the new firm became profitable, the quicker they could change hearts and minds and make believers out of the disillusioned.

Kenner Parker Toys

Jackson's first move was to dismiss Fifield's corporate staff in New York and close the expensive office there. He set up his much smaller staff in Beverly, moving into space left empty after the many layoffs that accompanied the gut-wrenching decline in video game sales. He did so because he favored living in his old neck of the woods and because he didn't want to lead remotely. He also did so to show everyone that he was serious about cost control. And by moving into the Beverly office building, as opposed to a separate building on the North Shore, he sent a message that Parker Brothers would be under his wing.

At first, Stearns thought it would be like the old times when Jackson had been his marketing boss. He did as Jackson asked and requested the resignation of Bruce Jones, who had become bitter and frustrated over the way his traditional games' business had been gutted and ignored by Fifield. Then Jackson asked Stearns to resign. Like Ranny, he regarded Stearns as not yet tempered by sufficient experience to manage the difficult rehabilitation of the firm—and as goods tainted by the Fifield experience.

The officers who had reported to Stearns, including Brett, Miller, and myself, were given the opportunity to state our case for reform and rebuilding. I was asked to put the pieces of R&D back together in one department. While other executives departed, several veterans, including Bracy and Marquez, were promoted to the corporate staff and lured back from competitors.

While General Mills wore goat horns for its mismanagement of the Toy Group, the indelible fact remained that the modern management practices and systems it had installed were beyond reproach. Parker Brothers had flourished for years by adhering to them. But like Parker Pride and George Parker's business principles, they too had been discredited during the video game mania. Now Jackson committed to restoring them.

One evening in June, Jackson assembled the Parker Brothers' officers in a small conference room, ordered in pizza, and had everyone speak about the principles that had once made Parker Brothers so uniquely great. We began to remember—we aimed for attainable goals; we built on past successes; we played by the rules, but we were aggressive and strove to be number one in our categories. We cared about our people. When adversity struck, we were patient and waited for the next good opportunity—we didn't try to force the numbers. In good times or bad, we were a team. Traditional values would guide our future, as they had guided our predecessors in the past.

Word began to spread throughout the company that it was all right to get excited about making games—games with boards and cards and dice and lots of pride. A product acquisition specialist (Laura Lemiesz) summed up the way many felt when she quipped, "We survivors felt like ugly ducklings one day, beautiful princesses the next."

John Moore and the Rebound

To replace Stearns, Jackson hired a toy industry pro, John Moore, who was then president of Parker Brothers Canada. Moore proved to be a sound choice because he excelled at signing onto a plan and executing it. It was soon clear to the managers at Parker Brothers that Jackson was setting the plan and goals and that Moore was the field officer responsible for achieving his objectives. And that was just fine with everyone. Moore was much like Ranny Barton in that he did not profess to have deep experience or interest in any one area of the firm. He relied explicitly on his officers to run their departments. However, he was a good coordinator, and his tall lean body and good looks made for a fine representative to the outside world. He and his family settled in Marblehead, not far from Robert Barton's home, and smoothly fit into Parker Brothers' culture and environment.

Henceforth, all new product effort would be concentrated on traditional games, some of which might have electronic chips inside, but which were mainly to be made of good old-fashioned cardboard, printing, and plastics. Fortunately, the core of R&D personnel had remained intact and relished the chance to again do what they did best. Throughout the firm, experienced people remained. Like their predecessors, most Parker Brothers employees still wished to work at the firm until retirement.

On November 1, 1985, Kenner Parker stock began trading on the New York Stock Exchange. It briefly rose, and then within weeks fell back because, as calendar 1985 closed, the firm lost an additional $14 million and Jackson wrote off a further $44 million in questionable assets in order to clean up the books.[6] The General Mills fiscal year reflected the grain cycle, which ended in May. This was awkward for a toy company, whose cycle peaked at year's end. Jackson filed an abbreviated year and, beginning in 1986, Kenner Parker adopted a calendar year cycle. Nevertheless, many pundits predicted another dismal year of losses for Kenner Parker. That was understandable, given the swagger and failed promises of the General Mills forecasts of recent years. Jackson himself was suggesting tough times, but what the pundits hadn't counted on was the return of Robert Barton–like conservatism. Jackson was a controller at heart. He felt most comfortable when expectations were held down, so that any surprise would be on the upside. He treasured a strong balance sheet with ample reserves for "rainy days." Reacting to his push to eliminate weak products and lines, it became a byword within the company that the key to increasing profits was to lower sales.

By the middle of 1986, profits were surging. People were smiling in the hallways. The stock was up a little. Parker Brothers' illustrious history was recognized when the American Toy Institute added George S. Parker to its newly founded Toy Industry Hall of Fame. Eddie Parker's name would join its growing ranks in 1990.

Flanker Products

One major board game had been acquired during the video game era, the aforementioned *Pente* game. It was a sleek adaptation of a Japanese game known as *Go Moku* ("five in a row"). Players tried to align five transparent glass stones in a line on its board, removing opposing stones by means of a clever capture principle. Its inventor, with the aid of a good sales partner, had built it into a top seller. Unfortunately, the largely inexperienced marketing team, assigned to traditional games back in 1984, made some poor merchandising choices and *Pente* failed to live up to its lofty expectations. In fact, Parker Brothers had not had a hit board game since 1978's *Bonkers* and 1979's clever *Mad Magazine Game*. Both of these games had since disappeared from the line. Nonetheless, consumers continued to bombard the company with questions about its traditional games. It was typical for the consumer response department to receive two mail baskets of letters a day—all of which were promptly answered. In all, sixty thousand consumer letters and phone calls were being handled each year.[7]

But it was becoming obvious that fewer and fewer people were looking for completely new board games. Kids, in particular, regarded them as "old-fashioned." This posed a formidable challenge to the current marketing staff. However, the success of *Trivial Pursuit* (which Parker Brothers had turned away back in 1982) revealed a surge of adult-level interest in games. This implied that the classic, tried-and-true games like *Monopoly, Clue, Sorry!,* and *Risk* might be more than single items—they might be *brands.*

In 1983, a clear-headed Fifield had first proposed this idea. It ran smack in the face of the very conservative attitude that prevailed at Parker Brothers during Jackson's first stint with the firm. Management had worried that "flankers" to the *Monopoly* games and other classics might endanger the reputation of the "family jewels" if they failed, or they might sap unit volume from the parent products if they succeeded. But times had changed. A flanker strategy was tried in 1985 via an innovative board game entitled *Advance to Boardwalk.* The idea of the game was to control the many hotels that rose, floor by floor, along the boardwalk (the player who owned the most floors in a hotel controlled it). Originally named "Atlantic City" when submitted by its inventor, its game board depicted the flavor of the real boardwalk in the city of *Monopoly* fame.[8] Its name was changed, and *Advance to Boardwalk* sold 400,000 units in 1985; sales rose further in 1986. Soon, games like *Castle Risk, Clue Jr.,* and *Boggle Jr.* were added to the line. Not only were sales of the "family jewels" unaffected, they rose from the added exposure their flankers gave them. People were reminded just how much fun the classics were. The "junior versions" prepared players for the main games at a younger age, making them eager to "graduate" to their play.

The *Nerf* brand, which had struggled after all popular field sports had been converted into safe, soft balls, found new hope with *Nerf Fencing.* Jackson was skeptical, because of the warlike play of the toy. War toys had been out of vogue since the Vietnam War. Their peak had come in the 1950s, in the afterglow of the victory in World War II and the nation's love affair with cowboy programs. Aside from some harmless cork-shooting games, Parker Brothers had steered clear of projectile games since World War I. But Jackson decided to let the Parker Brothers team make up its own mind. *Nerf Fencing* sold hundreds of thousands of units in 1986 and led to even bigger-selling safe-shooting toys such as *Nerf Blast-a-Ball* and the *Nerf Bow and Arrow.* Along with the *Nerf Turbo Football* (with spiral grooves on its surface), which became a huge seller in 1989, all three were internally designed. These four products added over $25 million in sales.

Based on the success Parker Brothers' competitors were having in acquiring Tokyo's best ideas for the U.S. market, it was clearly time for Parker Brothers to form closer ties with Japanese toy and game firms.

Relationships were vital to success in business dealings with Japan; the video game era had taught that. Currently, Parker Brothers had no interplay with Japanese toy companies, save one wholesaler. A Tokyo-based agent and his U.S. partner were contracted to help in the effort.[9] Three trips to Tokyo per year were organized, along with lessons in Japanese culture and language. Within a year, strong bonds were being built with leading firms Toybox, Sente, Tomy, and Takara. Top-selling children's action games soon came Parker Brothers' way.[10]

Games utilizing electronic technology made a comeback. In particular, the first games that included custom-made VCR "movies" were introduced as well as talking sports games (in which the statistics of real ball players, and their names, were programmed).[11] While these games did not last, they positioned the company to become a permanent maker of electronic and multimedia games after the 1990s dawned.

By the spring of 1987, Kenner Parker Toys was an indisputable success story. The return to classic values, conservative planning, and fiscal discipline provided the catalyst for strong growth in sales and new product innovation. Employee turnover ceased, aside from fluidity in the marketing department, where finding a strong leader became a reoccurring quest. The Salem plant received another infusion of new state-of-the-art production equipment, and a "just in time" inventory policy was adopted to meet the demands of retailers like Toys R Us, Wal-Mart, and Kmart. A growing sense of competence and achievement made the video era seem like a distant, disturbed dream.

When a global management conference was convened in late June 1987 at the Beverly office and the nearby Myopia Hunt Club, a sense of real unity of purpose pervaded everyone's thinking. Managers from the Asian and European companies, leaders from Kenner and Parker Brothers, plus the corporate staff were all on the same page, working together. The expressions on the faces of those present at the Myopia Club on the evening of June 24 spoke volumes. The machine they ran was finely tuned, well oiled, and ready to accelerate.

Takeover

At almost that precise moment, a force was poised to overwhelm the combined talent of Kenner Parker and wash away any possibility for continued independence.

It began innocently enough when product acquisition director Chris Campbell and I went to Los Angeles to meet Michael King of King World Productions, producers of the hit TV game shows *Jeopardy* and *Wheel of Fortune*. His desire was to adapt the *Monopoly* game to a TV quiz show. Over cocktails that evening at his home, King casually mentioned the intent of a Hollywood movie company named New World Productions to make a bid to take over Kenner Parker. He went on to say how flush with cash his firm was . . . and might it be possible to buy only Parker Brothers?

Upon my return, I told Jackson, reinforcing rumors that he had heard. Jackson convened his staff and started to investigate what might be done to thwart the action, if anything. In early July, New World launched its first hostile takeover bid, offering $44 a share to buy all the common shares of Kenner Parker. Our stock, languishing in the low $20's, zoomed to $46 by July 17.[12] Wall Street was buzzing about KPT being "in play" and was convinced that this would be but the first offer, because Kenner Parker's rapid success warranted a higher price. In this, the takeover era that preceded the big stock market crash of 1987, KPT was a juicy target. Not only had our firm made a miraculous recovery from the post–General Mills spin-off, but it had accumulated over $100 million in cash, and had millions more in its overfunded pension fund.[13] Jackson and team had looked at investing some of this horde by making an acquisition. But the cost of buying International Games (makers of the hugely popular *Uno* card game) seemed too dear (although Mattel didn't think so the next year). Tudor Games (makers of *Electric Football*) seemed out of vogue, and John Waddington Company Ltd—a natural partner since it held rights to sell the *Monopoly* game in the United Kingdom and had licensed *Clue* to Parker Brothers in the United States—was driving a hard bargain. So the money sat on the sidelines, making it possible for an acquiring company to pay for a deal, in part, with KPT's own cash.

Our firm's board of directors convened and tried to enact measures that would make it more difficult for any company charted outside the State of Massachusetts to pursue a takeover. But in response, New World raised its offer to $49 a share, knowing that no measure would stand in the face of shareholder desire to pocket a windfall.

Inside Parker Brothers, a numbed recognition of reality began to take hold. It was difficult for the average line worker, or foreman, or department manager, or vice president, to accept the likelihood of yet another outside owner so soon after surviving the havoc caused by the last one. The one thing that every Parker Brothers employee had in common with Jackson and his team was this: No one had been through a hostile takeover before. Nobody really knew what it meant, how it would feel during the battle, and more important, how it would play out if one succeeded.

The shareholders of Kenner Parker were, by and large, ecstatic. They did not want to see the firm ward off the takeover. That would send the stock back down to the $20's again. At the moment, virtually all the holders of KPT stock had more than doubled their investment—and they wanted to keep their gain. It wasn't possible for Jackson to echo Robert Barton by saying, "Well, we're not ready yet," as when General Mills had come courting, or, "It's up to the young guys to decide." No, this decision was already out of his hands. The only thing he could influence was *who* purchased Kenner Parker. It was decided that a "white knight" had to be found. Management feared that New World would gut the company beyond anything Fifield had contemplated. A better partner would be a company in the toy industry, for whom KPT provided real synergy, not just properties to turn into comic books and movies (New World owned Marvel Comics).

Tonka

Tonka, the maker of the famous metal toy trucks, turned out to be that white knight. Ironically, it was a Minneapolis-based company, like General Mills. In August, Tonka (which had once been discussed by Jackson and team as a potential KPT acquisition) came forward with an offer of $51 a share (over $600 million to buy them all) and KPT's board recommended to shareholders that they accept it, which they did. It was only a matter of time before all the documents could be put in order and the deal became official. On the Friday before the great stock market crash in October 1987, KPT ceased to exist. Tonka Kenner Parker was born.

Founded in 1946, Tonka was a relative newcomer to the toy industry. Boys of the 1950s became passionate about its durable metal trucks, and Tonka vehicles became "must have" toys thereafter. Tonka warded off a 1980 takeover bid by a rival, survived near-bankruptcy in 1982, and hit big in 1984 with *Gobots* transformable robots (licensed from Japan). Hasbro's line of *Transformers* robots soon did in *Gobots*, but Tonka rebounded with a line of adorable stuffed animals, called *Pound Puppies*, in 1985. *Pound Puppies* had provided just enough cash for Tonka to make its bid for Kenner Parker.

Steven G. Shank, a Harvard Law School graduate, was Tonka's CEO and, despite good intent and an honorable reputation, he never had a chance of making the deal work and fulfilling his promises to his shareholders. Tonka had to borrow $555 million to pay the shareholders of Kenner Parker, much of it in the form of junk bonds paying as much as 17 percent interest per annum.[14] So onerous was its leverage that the good ship Tonka began to sink immediately, even though the water rushing in had not yet tilted the bow downward. Tonka was smaller than Kenner Parker and much weaker financially. To pay for the annual interest bill and the cost of the corporate office, over $100 million of operating profit would be drained from Kenner, Parker, Tonka, and the international subsidiaries of the firm. The only way this outflow could be offset was if every division had a major success each year and cash poured into the company. With the economy damaged by the stock market debacle, a recession soon loomed and retailers restricted their purchases. And given the vagaries of the toy and game business, it was even more unlikely that the clouds swirling within each division's crystal ball would suddenly evaporate and clearly reveal which toys and games every kid would want come next year.

There was one person who might have made the deal work—the savvy cost-cutter and financial maestro named Ron Jackson. But, perhaps feeling threatened by Jackson's abilities, Shank decided to run the firm with his existing staff, despite their relative lack of experience. Jackson and most of KPT's corporate leaders soon departed, much richer but also very disappointed. Along with Jackson's exit went the carefully orchestrated return to management by principle. Tonka's preoccupation with financial survival mirrored Fifield's battle with the video game beast. It fought for survival by expedient means. Centralized control returned as an attempt to "will" results without the means to achieve them.

John Moore, who had been so effective as Jackson's standard-bearer, became ineffective as he tried, without success, to explain what made Parker Brothers tick and why its game characteristics set it apart from a toy company's character (the former relied on replay and structure—the latter succeeded via imagination and freeform play). A U.S. Army veteran, Shank had become president of Tonka in 1979. He was the company's highly respected attorney at the time, charged with the task of rebuilding his firm after the prior president was dismissed because of improprieties.[15] His greatest success came with the licensing of *Pound Puppies.* In a note of irony, Fifield had turned down this successful Canadian line of stuffed toys, invented by a U.S. automobile worker, after Brett had steered it to Parker Brothers in an act of desperation to find replacement sales as video games evaporated. As Brett later quipped, "*Pound Puppies* bit us in the backside—twice."[16]

Shortly after the takeover, Shank, mindful of the need to finance the interest burden, convened a meeting of Parker Brothers' management and offered this as his requirement for success: Double your sales and cut your advertising expenditures in half. The impossibility of this request undermined his credibility inside of Parker Brothers.

In the spring of 1989, hard work and an investor's road show led to a rise in the price of Tonka's stock. Tonka's management hoped to capitalize by selling additional shares, using the proceeds to pay off enough of the high-interest bonds to improve the corporation's alarming debt-to-equity ratio, and thereby grow profits. In the summer of 1989, the corporate staff prepared a new stock offering. But by the time the offering was ready in October, the stock had fallen from $24 to $16. Shortly after the offering, Tonka reported earnings that were less than promised. The new shareholders were fit to be tied as the stock sank back toward $10 a share.[17]

Parker Brothers had good years in 1988 and 1989, but the $20 million-plus in earnings it delivered to Tonka each year was insufficient to cover its share of the interest debt. Shank continued to pressure Moore to find a way to rapidly increase sales. Moore lacked an in-depth knowledge of Parker Brothers' history and its guiding principles, and without Jackson to guide him, could not press his case with Shank for attainable goals. Tonka's leader decided the solution was to hire an executive vice president to operate the firm under Moore. In a controversial move, Shank lured Milton Bradley's head of marketing, Lawrence Bernstein, for the position. (Reportedly, his coworkers cheered when they heard news of his departure because he was regarded as a self-centered tyrant.)

Milton Bradley had gained significant market share at Parker Brothers' expense while Parker Brothers was distracted by video games. But Shank did not grasp that Milton Bradley's success was due to the money supplied by parent Hasbro, Dave Wilson's sales strategy, and its excellent track record in selecting new games. In contrast, he was starving Parker Brothers, and restricting its ability to function. Within a few weeks of Bernstein's hiring, it was clear that he did not possess a magician's touch, as Shank had hoped. His past rivalry with Parker Brothers led to a seeming disregard for the firm, its products, and its proven way of doing business. Many questioned his business ethics; his decision making proved impulsive. He was given to sudden outbursts. The games he added in late 1989 to Parker Brothers' 1990 line failed to live up to expectations.[18]

The Trivial Pursuit Game

It was Moore who pulled off the biggest coup of the Tonka era. His Canadian roots helped him to snatch the rights for *Trivial Pursuit* when they became available in 1989 after the bankruptcy of Coleco, the U.S. toy company that had purchased Selchow & Righter (the venerable maker of *Parcheesi* and *Scrabble* and holders of the rights for the *Trivial Pursuit* game).

Trivial Pursuit began life in Canada on December 15, 1979. Scott Abbott, a sports writer, and Chris Haney, a photo editor, were engaged in a spirited argument over who was the better *Scrabble* player. The discussion led to a challenge to create a game of their own. Scott suggested trivia as its subject; that in turn led to the beginnings of *Trivial Pursuit*. But first they needed more help, and money. Haney's older brother John, an ex-hockey player, and Ed Werner, another ex-hockey player (turned lawyer), were recruited shortly thereafter, and *Trivial Pursuit* reached fruition. They licensed their game to a small Canadian firm, run by an ex–General Mills Toy Group manager named John Vernon. It was an immediate success.

Next, the *Trivial Pursuit* team turned to the United States for a manufacturing/marketing partner. Among the first companies they approached in 1981 was Parker Brothers. However, like other big game makers, Parker Brothers did not feel comfortable marketing an expensive game ($35 retail) with expendable software—especially at a time when electronic games were all the rage and traditional games seemed passé. However, Selchow & Righter decided to take a chance. In its first year of marketing the *Trivial Pursuit* game, an astounding 20 million copies were sold, which broke all sales records for board games in a single year.[19]

Two years later, Selchow & Righter was acquired by Coleco Industries, which had made substantial money with its Colecovision video game system and *Cabbage Patch Kids* dolls. But when its Adam home computer failed and video games waned, Coleco went bankrupt. The *Trivial Pursuit* contract was terminated and Moore was able to license the game for Kenner Parker on a long-term basis.

The End of Tonka Kenner Parker

Trivial Pursuit, Monopoly Jr., and the *Nerf Bow and Arrow* were the hits of the brief "Bernstein Era." All three had been developed before he arrived. At the end of 1990, desiring to call his own shots, Bernstein asked for and got the resignation of three vice presidents: Parker Brothers' current head of marketing, sales leader Bill Brett, and myself.

By the end of 1989, Tonka was on the verge of bankruptcy. Its stock was hovering around $4 a share. While it was known from the day Tonka purchased Kenner Parker that it faced long odds, given its huge debt burden, how had it collapsed so quickly?

Tonka's management had unknowingly violated most of George Parker's principles for success. Their decisions were driven by expedience, not by a desire to "make it last." In fairness, they never had the opportunity to run the firm debt-free, as had George Parker. But to the Parker Brothers' employees, it seemed painfully ironic that the house built by the *Monopoly* game found itself mortgaged to the hilt, unable to pay its own rent, forced to bow out and declare bankruptcy.

Necessity now compelled Tonka to utilize one of George Parker's principles: Seek help if the game threatens to overwhelm you.

The Hasbro Era

Coming to the rescue of Tonka was another toy and game company. But unlike Tonka, this one possessed a bank account Mr. Monopoly could envy.[20]

Hasbro Corporation—the owners of Milton Bradley, Parker Brothers' chief rival for more than seventy years—was about to claim ownership of the *Monopoly* game, *Clue, Sorry!, Trivial Pursuit, Tonka* trucks, *Play-Doh* modeling compound, and Kenner's *Easy Bake Oven*.

Hasbro, of Providence, Rhode Island, also began life as a family-owned company. In its seventy-five-year history, the firm grew from eight family members to a leisure time and entertainment company with thousands of employees worldwide and annual sales in excess of $2 billion. Two brothers, Henry and Hillel Hassenfeld, founded Hasbro in 1923. Known then as Hassenfeld Brothers, the company began by selling textile remnants and later pencil boxes and school supplies. In 1943, Henry's son, Merrill, was named president of Hassenfeld Brothers and the company expanded its product line to include toys such as paint sets and doctor and nurse kits. Merrill's sons Steven and later Alan took over the reins of command in the 1970s and were responsible for most of the firm's phenomenal growth.

Hasbro's most inimitable mascot was a toy named *Mr. Potato Head*. The brainchild of inventor George Lerner, Hasbro purchased his idea and launched it in 1952. It became a million-seller, thanks to the first advertising campaign on network TV for a toy product. The original *Mr. Potato Head* toy was just a bunch of pieces to press into a real potato! Although a Styrofoam "body" was provided, it wore out quickly and was primarily intended to hold the parts in the package.[21]

The toy industry underwent an amazing consolidation in the 1980s and 1990s. Hasbro began the 1980s as one of a dozen medium-sized toy firms. (It was often referred to as "Has-Been.") But megahits like *Transformers, My Little Pony,* and the rebirth of *GI Joe* filled its coffers with cash. Notable acquisitions followed, beginning with big game maker Milton Bradley (which already owned preschool giant Playskool). When CBS failed in its attempt to build a toy division through acquisition, Hasbro was there to pick up the most valued pieces, especially its best games (e.g., *Mousetrap*, acquired when it had purchased Ideal Toy). Other moves swept in enduring products made by former rivals Lakeside (*Trouble* and *Aggravation*), Knickerbocker (*Raggedy Ann*), Western Publishing (*Pictionary*), Schaper (*Cootie*), and Selchow & Righter (*Scrabble* and *Parcheesi*) after its parent—Coleco—went out of business. Hasbro also expanded overseas by acquiring the game business of Parker Brothers' longtime U.K. partner, John Waddington Company Ltd.[22]

Tonka had paid over $600 million to acquire the stock of Kenner Parker Toys in 1987. In contrast, Hasbro paid about $100 million to buy the shares of Tonka Kenner Parker in 1991.[23] After settling with the bondholders, the deal was sealed and Hasbro emerged with an 80 percent share of the nation's traditional game market.

Since Hasbro already owned Milton Bradley and its game line, it did not need to keep all of Parker Brothers' management. The Parker Brothers team, including Bernstein and Moore, became redundant and were let go. Bob Wann, of Hasbro's Playskool division, was appointed president of Parker Brothers. He brought in other executives from Hasbro and Milton Bradley to fill the gaps in his staff. (Wann also asked me to advise him on rebuilding Parker Brothers' new product efforts, teach him a bit about the firm's past, and help with the upcoming *Monopoly* world championship.)

Initially, Hasbro encouraged Milton Bradley and Parker Brothers to compete with each other. Parker Brothers kept up its winning ways, successfully launching *Monopoly Jr.*, the children's action board game *Don't Wake Daddy!*, and a button-pressing, lever twisting, handle-pulling electronic action game named *Bop-It!*. Parker Brothers also carefully rebuilt an electronic game line that featured handheld versions of many of its best traditional games. When CD-ROMs gained in popularity with home computer owners, they became the medium of choice for video games. Tom Dusenberry, the former loading dock worker from the Des Moines plant, now rose to vice president of new product acquisitions. He became the champion for the firm to enter the CD-ROM game category. Parker Brothers' first CD-ROM game was an audiovisual version of *Trivial Pursuit*.

The promise of this category sparked Hasbro's desire to build a new business devoted to CD-ROM games. In 1997, Dusenberry was appointed general manager of the new Hasbro Interactive Games division. Its prime mission was to convert Parker Brothers and Milton Bradley's best titles for play on home computers and video gaming systems. This new division set up shop in the Beverly office building. Dusenberry's staff occupied the space where Parker Brothers' programmers and engineers held forth during the wild years of the early 1980s.

Parker Brothers as a Brand

Hasbro's acquisition of Parker Brothers duplicated many of the assets already owned by Milton Bradley. It was inevitable that consolidation would occur. Both Milton Bradley and Parker Brothers would combine to form the Hasbro Games Group.

In a fitting touch of Parker Brothers irony, the executive placed in charge of Hasbro Games was E. David Wilson—the former head of sales at Parker Brothers who left in 1981 to become general manager of Milton Bradley. He was now leader of the world's largest non–video game company. Perhaps the most effective of all sales leaders who sold the Parker Brothers line, Wilson was very mindful of the hundred years of effort it took to establish the Parker Brothers name, and its legendary games, around the world. "I tip my hat to those who built Parker," he acknowledged. Wilson's great passion became the protection and fostering of Parker Brothers' legendary products, most especially the *Monopoly* brand. He felt honored to once again have a chance to contribute to the eternity of Parker Brothers games. Not only did sales of the *Monopoly* game continue to grow under his guidance, in 2002 *Trivial Pursuit*'s 20th Anniversary Edition became the number one new product in the toy industry.[24]

Wilson sought strong leaders to work for him. After unifying Hasbro Games, he invited Bill Dohrmann—the mastermind of so many Parker Brothers product successes of the 1970s—to return and head the R&D department. Dohrmann remained in place until his retirement.

But as consolidation wound inexorably to its most efficient conclusion, Parker Brothers disappeared from Salem and Beverly and became a name—a brand—within the Hasbro Games Group, located inside a sprawling building in East Longmeadow, Massachusetts.

Epilogue

1991–

O N OCTOBER 31, 1991, A FORTY-EIGHT-PAGE Parker Brothers booklet entitled *Family Album* was published in the Parker Brothers factory. It pictured the current employees, to whom the album was presented as a memento, plus many photos taken during the 108-year history of the great game company. The occasion was the closing of the Salem plant. Despite its modern equipment and cost effectiveness, it made poor economic sense to have two factories producing the same type of products. Milton Bradley's massive single-story factory was much newer and enjoyed a better location than transportation-constrained Salem, Massachusetts. After this booklet was made, the print shop was closed and game production ended for good in Salem. The Parker Brothers manufacturing equipment, once sponsored by Ranny Barton and his operations staff and paid for by General Mills, was packed and trucked across the state to the Milton Bradley factory. Soon, the Milton Bradley plant was running an added shift and producing over a million games and puzzles per day.[1]

Salem mourned the loss of its iconic game maker. A source of local pride for more than a century had been taken away. The city would have to endure higher unemployment and further reconfigure itself as a tourist attraction to compensate.

In 1994, after growing mightily in fits and starts during the prior 105 years, the Salem plant was torn down. Weeds consumed the ground for several years before a beautiful apartment complex named Jefferson at Salem Station was built on the site. A memorial is planned to honor the location as the original home of the *Monopoly* game.

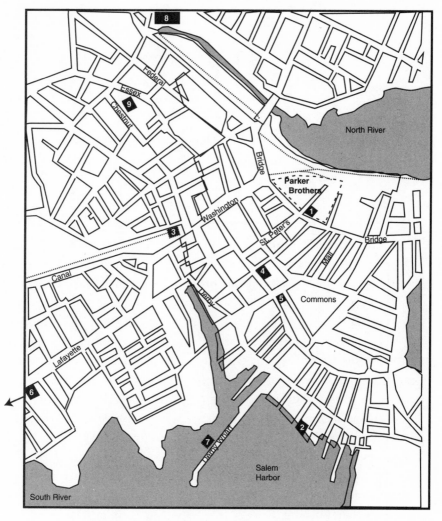

Salem, Massachusetts During the Parker Brothers' Years

1. *First building at site of Parker Brothers office/factory on Bridge Street*
(dotted line shows final extension)
2. *House of Seven Gables*
3. *Salem Railroad Station*
4. *Essex Institute/Peabody Museum (now the Peabody Essex Museum)*
5. *Hawthorne Hotel (where George Parker's first store was once located)*
6. *George Parker's home at the time of the Salem fire*
7. *Site of Smith & Parker fuel wholesalers*
8. *Blubber Hollow*
9. *Chestnut and Essex Streets, where the Parker and Barton families often lived*

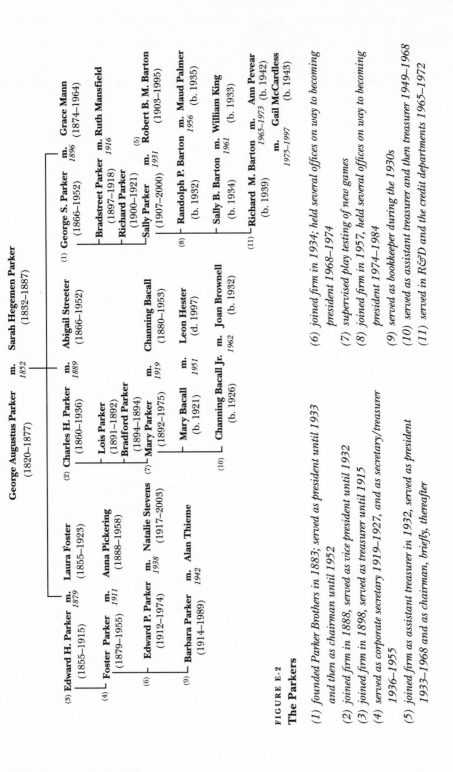

George Augustus Parker
(1820–1877)

m.
1852

Sarah Hegemen Parker
(1832–1887)

(3) **Edward H. Parker** m. **Laura Foster**
(1855–1915) 1879 (1855–1923)

(4) **Foster Parker** m. **Anna Pickering**
(1879–1955) 1911 (1888–1958)

(6) **Edward P. Parker** m. **Natalie Stevens**
(1912–1974) 1938 (1917–2003)

(9) **Barbara Parker** m. **Alan Thieme**
(1914–1989) 1942

(2) **Charles H. Parker** m. **Abigail Streeter**
(1860–1936) 1889 (1866–1952)

Lois Parker
(1891–1892)

Bradford Parker
(1894–1894)

(7) **Mary Parker** m. **Channing Bacall**
(1892–1975) 1919 (1880–1953)

Mary Bacall m. **Leon Hester**
(b. 1921) 1951 (d. 1997)

(10) **Channing Bacall Jr.** m. **Joan Brownell**
(b. 1926) 1962 (b. 1932)

(1) **George S. Parker** m. **Grace Mann**
(1866–1952) 1896 (1874–1964)

Bradstreet Parker m. **Ruth Mansfield**
(1897–1918) 1916

Richard Parker
(1900–1921)

(5) **Sally Parker** m. **Robert B. M. Barton**
(1907–2000) 1931 (1903–1995)

(8) **Randolph P. Barton** m. **Maud Palmer**
(b. 1932) 1956 (b. 1935)

Sally B. Barton m. **William King**
(b. 1934) 1961 (b. 1933)

(11) **Richard M. Barton** m. **Ann Pevear**
(b. 1939) 1965–1973 (b. 1942)

m. **Gail McCardless**
1975–1997 (b. 1943)

FIGURE E-2
The Parkers

(1) *founded Parker Brothers in 1883; served as president until 1933 and then as chairman until 1952*

(2) *joined firm in 1888, served as vice president until 1932*

(3) *joined firm in 1898, served as treasurer until 1915*

(4) *served as corporate secretary 1919–1927, and as secretary/treasurer 1936–1955*

(5) *joined firm as assistant treasurer in 1932, served as president 1933–1968 and as chairman, briefly, thereafter*

(6) *joined firm in 1934; held several offices on way to becoming president 1968–1974*

(7) *supervised play testing of new games*

(8) *joined firm in 1957, held several offices on way to becoming president 1974–1984*

(9) *served as bookkeeper during the 1930s*

(10) *served as assistant treasurer and then treasurer 1949–1968*

(11) *served in R&D and the credit departments 1965–1972*

The Beverly office building housed the Parker Brothers staff and Hasbro Interactive until 1999. Hasbro Interactive struggled to make money in the CD-ROM business, much as Parker Brothers had during the first wave of video games. So Hasbro decided to cut its losses by selling this division to a French firm named Infogrames (now Atari). Tom Dusenberry and the Beverly building went with the sale. Henceforth, employees assigned to the Parker Brothers brand would work out of the Milton Bradley facility in East Longmeadow. All Parker Brothers' employees were offered a transfer. Most declined (much as Robert Barton anticipated when considering a move out of Salem in the 1950s). The North Shore of Massachusetts was where they preferred to live. Many found jobs in industries where their talents applied. Some became independent contractors; others founded businesses. A few retired. Most look back on their years at Parker Brothers as the best years of their careers.

Among prior leaders, Rich Stearns went on to head Lenox China before becoming president of World Vision, the Christian charity organization. Bill Bracy served as president of Bell Sports before rejoining Lionel Trains, where he began his business career, this time as its president. Among Parker Brothers' other vice presidents, Joe Marquez served in Hong Kong for many years with a division of Mattel. He is now retired. Following his KPT days, Ron Jackson became chairman of Fisher-Price; many of his friends at Parker Brothers joined him there. After Fisher-Price was taken over by Mattel, Jackson retired. He devotes his time to community service and corporate boards.

In 1995, a new game company named Winning Moves, Inc., began business a few miles from Salem and Beverly. I became its president. In addition to developing select new games, our mission is to bring back to market former Parker Brothers and Milton Bradley classics. These include refreshed editions of *Pit*, *Flinch*, and *Mille Bornes*, plus card game versions of the *Monopoly* game and *Clue*. Winning Moves has also issued reproductions of the first 1935 deluxe edition of the *Monopoly* game and the 1949 edition of *Clue*.[2]

Today, Parker Brothers and Milton Bradley are coequal brands within Hasbro Games. George Burtch, a thirty-year veteran of Milton Bradley, heads the Parker Brothers marketing effort and is breathing new life into the pride and meaning of the brand.

In a sign of the times, Hasbro Games, Winning Moves, and most other game companies no longer accept unsolicited new game ideas from amateurs, as had George Parker and Robert Barton, due to intellectual property disputes and other legal concerns. However, the Toy Industry Association has taken this into account and has posted helpful advice for hopeful game inventors on its Web site, http://www.toy-tia.org.

The toy industry continues to evolve. While consolidation has created two giant toy firms (Hasbro and Mattel), many small firms leap to prominence on a regular basis. Hope springs eternal within the hearts of many toy and game entrepreneurs to one day become the next George Parker.

The Parker families have long since left the games business behind.

Channing Bacall—Charles Parker's grandson—and wife Joan are retired and reside in New Hampshire. Eddie Parker's wife Natalie remained in the same town near the Beverly office building where her husband spent his final days, until her own death in 2003. Robert B. M. Barton died in 1995 at the age of ninety-two. His wife Sally, George's daughter, died in 2000 at ninety-three.

Ranny Barton and wife Maud still reside in the seaside home where they hosted the annual Parker Brothers' celebrations. Ranny founded Corn Bay Associates, primarily to guide the family's trust.[3] He also became president of the Essex Institute and helped bring about its merger with the Peabody Museum of Salem. After his four-year term expired, he remained an active trustee and helped spur a dramatic expansion of the newly named Peabody Essex Museum. Like his father before him, he takes to the sea whenever possible and skippers his yacht from Nova Scotia to the Caribbean and the many points in between. Ranny often attends Parker Brothers alumni functions.

Parker Brothers graduates remain close, thanks to a vibrant alumni association. Their well-attended reunions are held annually, usually near the Beverly office building. A Web site links them, worldwide, in much the same way that interoffice memos and telephone extensions formerly did inside Parker Brothers.

Back in late 1991, the last copies of the *Monopoly* game came off the assembly line in the old Salem factory. They were numbered, included an extra token, and were given to the employees. These games became a lasting reminder of the spirit that glowed within Parker Brothers. The men and women in East Longmeadow who today make *Monopoly* and all the new games that bear the Parker Brothers logo carry forward the tradition that began with George S. Parker, perpetuating the product line he founded as a bright-eyed boy—a boy who built a business that lasted through the application of principles learned and a belief that games were meant to be fun.

For us all.

Notes

Note: "GSP" refers to George S. Parker.

Chapter 1

1. Gorton Carruth, *What Happened When* (New York: Signet, 1989); *Chronicle of America* (Mount Kisco, NY: Chronicle Publications Inc., 1990). Unless otherwise stated, these two chronological references were referred to verify the years and dates given throughout the text for historical events that occurred in the United States and which also had impact on the world at large. Also consulted was *Grolier Multimedia Encyclopedia* (New York: Grolier Interactive Inc., 1998).

2. The names, dates, places, quotes, and events throughout chapter 1 are taken from "Notes on the History of Parker Brothers," written by George S. Parker. It is composed of three documents written between 1932 and 1946. They cover, in overlapping detail, the origins and early years of his business, until about 1903. Parker did not leave a similar account for the years after 1903. However, he did highlight important products developed from 1903 to 1946 in the "Notes" documents. (His extant pocket diaries provide details for this period of time.)

3. Ink Mendelsohn, "Games Americans Play," *Smithsonian News Service*, 1986; Anthony Merrill, "Game Makers," *Pictorial Review Boston*, 25 March 1956; Pete Martin, "Game Maker," *Saturday Evening Post*, 6 October 1945. Game historian Bruce Whitehill has discovered two earlier American board games entitled *Traveller's Tour Through the United States*, and *Traveller's Tour Through Europe*, both made in 1822 by F. & R. Lockwood, a family of New York Booksellers.

4. GSP, historical notes; GSP, "Origin of Parker Brothers Inc." (undated), which details how he conceived *Banking*.

5. Charles Whittlesey, Arthur Freedman, and Edward Herman, *Money and Banking: Analysis and Policy* (New York: Macmillan, 1968), 15–30.

6. "Descriptive List of Games," George S. Parker Company, 1885.

7. Bruce Whitehill, *Games: American Boxed Games and Their Makers* (Radnor, PA: Wallace-Homestead Book Company, 1992).

8. *Chronicle of America.*

9. Robert B. M. Barton, interviews by author, 9 January 1988 and 13 October 1988.

10. GSP, historical notes.

11. Charles A. Parker, "Do You Nurse a Secret Ambition to Invent a Game?" draft of paper written for the *Boston Traveler*, circa 1933.

12. GSP pocket diary, appendix, 1888.

13. *Chronicle of America*.

14. <http://www.ci.beverly.ma.us/shoe> (accessed 14 July 2002).

15. Parker Brothers Partnership Agreements, 1889, 1891, 1893, 1894, 1895.

16. *Chronicle of America*.

17. Parker Brothers annual catalogs, 1888–1892.

18. Parker Brothers catalog, 1889.

19. Merrill, "Game Makers."

20. Parker Brothers Partnership Agreements, 1893, 1894, 1895.

21. *Gamester*, Parker Brothers, December 1949.

22. Stanley Appelbaum, *The Chicago World's Fair of 1893* (New York: Dover, 1980), 118.

23. London Topographical Society, *The A to Z of Victorian London* (London: London Topographical Society, 1987), v.

24. Maud P. Barton, interview by author, 22 November 2002.

25. GSP, pocket diary, 1896.

26. GSP, *Random Verse of Here and There*, self-published, 1944.

27. Channing Bacall, interview by author, 9 August 2002; Parker family biographical records.

28. GSP, pocket diary, 1898.

29. Harry Manning, interview by Professor John Fox, audiocassette, 18 November 1986.

30. Robert B. M. Barton, interview by author, 13 October 1988.

31. GSP, pocket diary, appendix, 1897, 1899.

Chapter 2

1. Parker Brothers catalog, 1996.

2. GSP, historical notes; Ink Mendelsohn, "Games Americans Play," *Smithsonian News Service*, 1986, 3.

3. GSP, historical notes.

4. *Chronicle of America* (Mount Kisco, NY: Chronicle Publications Inc., 1990).

5. Parker Brothers catalogs, 1898, 1899, 1900.

6. GSP, pocket diaries, 1897, 1898, 1899.

7. Patricia Johnson Beaulieu, "The Biography of My Grandfather, Albert Richardson," high school term paper, 1941.

8. Jim McAllister, *Salem: From Naumkeag to Witch City* (Beverly, MA: Commonwealth Editions, 2000).

9. <http:www.salemweb.com/history/maritime> (accessed 14 July 2002).

10. Joseph Flibbert et al., *Salem: Cornerstones of a Historic City* (Beverly, MA: Commonwealth Editions, 1999), 105–107.

11. Ibid., 32.

12. GSP, historical notes.

13. GSP, pocket diary, 1900; family photograph album.

14. GSP, pocket diary, appendix, 1901.

15. GSP, pocket diary, 1901.

16. Edmund Morris, *Theodore Rex* (New York: Random House, 2001), 14, 22.

17. Henry Ruoff, *Century Book of Facts* (Springfield, MA: King-Richardson, 1900), 597.

18. Gerald Gurney, *Table Tennis: The Early Years* (East Sussex, England: International Table Tennis Association, 1988), 11.

19. *Grolier Multimedia Encyclopedia* (New York: Grolier Interactive, Inc., 1998).

20. Coleman Clark, *Modern Ping-Pong And How To Play It* (New York: John Day Company, 1933), 2.

21. GSP, historical notes; GSP, pocket diary, 1901.

22. Fred French, telephone interview by author, 24 October 2002.

23. Channing Bacall, interview by author, 8 August 2002.

24. Rev. Jeffrey Barz-Snell, telephone interview by author, 7 November 2002.

25. GSP, pocket diary, 1903.

26. *Grolier Multimedia Encyclopedia.*

27. Chris Byrne, *Toys: Celebrating 100 Years of the Power of Play* (New York: TIA, 2003), 15.

28. Toy Industry Association, statistics, 2002.

29. GSP, pocket diary, appendix, 1903.

30. Gurney, *Table Tennis*, 11.

31. GSP, historical notes; Robert B. M. Barton, interview by author 9 January 1988.

32. Lee Dennis, *Antique American Games* (Elkins Park, PA: Warman, 1988), 35, 80, 91.

33. Parker Brothers catalog, 1902.

34. London Topographical Society, *The A to Z of Victorian London*, 34.

35. *Grolier Multimedia Encyclopedia.*

36. GSP, pocket diary, 1903.

37. GSP, historical notes.

38. GSP, pocket diaries, 1903, 1904.

39. GSP, pocket diary, 1904.

40. Louisiana Purchase Exposition Co., *Universal Exposition: St. Louis* (St. Louis: Louisiana Purchase Exposition Co., 1904).

41. GSP, pocket diary, 1904.

42. Robert B. M. Barton, interview by author 9 January 1988.

43. Bruce Whitehill, *Games: American Boxed Games and Their Makers* (Radnor, PA: Wallace-Homestead Book Company, 1992), 88.

44. GSP, pocket diaries, 1904 and 1905.

45. Edmund Gillon, *The Gibson Girl and Her America* (New York: Dover Publications, 1969), vii–xi.

46. Catherine Perry Hargrave, *A History of Playing Cards* (Boston: Houghton Mifflin, 1930), 22; Roger Tilley, *Playing Cards: Pleasures and Treasures* (New York: Putnam, 1967), 30.

47. GSP, historical notes.

48. GSP, pocket diary, 1908.

49. GSP, pocket diary, 1907.

50. Ibid.

51. Parker Brothers catalogs, 1907, 1908.

52. Anne Williams, "Parker Brothers and Pastime Puzzles," *Cutting a Fine Figure: The Art of the Jigsaw Puzzle* (Lexington, MA: Museum of Our National Heritage, 1996).

53. Ibid. Frank Ordway is the name of the Parker Brothers employee who applied for the patent.

54. Ibid.

55. Harry Manning, interview by Professor John Fox, audiocassette, 18 November 1986.

56. Robert B. M. Barton, interview by author, 9 January 1988.

57. Harry Manning, interview by Professor John Fox, audiocassette, 18 November 1986.

58. Ibid.

59. Ibid.

60. Pete Martin, "Game Maker," *Saturday Evening Post*, 6 October 1945.

61. <http://www.diaboloworld.41.com/history> (accessed 11 July 2002).

62. Harry Manning, interview by Professor John Fox, audiocassette, 18 November 1986.

63. <http://www.diaboloworld.41.com/history> (accessed 11 July 2002).

64. GSP, pocket diary, appendix, 1911.

65. Robert B. M. Barton, interview by author, 9 January 1988.

Chapter 3

1. Gorton Carruth, *What Happened When* (New York: Signet, 1989).

2. Chris Byrne, *Toys: Celebrating 100 Years of the Power of Play* (New York: Toy Industry Association, 2003), 34–41.

3. Harry Manning, interview by Professor John Fox, audiocassette, 18 November 1986.

4. Parker Brothers catalog, 1911.

5. Harry Manning, interview by Professor John Fox, audiocassette, 18 November 1986.

6. "The Story of the Britannica," *Encyclopaedia Britannica* (New York: Britannica, 13th ed., 1926); Grace Mann Parker, genealogical research, 1933.

7. Robert B. M. Barton, interview by author, 9 January 1988.

8. Channing Bacall, interview by author, 13 October 1988.

9. Helen Mitchell, interview by Professor John Fox, audiocassette, 5 December 1986.

10. Harry Manning, interview by Professor John Fox, audiocassette, 18 November 1986.

11. Ibid.

12. Ibid.

13. Ibid.

14. GSP, historical notes; Parker Brothers catalog, 1912.

15. Charles Whittlesey, Arthur Freedman, and Edward Herman, *Money and Banking: Analysis and Policy* (New York: Macmillan, 1968), 364.

16. Parker Brothers catalogs, 1911, 1912, 1913, 1914.

17. Anthony Merrill, "Game Makers," *Pictorial Review Boston*, 25 March 1956.

18. Robert B. M. Barton, interview by author, 9 January 1988.

19. Carruth, *What Happened When.*

20. Parker Brothers catalog, 1914.

21. London Topographical Society, *The A to Z of Victorian London* (London: London Topographical Society, 1987), 31–32.

22. Carruth, *What Happened When.*

23. Joseph Flibbert et al., *Salem: Cornerstones of a Historic City* (Beverly, MA: Commonwealth Editions, 1999), 109–111.

24. Ibid.

25. GSP, pocket diary, 1914.

26. Flibbert et al., *Salem*, 109–111.
27. GSP, pocket diary, 1921.
28. Parker Brothers catalog, 1916.
29. Randolph Barton, interview by author, 21 October 2002.
30. *Chronicle of America* (Mount Kisco, NY: Chronicle Publications Inc., 1990).
31. Randolph Barton, interview by author, 21 October 2002.
32. Parker family biographical records (undated).
33. GSP, *Random Verse of Here and There*, self-published, 1944.
34. Randolph Barton, interview by author, 21 October 2002.
35. *Freshman Red Book* (Cambridge, MA: Harvard University, 1919), iii, 76, 126, 162–163.
36. *Harvard Class Album* (Cambridge, MA: Harvard University, 1922), 4, 5, 207.
37. GSP, pocket diary, 1921.
38. <http://www.airdisaster.com> (accessed 8 August 2002).
39. *Harvard Class Album.*
40. Randolph Barton, interview by author, 21 October 2002.
41. Parker family biography (undated).
42. Robert B. M. Barton, interview by author, 9 January 1988.
43. GSP, pocket diary, 1922.
44. James J. Shea, *It's All in the Game* (New York: Putnam, 1960), 204–205.
45. <http://www.mahjonggmuseum.com> (accessed 20 July 2002).
46. Charles Babcock, "Rules of Mah-Jongg," Mah-Jongg Sales Company, 1923.
47. <http://www.mahjongmuseum.com> (accessed 12 July 2002).
48. Ibid.
49. Babcock, "Rules of Mah-Jongg."
50. <http://www.mahjongmuseum.com> (accessed 12 July 2002).
51. GSP, pocket diary, 1922.
52. Parker Brothers catalog, 1923.
53. <http://www.mahjongmuseum.com> (accessed 12 July 2002).
54. GSP, pocket diary, 1922.
55. *Grolier Multimedia Encyclopedia* (New York: Grolier Interactive Inc., 1998).
56. Babcock, "Rules of Mah-Jongg."
57. "Shinbones are used for Mahjongg sets," *London Daily Mail*, 9 October 1923.
58. <http://www.mahjongmuseum.com> (accessed 12 July 2002).
59. Ibid.
60. "Parker Brothers to Build New Plant," *Salem News*, 10 March 1924.
61. *Chronicle of America.*
62. Carruth, *What Happened When.*
63. GSP, pocket diary, 1927.
64. Robert Lacey, *Ford: The Men and the Machine* (Boston: Little, Brown, 1986), 98–106.
65. *Grolier Multimedia Encyclopedia.*
66. Parker Brothers catalogs, 1926, 1927.
67. Parker Brothers catalog, 1928.
68. GSP, pocket diary, appendix, 1928.
69. Grace Mann Parker, "Brookwood," biographical notes, unpublished, 1933.
70. GSP, pocket diary, 1929.
71. Pete Martin, "Game Maker," *Saturday Evening Post*, 6 October 1945.
72. Parker Brothers catalog, 1935.
73. Gene Smiley, *Rethinking the Great Depression* (Chicago: Ivan Dee, 2002), 28.
74. GSP, pocket diary, 1930.

75. Angie Gagnon, interview by Professor John Fox, audiocassette, 4 November 1986.

76. Ibid.

77. Ibid.

78. Parker Brothers catalog, 1932.

79. Channing Bacall, interview by author, 9 August 2002.

80. Robert B. M. Barton, interview by author, 13 October 1988.

81. Robert B. M. Barton, interview by Professor John Fox, audiocassette, 27 December 1986.

82. Robert B. M. Barton, interview by author, 13 October 1988.

83. Ibid.

84. GSP, pocket diary, 1932.

85. Robert B. M. Barton, interview by author, 13 October 1988.

86. Robert B. M. Barton, *Memoirs* (Beverly, MA: Memories Unlimited, 1989), 30–31.

87. Robert B. M. Barton, interview by author, 13 October 1988.

88. Barton, *Memoirs*, 33.

89. Louis Vanne, interview by author, 14 December 1987.

90. Robert B. M. Barton, interview by author, 9 January 1988.

91. John J. Fox, "Parker Pride," *Essex Institute Historical Collections* 123, no. 2, April 1987.

92. Helen Mitchell, interview by Professor John Fox, audiocassette, 5 December 1986.

93. Ibid.; Channing Bacall, interview by author, 9 August 2002.

94. Henry Sullivan, interview by Professor John Fox, 12 November 1986.

95. *Gamester*, Parker Brothers, winter issue, 1949.

96. Robert B. M. Barton, interview by Professor John Fox, 27 December 1986.

97. Patricia Beaulieu, interview by author, 10 March 2003.

98. Patricia Beaulieu, "Biography of My Grandfather, Albert Richardson," high school term paper, 1941; *Ninety Years of Fun*, Parker Brothers, 1978.

99. Robert B. M. Barton, interview by Professor John Fox, audiocassette, 27 December 1986; Robert B. M. Barton, interview by author, 9 January 1988.

100. Biography of Hendrik van Loon, <http://www.encyclopedia.com> (accessed 29 July 2002).

101. Parker Brothers catalog, 1933; GSP, pocket diary, 1933.

102. John Chartres, "A History of Waddington's," *Leeds Business History* (Leeds, U.K: Leeds University, 1952).

103. GSP, pocket diary, 1935.

104. Robert B. M. Barton, interview by author, 9 January 1988.

Chapter 4

1. Robert B. M. Barton spelled out the details of Black Monday in my interview with him on 1 November 1988; he also mentions it in Robert B. M. Barton, *Memoirs* (Beverly, MA: Memories Unlimited, 1989).

2. John J. Fox, "Parker Pride," *Essex Institute Historical Collections* 123, no. 2, April 1987.

3. Robert B. M. Barton, interview by author, 9 January 1988.

4. Robert B. M. Barton, interview by author, 13 October 1988.

5. GSP, pocket diary, appendix, 1935.

6. The lady who placed the call was Helen Coolidge. Helen Coolidge, telephone interview by author, January 1988.

7. George McDonald, interview by Andy Eggendorf, 15 September 1988.

8. Darrow–Parker Brothers contract, 19 March 1935.

9. GSP, pocket diary, 1935. George and Sally Parker left for Europe on 20 March 1935, the day after Barton signed the deal with Darrow.

10. The main issue was the choice of the word "if" or "when" doubles are thrown. Roy Howard persuaded George to adopt "when doubles are thrown" because it was inevitable they would occur many times in a game.

11. Robert B. M. Barton, interview by author, 9 January 1988.

12. Robert B. M. Barton, interview by Professor John Fox, audiocassette, 27 December 1986.

13. GSP, pocket diary, 1935. The *Landlord's Game* patent # is 1,509,312. The *Monopoly* game's patent # is 2,026,082.

14. Robert B. M. Barton, interview by author, 8 January 1988.

15. GSP, pocket diary, 1935.

16. Darrow–Parker Brothers contract, 27 January 1936.

17. Robert B. M. Barton, interview with Professor John Fox, audiocassette, 27 December 1986; Barton, letter to author, 8 February 1988.

18. John Chartres, "A History of Waddington's," *Leeds Business History* (Leeds, U.K.: Leeds University, 1952), 198; Victor Watson, telephone interview by author, 12 September 2002.

19. Helen Mitchell, interview by Professor John Fox, audiocassette, 5 December 1986.

20. Louis Vanne, interview by author, 14 December 1987; Louis Vanne, interview by Professor John Fox, audiocassette, 4 November 1986.

21. Fox, "Parker Pride."

22. Robert B. M. Barton, interview by author, 13 January 1988; Robert B. M. Barton, interview with Professor John Fox, audiocassette, 27 December 1986.

23. Ibid.

24. Ibid.

25. Parker Brothers catalog, 1936.

26. GSP, pocket diary, appendix, 1937.

27. Robert B. M. Barton, interview by author, 9 January 1988.

28. *Grolier Multimedia Encyclopedia* (New York: Grolier Interactive, Inc., 1998).

29. Michel Matschoss, interview by author, 17 October 2002; Dan Glimne, interview by author, 23–24 March 2003. See also <http://www.muurKrant.nl/monopoly> (accessed 11 July 2003).

30. Louis Vanne, interview by author, 14 December 1987.

31. Parker Brothers catalog, 1937.

32. GSP, pocket diary, 1939.

33. GSP, pocket diary, 1937.

34. Lowell Thomas, <http://www.horatioalger.com>; <http://www.creativequotations.com>. Melvin Purvis, <http://www.foia.fbi.gov>. S. S. van Dine, <http://www.mysterylist.com>; <http://www.npg.si.edu>. Boake Carter, <http://www.findagrave.com>; <http://www.otr.com> (all accessed 3 August 2002).

35. Patricia Beaulieu, "Biography of My Grandfather, Albert Richardson," high school term paper, 1941; *Ninety Years of Fun*, Parker Brothers, 1978.

36. Robert B. M. Barton, interview by author, 9 January 1988.

37. Lou Gody, *The Federal Writers Project Guide to 1930s New York* (New York: Random House, 1939).

38. Parker Brothers catalog, 1941; Channing Bacall, interview by author, 9 August 2002.

39. Parker Brothers catalog, 1939.

40. Barton, *Memoirs*, 177.

41. Helen Mitchell, interview by Professor John Fox, 5 December 1986.

42. GSP, pocket diaries, 1938, 1939; Grace Mann Parker, travel diaries, 1938, 1939.

43. Chartres, "A History of Waddington's."

44. Helen Mitchell, interview by Professor John Fox, 5 December 1986.

45. *Gamester*, Parker Brothers, 1941.

46. Parker Brothers catalogs, 1940, 1941.

47. GSP, pocket diary, appendix, 1941.

48. Edward P. Parker, Parker family biographies, (undated).

49. Robert B. M. Barton, interview by Professor John Fox, audiocassette, 27 December 1986.

50. Diane Bolman, letter to author, 23 September 2002.

51. Robert B. M. Barton, interview by author, 9 January 1988.

52. Parker Brothers catalog, 1943.

53. George S. Parker, Wartime Scrapbook, 1944, Randolph Barton Archives.

54. Louis Vanne, interview by author, 14 December 1987.

55. Norman V. Watson, "M.I.5 & No. 40, Wakefield Road," biographical memoirs, 1946; Foot and Langley, *MI5*, 1946. John Waddington Company Ltd Archives, courtesy of Victor Watson.

56. GSP, pocket diary, 1946.

57. Barton, *Memoirs*; GSP, letter to Robert Barton, 30 March 1945.

58. Pete Martin, "Game Maker," *Saturday Evening Post*, 6 October 1945.

59. H. O. Todd, patent, *Rich Uncle*, #2,526,300.

60. Maud Barton, interview by author, 22 November 2002.

61. Randolph Barton, interview by author, 21 October 2002.

62. Helen Mitchell, interview by Professor John Fox, audiocassette, 5 December 1986.

63. Robert B. M. Barton, interview by Professor John Fox, audiocassette, 27 December 1986; Louis Vanne, interview by author, 14 December 1987; Barton, *Memoirs*, 42–43.

64. Louis Vanne, interview by author, 14 December 1987.

65. Robert B. M. Barton, interview by Professor John Fox, audiocassette, 27 December 1986.

66. Ibid.

67. Parker Brothers catalog, 1946.

68. Robert B. M. Barton, interview by author, 9 January 1988.

69. Parker Brothers Company Scrapbook, 1950; Parker Brothers Archives.

70. Barton, *Memoirs*, 78–79.

71. James J. Shea, *It's All in the Game* (New York: Putnam, 1960), 268–274.

72. Bruce Whitehill, *Games: American Boxed Games and Their Makers* (Radnor, PA: Wallace-Homestead Book Company, 1992), 128.

73. Channing Bacall, interview by author, 9 August 2002.

74. Ibid.

75. Fred French, telephone interview by author, 24 October 2002.

76. Helen Mitchell, interview by Professor John Fox, audiocassette, 5 December 1986.

77. *Peterborough Record*, 2 October 1952, is an example.

78. Helen Mitchell, interview by Professor John Fox, audiocassette, 5 December 1986.

Chapter 5

1. *Chronicle of America* (Mount Kisco, NY: Chronicle Publications Inc., 1990).

2. Channing Bacall, interview by author, 13 October 1988.

3. "Historical Sales of Monopoly," Parker Brothers report, 1984.

4. Channing Bacall, interview by author, 13 October 1988.

5. Ibid.

6. <http://www.richsamuels.com/nbcmm/garroway> (accessed 6 August 2002).

7. Randolph Barton, interview by author, 5 November 2002.

8. *Ninety Years of Fun*, Parker Brothers, 1978.

9. *Salem Record*, Parker Brothers, 1960.

10. Preston Gise, Parker Brothers—Acquisition Review memorandum for General Mills, 16 January 1968.

11. Randolph Barton, interview by author, 5 November 2002.

12. Channing Bacall, telephone interview by author, 23 October 2002.

13. Chris Byrne, *Toys: Celebrating 100 Years of the Power of Play* (New York: Toy Industry Association, 2003), 128–135.

14. Robert B. M. Barton, interview by author, 13 October 1988.

15. Channing Bacall, interview by author, 23 October 2002.

16. Robert B. M. Barton, interview by author, 9 January 1988.

17. Channing Bacall, interview by author, 9 August 2002.

18. Channing Bacall, telephone interview by author, 23 October 2002.

19. Channing Bacall, interview by author, 9 August 2002.

20. "The Civil War," *Life* magazine, 6 January to 17 March, 1961.

21. Robert Barton, *Memoirs* (Beverly, MA: Memories Unlimited, 1989), 93–95.

22. George Fox, interview by Professor John Fox, audiocassette, 25 November 1986.

23. Anne Parker-Pollock, letter to author, 17 October 2002.

24. Fred French, interview by author, 24 October 2002.

25. Anne Parker-Pollock, interview by author, 22 November 2002.

26. Helen Mitchell, interview by Professor John Fox, audiocassette, 5 December 1986.

27. Randolph Barton, interview by author, 7 October 2002.

28. Robert B. M. Barton, interview by author, 9 January 1988.

29. Ibid.

30. Gise, Acquisition Review memorandum.

31. Channing Bacall, interview by author, 13 October 1988.

32. Robert B. M. Barton, interview by Professor John Fox, audiocassette, 27 December 1986.

33. Gise, Acquisition Review memorandum.

34. Ibid.

35. <http://www.museumoftalkingboards.com> (accessed 12 October 2002).

36. Robert B. M. Barton, interview by Professor John Fox, audiocassette, 27 December 1986.

37. Craig Nalen, telephone interview by author, 10 October 2002.

38. Ellen Wojahn, *Playing by Different Rules* (New York: Amacom, 1988), 25.

39. Randolph Barton, interview by author, 12 June 2002.

40. Ibid.

41. Robert B. M. Barton, interview by Professor John Fox, audiocassette, 27 December 1986; Randolph Barton, interview by author, 19 June 2002.

42. Channing Bacall, interview by author, 9 August 2002.

43. Craig Nalen, telephone interview by author, 10 October 2002.

44. <http://chnm.gmu.edu/features/sidelights/crocker>; <http://www.general mills.com/corporate/about/history> (both accessed 30 July 2002).

45. Randolph Barton, interview by author, 19 June 2002.

46. George Fox, interview by Professor John Fox, audiocassette, 25 November, 1986.

47. Ibid.

48. Randolph Barton, interview by author, 19 June 2002.

Chapter 6

1. Preston Gise, Parker Brothers—Acquisition Review memorandum for General Mills, 12 January 1968.

2. Fred French, telephone interview by author, 14 October 2002.

3. Randolph Barton, interview by author, 21 October 2002; Robert B. M. Barton, interview with Professor John Fox, audiocassette, 27 December, 1986.

4. Channing Bacall, interview by author, 9 August 2002.

5. Ibid.

6. Despite these advertising successes, General Mills did not think Frank Browning Jr.'s agency had the right stature or capabilities to serve Parker Brothers long term. But at almost the same moment it planned to confront Eddie Parker and force a change, Browning beefed up his agency by hiring a copywriting whiz (Mal McDougall) and merging with another competent agency (owned by Rick Humphrey). The new firm—Humphrey, Browning and McDougall—had the kind of clout General Mills approved of and "HBM" endured as Parker's agency.

7. William Dohrmann, interview by author, 22 September 2002.

8. Their names were Dave Laughridge and Arthur Venditti.

9. Channing Bacall, interview by author, 9 August 2002.

10. Thirty-one-year-old Cheng Sang Kwa, a sales executive from Singapore, won the prize.

11. William Dohrmann, interview by author, 22 September 2002.

12. Jack McMahon became an employee after having designed packaging for Parker Brothers as a freelancer since 1962. Artist Nancy Babson also joined the firm at this time.

13. William Dohrmann, interview by author, 22 September 2002.

14. One of the annoying uses for *Oobi* was the passing of one to a female flight attendant ("stewardess" then) by a male airline passenger.

15. William Dohrmann, interview by author, 22 September 2002.

16. Ibid.

17. Ibid.

18. *Ninety Years of Fun*, Parker Brothers, 1978; Randolph Barton, interview by author, 5 November 2002.

19. Randolph Barton, interview by author, 19 June 2002.

20. Ibid.; Ellen Wojahn, *Playing by Different Rules* (New York: Amacom, 1988), 55–59.

21. It adjoined the property of the *Beverly Times*. Bill Dohrmann found the site through a friend who worked there.

22. This was a frequent topic in the *Salem Evening News* in 1977.

23. Annual Report, Milton Bradley, 1963.

24. Laurie Curran managed Dohrmann's licensing and inventor relations efforts.

25. Randolph Barton, interview by author, 5 November 2002.

26. E. David Wilson, interview by author, 13 March 2002.

27. For Professor Anspach's perspective, see his book *The Billion Dollar Monopoly*® *Swindle*, self-published, 1998.

28. Robert B. M. Barton, interview by Professor John Fox, audiocassette, 27 December 1986.

29. Oliver Howes, interview by author, 1 December 1987.

30. Wojahn, *Playing by Different Rules*, 76.

31. Ibid.

32. William Dohrmann, interview by author, 22 September 2002.

33. Ibid.

34. Ibid.

35. *Merlin* was styled by Parker Brothers industrial designer Sam Kjellman.

36. Wojahn, *Playing by Different Rules*, 84–85.

37. The music-playing aliens in the movie *Close Encounters of the Third Kind* enhanced *Simon*'s even greater sales success.

38. Tony Lemone, telephone interview by author, 11 October 2002.

39. Report of Operations, Parker Brothers, December 1979.

40. Randolph Barton, interview by author, 5 November 2002; personal recollection.

41. Among them were *Wildfire, Split Second*, and *Bank Shot*. A novel electronic action figure named *ROM* was also marketed.

42. Report of Operations, Parker Brothers, January 1981 and January 1982.

43. Joseph Marquez, telephone interview by author, 13 October 2002.

44. Randolph Barton, interview by author, 5 November 2002.

45. These included Frank Ventura, Jim Tinguely, Rene Soriano, Randy Moorman, and Walter Friedman.

46. Randolph Barton, interview by author, 5 November 2002.

47. Ralph Baer, interview by author, 11 July 2002.

48. The engineer was John Gates, not to be confused with plastic molding expert John Gates, who had joined Parker Brothers years earlier with the acquisition of Boyden Plastics.

49. Don Swanson of General Mills had absorbed Ranny's concerns regarding Loomis's management style, especially when Ranny threatened to quit if a change wasn't made. Swanson valued Bernie and gave him what he asked for, responsibility for a creative center that would service the entire Toy Group. Then he handed up-and-coming young James Fifield—a favorite of General Mills' current chairman—the reins of the New York–based Toy Group.

50. Miffitt's growing programming group was headed at this time by Jim McGinnis.

51. Ed English was the programmer.

52. E. David Wilson, interview by author, 13 March 2002.

53. Wojahn, *Playing by Different Rules*, 173–174.

54. Randolph Barton, interview by author, 5 November 2002.

Chapter 7

1. William Bracy, interview by author, 19 February 2003.

2. Joseph Marquez, interview by author, 13 October 2002.

3. This executive was Tony Lemone. Tony Lemone, telephone interview by author, 11 October 2002.

4. William Bracy, interview by author, 19 February 2003.

5. William Brett, interview by author, 8 November 2002.

6. Annual Report, Kenner Parker Toys, 1985.

7. Laura Pecci, interview by author, 28 October 2002.

8. Charles Phillips brought the game to Parker Brothers.

9. Hiro Fukami and Sandy Strichard, respectively.

10. *Don't Wake the Dragon, Monster Mash,* and *Spinjas* were three.

11. *Clue VCR, Rich Little's Charades,* and *Starting Lineup Talking Baseball.*

12. *Wall Street Journal,* 17 July 1987.

13. Annual Report, Kenner Parker Toys, 1986.

14. John Goff, "Tonka Toys with the Equity Market," *Corporate Finance,* December 1989.

15. Bear Stearns, Speaker Profiles, Toy Conference, 1990.

16. William Brett, interview by author, 8 November 2002.

17. Memorandum on potential lawsuits, Tonka, 22 November 1988.

18. Annual Report, Tonka, 1990.

19. <http://www.trivialpursuit.com> (accessed 20 July 2002).

20. Annual Reports, Hasbro, 1989, 1990.

21. <http://www.kingbolo.com> (accessed 22 July 2002).

22. <http://www.hasbro.com/pl/page.corporate_history_hasbro> (accessed 22 July 2002).

23. "Merger Agreement," Tonka Corp. with Hasbro, Inc., 31 January 1991; "Offer to Purchase Shares of Tonka," Hasbro, 6 February 1991.

24. E. David Wilson, interview by author, 13 March 2002.

Epilogue

1. E. David Wilson, interview by author, 13 March 2002.

2. Information on all Winning Moves' games can be found at <http://www.winning-moves.com> (accessed 5 May 2003).

3. It was named for the cove in the Bahamas where his parents had purchased a winter home.

Index

Photo Credits

Black-and-White Illustrations/Photographs

All black-and-white illustrations and photographs are from Parker Brothers catalogs in the author's collection, except for:

Invoice for *Banking* (p. 3), courtesy of the archives of Randolph P. Barton; *Pastime Puzzle* package (p. 42), courtesy of the archives of Anne Williams; John Waddington factory (p. 104), courtesy of the archives of Penny Melling; Holiday cheer ad (p. 127), *Risk* ad (p. 135), *Mah-Jongg* trade ad (p. 66), and cartoon (p. 68), courtesy of the Parker Brothers archives; World's Fair booth 1904 (p. 37), *Merlin* (p. 153), and Parker plant development (p. 139), created by the author based on photos from Parker catalogs; *Monopoly* ad (p. 94), archives of author.

Color Photographs

Young George Parker, 1878, graduation photo of George Parker, 1884; Parker Brothers' stationery and original factory building, 1892; Parker brothers, 1901, carriage photo,1902, and three Parker children, Foster, Richard, and Bradstreet, 1903; George Parker's business cards; George and children Sally (1910), Bradstreet (1918), and Richard Parker (1919); Field Day program, 1927, Tuck's Point, 1928; Sally Parker, Robert Barton; plaque on desk, 1933, Parkers in Egypt and at Pyramids, 1929; Parker management, 1935; Robert Barton onboard ship, "Brookwood"; Robert Barton; Craig Nalen, Robert Barton, and check, 1968; Eddie Parker; Michael Habourdin, Ranny Barton, and Victor Watson. Courtesy of the archives of Randolph P. Barton.

Charles and Edward Parker, 1878; George and Charles Parker, 1892; Charles Parker, 1925; Channing Bacall, 1952 (a); Channing Bacall (b). Courtesy of the archives of Channing Bacall.

Edward P. Parker, 1934; Edward P. Parker and Destroyer Escort (DE) *USS Wyman* painting. Courtesy of the archives of Diane Bolman.

Edward H. Parker, 1914. Courtesy of the archives of Edward Bolman.

William Dohrmann, R &D department, 1974, and *Oobi* package. Courtesy of the archives of William F. Dohrmann.

Pastime Girl, 1909, *Pit* postcard, 1905; Parker factory; *Mah-Jongg* assembly, 1924; Parker warehouse, 1925; back of plaque; Louis Vanne at press, 1937; *Monopoly* chimneys, cutting *Monopoly* money, 1934; three Parker presidents, 1958, Ranny Barton with *Risk*, 1960; Richard Stearns and John Moore. Courtesy of the Parker Brothers' archives.

Salem plant, 1984; David Wilson. Courtesy of the Hasbro Games archives.

Albert Richardson's card. Courtesy of the archives of Patricia Johnson Beaulieu.

Kenner Parker Toys management photo, 1985. Courtesy of the archives of William Brett.

Billy Bumps game. Courtesy of the collection of Bruce Whitehill.

Mansion of Happiness, Battle of Manila and *United States* games; *Motor Carriage* and *Merry Christmas* games; *European War* game and *Militac* games. Photographs in the author's collection and through the courtesy of the Parker Brothers' archives.

About the Author

Philip Edward Orbanes is currently president of Winning Moves, Inc., a specialty game company that markets retro games and select new titles. He's been a game executive and historian for more than thirty years. He held the position of senior vice president of research and development at Parker Brothers during the 1980s and also served as chief judge at Parker Brothers' U.S. and world *Monopoly* championships.

He is the author of *The Monopoly Companion* and *Rook in a Book* and is the inventor of many board and card games.